The Origins of the American Income Tax

The Origins of the American Income Tax

The Revenue Act of 1894 and Its Aftermath

Richard J. Joseph

Syracuse University Press

Syracuse, New York 13244–5160

First Edition 2004

04 05 06 07 08 09   6 5 4 3 2 1

The paper used in this publication meets the minimum requirements of American National Standard for Information Sciences—Permanence of Paper for Printed Library Materials, ANSI Z39.48–1984.∞™

Library of Congress Cataloging-in-Publication Data

Joseph, Richard J.
The origins of the American income tax : the Revenue Act of 1894 and
its aftermath / Richard J. Joseph.—1st ed.
p. cm.
Includes bibliographical references and index.
ISBN 0–8156–3021–2 (alk. paper)
1. Income tax—Law and legislation—United States—History. I. Title.
KF6369 .J67 2004
343.7305'2'09—dc22
2003022296

Manufactured in the United States of America

To the women who have inspired me

Kathy, Salwa, Gabriella, Stephanie, Julia

It must be admitted that the history of all taxation reveals a constant struggle between classes, each striving to shift the chief burden of taxation upon the other. Taxation is coeval with organized society. The income tax is the outgrowth of centuries of tax legislation throughout the world. By universal consent it more nearly approximates justice in taxation than any other general tax method yet devised. . . . The incorporation of this tax as a part of the newly adopted fiscal policy of the country marks the culmination of a contest that has been waged in its behalf throughout the Nation for 20 years.

—Democratic representative Cordell Hull
of Tennessee, January 1914

Richard J. Joseph is a senior lecturer in federal income taxation at the University of Texas at Austin. A graduate of Harvard, Oxford, and the University of Texas School of Law, he is a coauthor of *Prentice Hall's Federal Taxation* series and has published numerous articles on tax equity, the consumption and flat taxes, the theory of contract formation, and U.S. foreign policy. Before embarking on an academic career, Mr. Joseph worked as an investment banker and securities trader on Wall Street and as a mergers and acquisitions lawyer in Texas.

Contents

Illustrations

Tables

Preface

This book marks the culmination of several years' inquiry into the social origins of the American income tax. It was written in response to the cries on the part of some congressional critics to "pull up the income tax by its roots." It addresses the fundamental questions, "What are these roots, and why do we have an income tax in the first place?" It purports to shed light on the original intent, rationale, and effect of the early income tax and thus stimulate discussion and debate on the philosophical underpinnings of our present tax system.

In conducting this inquiry, I initially consulted the *Congressional Record* for 1913. It was in that year that the Sixty-third Congress enacted a permanent tax on individual incomes. This tax, merged with a corporate tax instituted in 1909, laid the foundation for our modern system of income taxation. I soon discovered that relatively little is revealed in the way of why Congress wanted to institute a broad-based tax on net income. Indeed, I learned, the central issue in the debates of 1913 was not the impending shift to a new tax base, but rather the degree to which tax rates should be progressive.

So I went back in time to events preceding passage of the Sixteenth Amendment, which authorized the imposition of an unapportioned income tax. I observed that opponents of the amendment, and by implication opponents of the tax, persistently invoked constitutionality as a means of obstructing institution of the tax, and furthermore that this obstructionism was part of a wider controversy over who should bear the tax burden and how. This controversy, this "struggle," if you will, extended back to the late nineteenth century, when America was in the throes of industrialization. Many of the legislative actors, political parties, and socioeconomic groups that pushed for the tax in the 1890s (as well as many that opposed the tax) were essentially the same ones that pushed for (and respectively opposed) the tax in the 1910s.

Furthermore, most of the arguments advanced in favor of, and against, the tax in both periods were also the same.

I focused on the years 1893–95, when the controversy seems to have peaked. I discovered that during this period, the political philosophy of income taxation was more fully articulated and that the central issue in the congressional debates of 1894 was precisely whether to base federal taxation on net income. This finding led me to believe that the social origins of the American income tax lay not in the twentieth century, as some might suppose, but rather in the nineteenth century, and furthermore that although the legislative outcome of the 1913 debates shaped the essential contours of the tax rate, in favor of graduation, the legislative outcome of the 1894 debates defined the "core structure" of the tax base, in favor of net income.

It was in the latter year that the Fifty-third Congress adopted an integrated corporate-individual income tax scheme. Congress intended for this scheme to coexist with the preexisting system of tariff taxation. Democratic legislators structured the Income Tax of 1894 to meet only a fraction of the government's annual revenue needs. Nonetheless, and notwithstanding a brutal constitutional assault in 1895, this tax served as a prototype for what ultimately became our modern system of income taxation and represents a monumental shift in thinking over how the federal tax burden should be distributed.

Ratification of the Sixteenth Amendment, I came to realize, paved the way for the institutionalization of a tax base that had been fundamentally structured in 1894. Furthermore, this constitutional outcome vindicated the efforts of income tax proponents, who as individuals and as a collectivity, had pushed for institutionalization as early as the 1890s. Thus, by the time the Sixty-third Congress took up income tax legislation in 1913, the question of whether federal taxation could, and should, be based on net income had already been resolved. The central issues remaining were how to refine the withholding mechanism and the degree of graduation to be embodied in the tax rate schedule.

For the foregoing reasons, this book focuses on the Income Tax of 1894, which defined the core structure of the modern income tax base. It explores the socioeconomic trends underlying enactment of the 1894 tax, the political and institutional context of enactment, the legislative and judicial history of the early income tax, and the original intent, rationale, and effect of the levy. The book is designed to appeal to the policy maker, the legislator, the tax scholar, and the intelligent laymen, with the hope that it will enhance their understanding of why we are where we are institutionally today. It is intended to offer *not* a comprehensive history of American income taxation, but rather a brief, but illuminating, glimpse of a critical moment in its early formation.

In concluding this inquiry, I would like to thank the students and faculty of the University of Texas at Austin for providing me with an intellectually stimulating environment; Professor Steve Limberg of the McCombs School of Business for his personal backing; Associate Dean Patricia Cain of the University of Iowa School of Law for her helpful pointers; Syracuse University Press for its commitment, professionalism, assistance, and advice; and most important of all, my wife and children for so patiently enduring the writing of this book, for their heartwarming encouragement, their unwavering support, and their uplifting smiles.

The Origins of the American Income Tax

Prologue

History and the Income Tax

> *The spirit of a people, its cultural level, its social structure, the deeds its policy may prepare—all this and more is written in its fiscal history, stripped of all phrases. He who knows how to listen to its message here discerns the thunder of world history more clearly than anywhere else.*
>
> —Joseph Schumpeter,
> "The Crisis of the Tax State"

That history is relevant to the meaning of the income tax is widely accepted among tax scholars. History reveals the legislative intent behind particular tax provisions. It dispels ambiguities in the statutory language. It offers clues as to why one judicial interpretation is to be preferred over another. Indeed, without history, scholars would agree, disentangling the complex web of sections, subsections, and paragraphs of our internal revenue laws would be virtually impossible.

Where tax scholars tend to disagree is on the *scope* of the relevant history. Most believe that *case history* is relevant in deciphering the meaning of the statutory language. Others view the *legislative history* of particular code provisions as pertinent. Still others find revealing the *administrative history* of the tax. Few, if any, attach significance to the *social history* of the tax, for it is law, not society, that supplies the substance of income taxation—or so it seems.

This approach was not the case some time ago. When the income tax was first instituted, the most preeminent of tax scholars—Richard T. Ely, Arthur L. Perry, Francis A. Walker, William G. Sumner—were political economists, "social historians" of sorts.[1] They viewed the income tax as an institution, not merely an amalgamation of precepts. They explained its historical development in terms of the transformation of society, not just the meaning ascribed to it by the courts. They analyzed its peculiar features in terms of competing class claims and group interests, not abstract juridical norms and complex accounting principles. They saw their task as unmasking and reforming its distributive impact, not deciphering and revising its technical language.

These early scholars were disciples of Adam Smith, John Stuart Mill, and Henry George. They recognized that the key ideas that went into the making of the income tax were the product of philosophy, not accounting. They defined the central issue in taxation to be, "Who should bear the burden, and why?" They set forth three basic principles for resolving the issue: ability to pay, equality of sacrifice, and the imposition of burdens commensurate with benefits. And they regarded themselves not only as analysts of change, but also as catalysts.

What has happened over the years has been the transformation of tax scholarship from the social and philosophical to the legalistic and technical. This transformation has coincided with the institutionalization of the tax—its widespread acceptance as a permanent feature of the U.S. political landscape. Indeed, as the tax has become ingrained in the American mind, tax scholars have come to attach less significance to its historical roots and greater significance to its policy implications. They have transformed the nature of the inquiry from the social and the metaphysical to the doctrinal, the interpretive, the procedural, the administrative.

This trend became particularly pronounced in the 1920s and 1930s. The tax having taken hold in U.S. society, scholars began to turn their attention away from its institutionalization toward its "rationalization"—rationalization not in terms of its original social and political objectives, but rather in terms of broad economic policy aims and abstract legal and accounting norms. It was during this period that Edwin Seligman belabored the issue of double taxation, T. S. Adams perfected his foreign tax credit, and Henry Simons redefined the concept of income. It was also during this period that the locus of academic thought shifted from the merits of the tax as an institution to the theoretical implications of its individual provisions.[2]

In the process, there was always a tendency to reify the tax, to purge it of its social and political content. Thus, in the academic literature, "class" and "group" gave way to "the taxpayer," a nonidentity who consumes, saves, and otherwise behaves "rationally" in an atomistic society. Tax law came to reflect not particularistic interests, but rather "essential tenets," "basic doctrines," and "equitable principles." Institutional development stemmed not from social transformation, but rather from legislative process and judicial interpretation. Social history lost ground to econometric models, as society became more static, the system more abstract, and the discipline more "scientific."

Today, as prospects for deinstitutionalization become real, the social history of the income tax has taken on a new significance—for it is the social history of the tax that reveals its *original intent.* Understanding this intent is critical to the issue of tax reform. Indeed, if the original intent of the income tax is no longer valid, if the tax no longer performs its historical function, then the argument for abandoning it in favor of a broad-based sales or consumption tax is strengthened. On the other hand, if the original intent is still valid, if the tax continues to perform its historical function, then the argument for abandoning it is considerably weakened. With these implications in mind, let us turn to the sociohistorical roots of the modern U.S. income tax. Perhaps in the process, we can shed light on issues that impact the current debate on tax reform.

Our focal point is the Income Tax of 1894. Why this levy? The Income Tax of 1894 served as a model for the Income Tax of 1913. The latter measure laid the foundation for our present tax scheme. Key provisions of the 1894 act were extensively debated in the Fifty-third Congress. This debate sheds light on the original intent of the income tax *as an institution.*

But were not the arguments put forth in the debate rendered moot by the decision in *Pollock v. Farmers' Loan & Trust Company*? Is not the intent of the 1894 act irrelevant to the aim of the 1913 act? I argue the contrary for four reasons. First, the basic structure of the 1913 tax is similar to the structure of the 1894 tax. Both measures carved out a generous exemption for amounts required for basic consumption. Both allowed deductions for taxes, interest, and operating expenses. Both treated the corporation as a taxable entity. These likenesses point to a *similarity of purpose.* They suggest that the ideas that inspired the structuring of the 1894 tax parallel the ideas that inspired the structuring of the 1913 tax, implying a similar motive. Second, the socioinstitutional circumstances surrounding enactment of the 1913 tax are comparable to the ones surrounding enactment of the 1894 tax. Specifically, both were enacted in the throes of U.S. industrialization; the emergence of the corporation as the nation's principal mode of business association; the rise of the mercantile, industrial, and financial classes; and the inability of the preexisting tax regime to reach income derived from intangibles. These likenesses point to a *comparability of purpose.* They suggest that the historical context that gave rise to enactment of the 1894 tax is analogous to that which gave rise to enactment of the 1913 tax, implying that the two measures may have been inspired by similar contextual considerations. Third, protax arguments advanced in the Sixty-third Congress essentially echo the arguments advanced in the Fifty-third Congress.[3] In the aftermath of *Pollock*, the latter arguments were taken up by subsequent Congresses—by the same political parties that propounded them in 1894 and by many of the same legislators. These parallels point to a *continuity of purpose*. They suggest that what philosophically compelled the tax at the time of its inception remained prevalent up to the time of its institutionalization. (Significantly, because the Fifty-third Congress more fully articulated these arguments, this book focuses on the debates of the latter legislative body.) Finally, the principal author of the 1913 legislation (a protégé of the chief author of the 1894 legislation) borrowed provisions from the 1894 act without substantial modification; the Sixty-third Congress adopted these provisions without significant debate.[4] These omissions point to a *ratification of purpose*. They suggest that both this author and this Congress implicitly endorsed the intent of the Fifty-third Congress in enacting these provisions, and furthermore that both accepted the underlying rationale for the 1894 tax. Thus, by logical inference, if not by direct observation, one can reasonably conclude that the intent behind the 1894 tax *is* relevant to a study of the 1913 act; furthermore, because the 1913 act supplies the core structure of our present tax code, the intent behind the 1894 tax also is relevant to a study of our current tax system.

In the social history of the income tax, the dominant scholarly tradition is progressive.[5] This tradition is predicated upon a peculiar conception of society, state, law, and history. For progressives, society is divided primarily into classes. These classes have conflicting economic interests and vie for political power to realize these interests.[6] Class divisions generally crystallize in times of economic crisis. They translate into sectional and partisan alignments over issues of allocative significance. Class conflict typically is seen as an endless political struggle. The ultimate aim of this struggle is control of the state.[7]

Thus, in the progressive literature, the agrarian and working classes compete for political power with the mercantile and industrial classes.[8] The former are grouped as populist Democrats, principally from the South and West. The latter are aligned as conservative Republicans, primarily from the industrial East. The populists put forth a reformist agenda, typified by the progressive income tax. The conservatives defend the status quo, symbolized by the protective tariff. These measures are important because they ultimately determine the allocation of society's wealth. The income tax redistributes it in favor of agriculture and labor. The protective tariff preserves it in the interests of trade and industry.

Progressives often depict social classes as political forces, moving toward the realization (or subversion) of some abstract ideal. Thus, they portray the agrarian and working classes as "popular forces," moving toward the realization of democracy. They portray the mercantile and industrial classes as "the moneyed interests," defending the interests of capitalism. In a passage from *Taxation and Democracy* illustrative of this approach, progressive historian Sidney Ratner writes:

> The farmers and workers upon whose shoulders the business groups attempted to place the tax load resisted, as best they could, the repudiation of the program of economic and social equality with which they had been won to the support of the middle classes' revolution against the landed aristocracy. The republican form of government furnished at least the basis on which the agrarian and laboring classes could build their movements of the realization of democracy as they understood it. To counteract the supremacy of both the small and the big business groups, new tax instruments were forged which would rest most heavily on those with high incomes and large fortunes. The thrust for social justice and the counterthrust for private gain have marked the conjoined spiral movements of political democracy and the concentrated economic power of big business and high finance.[9]

For progressives, the state is an extension of society. It depends upon society for its existence. It is the "instrument" or "tool" of the dominant social groups.[10] Within the public sphere, class conflict is played out through partisan politics. It engulfs all branches of government and all institutional processes. In their capacity as legislators, judges, and public administrators, political elites promote the interests of the powerful. They serve more as passive agents of society than as active agents of the state. Continues Ratner:

> The historic struggle for control of the state by the middle classes in England, France, and America during the seventeenth and eighteenth centuries was inspired to some degree by their desire to secure a more equitable tax system, one in which they would not bear the major tax burden without receiving

> commensurate benefits. The governments which these middle classes succeeded in establishing were chiefly representative of business interests. The new ruling groups in turn attempted to obtain for themselves the maximum gain at the least cost from the services of the state they controlled.[11]

Thus, in the progressive scheme, the drive for the income tax involves a virulent struggle.[12] In this struggle, liberal Democrats propose legislation in the interests of the popular forces. Conservative Republicans erect a protective tariff in defense of the moneyed interests. Political battles ensue, characterized by uncanny alliances, intense lobbying, and heated debates. The Democrats ultimately prevail, marking the triumph of democracy over capitalism. T. S. Adams describes the classist character of U.S. tax politics in this manner:

> While taxation may not have started as a class struggle, and while the class element is modified in the United States by the operation of constitutional inhibitions, modern taxation or tax-making in its most characteristic aspect is a group contest in which powerful interests vigorously endeavor to rid themselves of present or proposed tax burdens. It is, first of all, a hard game in which he who trusts wholly to economics, reason, and justice, will in the end retire beaten and disillusioned. Class politics is the essence of taxation.[13]

Laws and institutions, in the progressive scheme, are at once reflective, instrumental, and allocative. They are reflective in the sense that they are molded by class interests. They are instrumental in that they ultimately serve these interests. They are allocative in that they redistribute national wealth from subordinate to dominant social groups. This latter effect has profound implications for the workings of democracy. Democracy requires the broad dispersion of national wealth. Laws and institutions either concentrate this wealth in the hands of a few or redistribute it among the many.[14] In the progressive estimation, the allocative impact of laws and institutions is particularly true of tax laws and institutions—for tax laws and institutions involve the compulsory appropriation of private wealth, hence the *direct* allocation of society's resources. "Some have sought to create and to use a tax system which would be an important instrument for concentrating wealth and income in their own hands and that of their class and section," explains Ratner.

> Others have striven for a society free of glaring inequalities and have tried to develop and control a revenue system which would counteract the centralization of economic power.
>
> The success or failure of these campaigns has been bound up with the fate of democracy. . . . A high concentration of economic power has tended to be associated with the political and social rule of a business oligarchy. Democracy in both its political and economic phases has been dependent upon a sufficient diffusion of wealth and income to enable most individuals within a society to maintain their sense of independence.[15]

History, for progressives, is a confluence of all these factors. It is struggle toward the realization of a democratic ideal.[16] It is steady advancement, occasional setback, and inevitable triumph over the forces of darkness and evil. In this struggle, competing social classes vie for control of the state. Through the agency of their political elites, they create laws and institutions that advance their specific interests. The driving force in this process, almost invariably, is the transformation of the economy. It not only determines the basic structure of society but also shapes the essential character of the political battles that ensue.[17] History, for progressives, is movement toward the realization of the virtuous idea. It is metamorphosis in the direction of human progress, social equality, and the emancipation of the individual from the shackles of tradition.

Thus, in the progressive worldview, the drive for the income tax is part of a broader social movement toward greater equality and democracy.[18] Propelling this movement forward is the industrialization of the United States. Marking its culmination are the Sixteenth Amendment, the Income Tax of 1913, and the emergence of the modern welfare state. Critical milestones along the way are the Income Tax of 1894, the Corporations Tax of 1909, and *Pollock v. Farmers' Loan & Trust Company.* The former signify the victory of the popular forces over the moneyed interests, the latter a temporary setback. At the end of their historic march, we are told, the popular forces succeed in installing an order of equality. Democracy, at last, is vindicated. The outcome is at once triumphant, enlightening, and liberating. Proclaim progressive historians Roy and Gladys Blakey:

> The abortive income tax of 1894 . . . was really the result of a great egalitarian movement generated by two prolonged post-war depressions of great

> severity. Although frustrated for nearly two more decades, the leaders of this democratic movement won in 1909 what later proved to be a decisive victory by forcing a conservative President and even more conservative congressional leaders to submit a Constitutional amendment to the states and, also, by forcing them to authorize an entering-wedge income tax under the guise of an excise tax on corporations. These two 1909 income tax measures were not originated by immediate and urgent fiscal pressures, rather they were results of a no longer postponable conflict between holders of opposing economic interests and political philosophies. The ratification of the amendment by three fourths of the states—contrary to the expectations of the conservative leaders—showed on which side the victory lay, and was followed promptly by the adoption of a general income tax which included the previous tax on corporations and much more besides.[19]

The merits of the progressive view are many. First, it is founded on a *unified* and *coherent* conception of reality. This conception presupposes the interrelationship of economy, society, state, and law. It avoids compartmentalizing phenomena into mutually exclusive spheres or disciplines that limit the scope of inquiry. Second, it is built on a *dynamic* and *ever changing* conception of fact. This conception depicts economic, social, and institutional development as an integrated historical process. It embodies the Hegelian idea of *phenomena as they unfold,* thus facilitating transformational analysis. Third, the progressive view embraces a vision of society based on relations of production, not metaphysical concepts. These relations are grounded in reality. They do not depend for their existence on epistemological categories superimposed by the historian. Fourth, the view incorporates a dynamic mechanism for change. This mechanism, the capitalist economy, it sees as a driving force in history. Finally, the progressive view recognizes the *social element* in institutional change. Thus, it avoids reifying laws and institutions and attributes their existence to social phenomena, not transcendental ideals.

The problems with this view, however, are numerous. First, carried to a logical extreme, it is overly deterministic. It attributes institutional development to impersonal forces over which the individual has no control. It leaves little room, if any, for human judgment, reason, and free will. To be sure, under vulgar variants of this view, the human thought process itself is a function of where one sits in the production process. Social classes, not individuals, shape the structure of laws and institutions. Economic forces, not heroic actors, determine the fate of mankind. Second, the view depicts government as passive, ineffective. In the progressive order of things, but for social classes government would not exist. It subsists solely for their purposes and precariously at their whim. It has no life of its own and no will to impact. This conception truly is difficult to reconcile with reality. In modern times, government has been an actor in the political arena. It has not only shaped the course of economic development—hence the structure of society—but also *regulated* the conduct of competing social groups. Third, and most important, the progressive conclusion is flatly wrong. Contrary to progressive assertions, the income tax has not led to greater democracy. Nor did it substantially change the basic pattern of national wealth distribution, particularly in its early days of operation. Nor, for that matter, has it served as the "great social equalizer" that progressives have made it out to be. These contradictions cast doubt on the entire progressive thesis. Indeed, one must ask, *Was the income tax meant to eliminate social disparities, or to preserve them under the guise of reform?*

A somewhat different view of income tax development is presented by pluralist John Witte. This view accepts the progressive premise that social forces instigate institutional reform. It, however, rejects the progressive supposition that society is fundamentally classist in character. In the pluralist order, society consists of diverse social groups, each with particularistic aims. These aims are advanced by political elites, who formulate public policy. Intermediating between these elites and the groups they represent are diverse, competing organizations. They facilitate the upward flow of information on political preferences and the downward flow of information on legislative process. This "social system," if you will, both thrives in an environment of political freedom and is conducive to representative government. Among its platitudes are the furtherance of broad-based participation in the legislative process, private access to public decision making, and government access to the opinions of private citizens.[20] In *The Politics and Development of the Federal Income Tax,* Witte illustrates how the system works:

> Major tax subsidies are often supported by powerful organizations: councils of mayors, governors, and state legislators protect the interest exclusion of state and local bonds (to the advantage of the very wealthy); a range of groups representing the elderly reject even the mildest suggestion that retire-

> ment benefits and Social Security be further taxed; and the Chamber of Commerce, the National Association of Manufacturers, and the Business Council variously promote higher depreciation allowances, investment credits, and other business provisions. Similarly, smaller-scale lobbying efforts representing much narrower groups are often successful in altering minor legislative provisions or IRS rulings.[21]

Complicating pluralist society is a multitude of "nonsystemic" factors. Groups that constitute this society may be economic or sectional in character. Intermediaries that espouse group interests may be ideological in orientation. Elites that advance organizational goals often promote their own personal agenda. All act in peculiar sociohistorical circumstances.

Thus, in the pluralist scheme, although Congress enacts the income tax, the Democratic and Populist Parties lead the drive for its enactment. They convey the demands of southern and western groups to the government and apprise these groups of the progress of legislation. Fueling these demands are the debilitating effects of tariff taxation compounded by a severe financial crisis.[22] Propelling these parties to act is an earnest desire to rectify these defects and at the same time solidify their base of support. Witte gives an example:

> The financial situation, combined with the Democratic Party's fear of losing ground to the Populists in the West and South, created a precarious tax position that led to the introduction of the income tax. At the same time that there was a need to increase revenue, there was also pressure to lower the extremely high rates of the McKinley tariff (1890), particularly on necessities. It was this combination of forces plus the decisive actions of a few men in the House and Senate that led to the passage of an income tax as an amendment to the tariff bill of 1894.[23]

The state, in the pluralist order, reflects a myriad of interests. As these interests crystallize in the form of law, the state grows more complex. It devotes more time, energy, and resources to administer this law. Within the public sphere, political elites take on the task of formulating public policy. In this their essential role, they are competent, accommodating, willing to compromise, and deferential to precedent. Almost instinctively, they prefer practical results to lofty ideals. They are inspired less by a grand vision of society than by hard-nosed notions of what is required and what is doable. They tend to distinguish themselves from one another through symbol and rhetoric. Thus, the conflict that seems to cloud their relations is more apparent than real. Behind the mask of discord is a broad consensus over particulars.[24] These particulars relate to "tax expenditures," that is, revenue concessions made by politicians to broad-based constituents and special-interest groups. In the words of Witte:

> Politicians move away from the unpleasant consequences of high tax levels and toward a distribution of benefits to their constituents. Rather than adhering to an abstract ideal of equality, they treat issues on a piecemeal basis, each within its own incremental orbit. Rather than instigating conflict-producing philosophical debates over economic distribution, they resolve differences through particularistic negotiations on narrow, distributive grounds. And rather than promoting some vision of a future state, they act pragmatically in terms of temporary needs and evils.[25]

Consistent with this view, Congress structures the income tax to accommodate the interests of these groups and constituents. It creates the spousal exemption to accommodate the interests of married persons. It exempts life insurance proceeds to accommodate the interests of insurance companies. It grants depletion allowances to accommodate the interests of the extractive industries. It allows a deduction for operating expenses to accommodate the interests of businesses in general. At the same time, Congress defers to longstanding precedent. It borrows provisions from earlier statutes to address group concerns. It looks to foreign laws and institutions for guidance. It weighs the degree to which its acts comport with the Constitution.[26]

> The final income tax provisions that emerged from conference and became law on October 3, 1913, were a blend of compromises and adjustments to accommodate legal precedents, political divisions, and the demands of several interest groups. The exemption for dependent children was dropped, but the marriage differential remained, as did the graduated rate structure that the radicals forced through the Senate. . . . A number of sources of income were excluded: interest on state and local bonds, salaries of all state and local employees, and the income of the president and federal judges were excluded out of deference to previous court rulings. . . ,and proceeds of life insurance policies were excluded to appease the life insurance lobby. A series of deductions were also allowed as "expenses" of doing business. . . .

> . . . The final legislation was borrowed from past experience and the experience of states and other countries, and it was carefully adapted to the political and constitutional restraints that had developed over time.[27]

As a result, pluralist laws and institutions are the embodiment of these interests. They are structural devices designed to influence behavior, subsidize industries, and benefit constituents. They are malleable instruments of public policy subject to political dickering, legislative tinkering, and administrative fine-tuning. Far from mirroring the interests of dominant social classes, they reflect the self-serving aims of broad segments of the population. Far from redistributing national wealth, they dole out benefits to special-interest groups. An essential feature of these instruments is their enormous complexity. In catering to client needs, they expand in scope, cost, and structure. In rectifying client abuses, they grow convoluted and unmanageable. An unintended result of this complexity is the striking inability of these devices to meet future needs, as well as their stubborn resistance to structural reform. In a sense, the system grows dysfunctional as elites transform it into a multifaceted tool of public policy. It strays away from its original purpose as it comes to serve a multiplicity of aims.[28] The pluralist prognosis is grim:

> Over the years, in trying to respond to the demands of diverse groups, to meet the political needs of decision makers, and—so very important—to correct, adjust, and fine-tune the system, the income tax as a fundamental and ostensibly equitable means of raising revenue has been slowly but continuously eroded. In the process, any possibility of using the tax system to redistribute income—now or, I believe, in the future—has been lost. What has emerged may be a versatile and flexible policy tool, but it is also a devastatingly complex tangle of diverse legislative provisions and administrative rules. These problems are interrelated.[29]

Thus, in the pluralist scheme, although the income tax starts out *redistributive,* it ends up *distributive*. Although it begins as class legislation, it evolves into a hodgepodge of policy-based measures. Although it is forged by populist idealists, it is undermined by pragmatic elites. Although it is inspired by egalitarian ideals, it is transformed by particularistic needs. Accompanying this transformation are two significant developments. First, as the tax becomes institutionalized, revenue legislation grows more piecemeal. Individual provisions take on a logic of their own, unrelated to any standard of redistributive justice. Second, as the tax expenditure system expands, so does congressional emphasis on revenue concessions. The focus of tax policy shifts from general welfare to specific benefit. Social equality takes a backseat to group wants and client needs.

> [T]ax bills began to resemble large jigsaw puzzles, the components of which rarely fit into a consistent pattern. This meant that individual provisions were determined piecemeal, determined more by their individual provisions than by reference to any standard of redistribution. . . .
>
> [A]s the tax expenditure system grew, the problem of redistribution, which was often raised in connection with rate changes, was displaced in importance by tax expenditure debates that were essentially distributive in nature. . . . As the use of the tax code for varying purposes expanded, redistribution simply took a back seat to distributive requirements based on need or incentive effects.[30]

History, in the pluralist view, is incremental change. It involves a multiplicity of actors and a wide spectrum of interests. It leads to marginal adjustments in existing institutional structures. In its course, social groups advance their self-serving aims. Initially, these aims are resisted by the opposition. Eventually, however, the resistance wears thin, giving rise to political concessions. As the concessions accumulate over time, complexity clogs the system. It grows dysfunctional, less redistributive, and incapable of overhaul. Within this broad trend of gradual reform are minor cycles of rapid advancement and sudden retreat. Peace and prosperity create a propitious climate for group concessions. Wars and economic crises provide fertile ground for progressive legislation. This legislation, almost by nature, is never radical, or upsetting, or unprecedented. Continuity is ensured as new laws are forged on the basis of the old. Stability is preserved as these laws are adapted to preexisting circumstances.[31] "Thus, at any point in time," Witte informs us,

> decisions on tax policy fulfill most of the conditions of the incremental model. They lead to primarily marginal variations in existing structures, with little time spent in consideration of radical proposals; they are remedial in nature, responding to general or particular needs or problems, either within the tax system or without; innovations are often based on or are direct copies of old proposals; and there appears to be an ongoing process of adjustment as

> new values and objectives are introduced or unforeseen consequences emerge. In all of these respects the structure of the tax code is well suited to the incremental process.[32]

Accordingly, the income tax emerges from a tedious process of group pressure and political capitulation. Bearing the banner of egalitarianism, rural groups from the South and West demand a progressive income tax. Their cause is taken up by populist and progressive congressmen, who propose concrete legislation. Eastern conservatives oppose this legislation because it disproportionately burdens their principal clients. They stonewall the measure in Congress and delay enactment for decades. Eventually, however, conservative opposition crumbles and the progressives succeed in levying a modest tax on a narrow base.[33] They carve out a broad exemption for their constituents. They borrow operative provisions from earlier statutes.

> [The income tax] was created in the best tradition of incremental politics. The process was torturously slow, including four major political tests involving all branches of the federal government, states, and localities. The final legislation was borrowed from past experience and the experience of states and other countries, and it was carefully adapted to the political and constitutional restraints that had developed over time. Through its varied provisions the law acknowledged particular circumstances of ability to pay as well as conditions and expenses affecting the creation of income. The final rates were a very modest expression of the Progressive ethic that had captured at least part of the nation.[34]

With time, however, the progressivity of the tax is eroded through new social pressures and additional legislative concessions. In the postwar years, special-interest groups emerge to seek special favors from their congressmen. The latter, eager to please them, enact a series of piecemeal measures that cater to their clients' needs. These measures create new exclusions, carve out minor exemptions, expand the list of deductions, and offer broader credits. The result, alas, is a multifaceted tax code, convoluted in character and incapable of reform.[35]

The merits of the pluralist view are as follows: First, like the progressive view, it links society with state. It explains institutional development in terms of group pressures and political responses. It interprets state action in terms of underlying social impulses. Second, it offers a cogent theory of democratic government. This theory emphasizes the functionality of political organization and the instrumentality of political elites. It recognizes the vitality of information flow for both policy formulation and mass education. Third, the view attaches a positive value to political freedom and popular representation. In so doing, it defines a normative standard by which the results of historical action can be measured. Finally, the view offers a compelling explanation of the evolution of democratic laws and institutions. It postulates, quite correctly, that this evolution stems from the realization of group wants and elite aspirations. Thus, it both demystifies historical process and humanizes institutional development.

The principal weaknesses of the view are the following: First, it pays scant attention to the element of power in society. As a result, it underplays a critical factor that frequently determines political outcome. No doubt, elected officials attach great weight to constituent demands. But they attach even greater weight to constituent demands backed by political force. The pluralist view gives the impression that all group demands are of equal force, hence of equal consideration. That they are not is implied by the unequal distribution of wealth and power in society. Second, the pluralist view neglects group *relations*. Specifically, it discounts the ability of some groups to impose their will on others. In the pluralist order of things, civil society consists of an amalgamation of diverse social elements. Far from dominating one another, these elements peacefully compete and coexist. This vision ignores the strategic position that some groups occupy in the economy. It ignores their commercial and financial dealings with one another. It ignores their eminent ability, by virtue of this position and these dealings, to mold public opinion, inculcate political values, define national priorities, and influence legislative outcome. Third, the pluralist view fails to address the issue of social transformation. Though providing a mechanism for institutional development, it omits a mechanism for social change. This omission raises several troubling questions. Does pluralist society change at all? If so, how and under what circumstances? Are institutional development and social change an integral historical process? Is the one dependent on the other? These gaps render the theory deficient in accounting for the timing and direction of institutional development. They leave one to surmise that such development occurs not in tandem with social transformation, nor as a result of such transformation, but rather in tandem with, and as a result of, the vagaries of group pressure and elite response. Finally, the pluralist view presupposes the existence of specialized industries and pressure groups that are more characteristic of an industrialized nation than of a developing country. Yet the income tax emerged precisely in the latter context. This anomaly leads one to conclude that pluralism is more suited for the analysis of *modern* institutional development than of *early* structural formation. In other words, it more adequately explains the emergence of the tax expenditure system than it does the origins of the modern income tax.

The progressive and pluralist views have recently come under attack by historian Robert Stanley. The principal grounds for attack are two. First, the views cannot explain the occurrence of events that under their premises should *not* have occurred. Second, they cannot account for the nonoccurrence of events that under their premises *should* have occurred. Stanley's specific allegations are the following: The progressive and pluralist views cannot explain why there was virtually no opposition to the income tax during the Civil War. They cannot explain why protectionists were unable to kill the tax during and after the war. They cannot explain why during the depression of 1878 southern congressmen voted to quash the tax. They cannot explain why the public pressed Congress only sporadically for an income tax. Finally, their ultimate conclusions are at odds with the actual distribution of wealth and opportunity in society. As for the Income Tax of 1894, Stanley contends that the limited scope of this levy cannot be reconciled with progressive claims regarding its intended result. Indeed, he queries, if the 1894 tax was intended as an allocative measure, why did it reach less than 1 percent of the population and account for only 2 percent of government revenues?[36]

This bill of objections in hand, Stanley presents his version of U.S. income tax development, founded on what he coins *centrism*. Centrism, for Stanley, characterizes the operation of the state and the ideology of lawmakers who compose it. It includes, first, an inertial commitment to "statist capitalism" and, second, a vision of courts and legislatures as the gatekeepers of allocative authority. The first attribute embodies the idea that the law is ultimately used to support privately held enterprise. The second portrays government as an intermediary between groups from whom resources are appropriated and groups to whom the resources are channeled. Centrism, says Stanley, is expressed through patterns of political organization, such as the party, and through institutional devices, such as the protective tariff. Its primary functions are to reconcile public lawmaking with private concerns, to unite diverse political elements in a common calling, and to mollify popular discontent with rhetoric.[37]

From these premises, Stanley proceeds to articulate his view of society, state, law, and history. He accepts the progressive division of society into classes, but divests these classes of political power. Real political power, for Stanley, resides with the state. Although social classes both react to and prompt political action, the state actually takes this action. Stanley radically inverts the relationship between state and society. For progressives and pluralists, society impacts the state, while *competing social groups* influence the course of *political* development. For Stanley, the state impacts society, while *consensual political elites* influence the course of *social* development. Likewise, Stanley redefines the body politic. For progressives, the body politic is defined by relations of production, that is, economic substructure. For Stanley, it is defined by laws and institutions, that is, political superstructure. Finally, Stanley accepts the progressive premise that economic development dramatically transforms society. But he rejects the progressive conclusion that this transformation somehow changes the nature of the state.[38]

Thus, in the centrist scheme, industrialization gives rise to new social classes—but these classes have little impact upon the course of institutional development. Social groups vie for political power—but they never actually succeed in controlling the state. Popular forces seek to redistribute society's wealth—but they end up with laws and institutions that in actuality are only token. Political parties aspire to shape the nation's destiny—but they stand at the mercy of statist elites who determine what political concessions, if any, are to be granted. Thus, writes Stanley in *Dimensions of Law in the Service of Order,* "[F]rom society . . . there was little direct pressure to establish income taxation; only intellectuals offered sporadic assessment of its value in non-crisis periods. In terms of the timing, form, and conflict over the issue, it was society, not the state, that reacted to pressure, and the state, not society, which shaped the issue and its environment."[39]

At the heart of the centrist order is the state. It is not an extension of society, but rather a separate and autonomous unit. It is not controlled by forces external to it, but rather controls them. It is not a passive instrument of the dominant social groups, but rather an active player. It, not society, determines political outcome. Within this order, class conflict is manifest not from within the state but rather from without. Its ultimate impact is to prompt state action and thus increase state power relative to competing social classes. In the public domain, political elites tend to identify more with one another than with their respective constituents. This orientation produces four significant consequences for historical action. First, these elites develop political interests separate and distinct from the concerns of the "masses." Second, they become the "trustees" of the dominant social groups, not merely their "agents." Third, their relations among one another become less conflicting and more consensual. Finally, their roles are transformed from "political representatives" to "social managers." Although political elites attach significance to the aims of their constituents, they attach even greater significance to their own aims. What are these aims? To ensure political stability, to promote statist capitalism, and, ultimately, to advance the interests of the dominant social groups.[40]

Accordingly, in the centrist scheme, the state, not society, institutes the income tax. It does so not to redistribute society's wealth, but rather to palliate discontents with rhetoric so as to preserve the existing status quo. Populist Democrats and conservative Republicans join forces to enact the requisite legislation. They see it as a means to diffuse class tensions, achieve political stability, and enhance their own personal power to boot.[41] Stanley illustrates:

> [T]he key to the power of the state on this question was that it acted as trustee, rather than agent, for the powerful in society. From John Sherman to Benton McMillin, from William Howard Taft to Woodrow Wilson, the tax was above all *useful.* It provided ideological insurance against the rampant disparities that split society. Before the era of entitlements, it was the only direct way to address the class gap. It could be used to protect the wealthy against the short-sighted greed that McMillin warned would otherwise result in grassroots "violence" that "threatens the very foundations upon which our whole institutions rest."[42]

Elsewhere, Stanley states: "Congress had debated the income tax during the Civil War, during the depressions of the 1870s and 1890s, and would do so again briefly in the battles over the finance of the Spanish-American War, and extensively in the wake of the Panic of 1907. On each occasion, contrary to progressive implications, the issue was congressionally created and not in response to any ascertainable 'public' pressure or opinion about the measure."[43]

Laws and institutions, in the centrist view, are rhetorical, deflective, and symbolic. They are rhetorical in the sense that they diffuse class tensions with hollow words. These words have little or no bearing on the actual distribution of wealth and opportunity in society. They are deflective in the sense that they deflect public opinion from the narrow interests served by the state. If anything, they reflect *not* the will of the people, but rather the will of statist elites. They are symbolic in the sense that they represent the voice, the ideology, the language of the state. This language permeates political culture. It shapes public perceptions, beliefs, behavior. As well, centrist laws and institutions serve important integrating, stabilizing, and legitimating functions. They unify a fragmented society in a common political vision. They stabilize the uncertain course of institutional development. They add an aura of legitimacy to statist authority.[44]

Thus, in the centrist scheme, statist elites hoist the banner of income taxation upon the mast of society not to democratize it, but rather to forestall popular dissent against the "course of centrism." They keep the allocative content of the tax negligible, all the while maximizing its rhetorical impact. Their ostensible aim is to lead political discontents to believe that the "system" is essentially fair. Elites find solace in income tax legislation because it addresses class anxieties with symbols that differentiate on the basis of wealth. By instituting the tax, they at once avert more drastic redistributive measures, increase their own political clout, and unite diverse elements in a myth of equality so as to preserve an order of inequality.[45] Hence, we are advised at the onset:

> This analysis seeks to explain the apparent contradiction between the reformist promise of income taxation and its fitful history by demonstrating that it is the vision of law in society held by the dominant tradition which has led to our perception that a contradiction exists at all. Proceeding from changed assumptions about the nature of society, the state, law, and history, the analysis contends that there was no contradiction. It reveals that income taxation was not created as a vehicle for the authentic expansion of wealth and opportunity through a redirection of the continuous flow of legally channeled largesse. Rather as a product of the center's efforts to protect itself against dissent, income taxation served as an important element in the maintenance of the traditional order.[46]

History, in the centrist worldview, is not movement, but rather inertia. It is *not* progress toward the realization of the virtuous idea, but rather "transformation without a particular destination." It is *not* social democracy in the making, but rather statist capitalism in the course of its consolidation. Peculiarly, the driving force in this "journey to nowhere" is not the economy, but rather the state. In rationalizing its allocative function, it augments its political power. In broadening its decision-making authority, it expands its administrative autonomy. Granted, economic transformation plays a role in this process, but only indirectly. By threatening social upheaval, it prompts state action. By strengthening the hand of the "trustees," it entrenches the position of the "beneficiaries." Centrist history, in sum, is enhancement of the center at the expense of the periphery. It is social transformation without institutional result; alternatively, it is institutional transformation without social result.[47]

Accordingly, in the centrist scheme, the drive for the income tax leads *not* to greater equality, but rather to perpetual inequality. It leads *not* to flourishing democracy, but rather to the reinforcement of government control. It leads *not* to broader freedom, but rather to continued state domination. It leads *not* to social justice, but rather to a *spectacle* of justice. In its path, the Sixteenth Amendment, the Income Tax of 1913, and its institutional predecessors are not monumental reforms, but rather *symbols* of reform. They are rhetorical devices installed by statist elites to contain social discontent, distract a gullible populace, and stifle human progress.[48] They are emblems of what society aspires to be, not what it actually is. Centrist history, in sum, is institutional stability *in spite of* social transformation. It is neither triumphant nor defeating, neither enlightening nor perplexing, neither emancipating nor enslaving. It is static.

> [H]istory is transformation without a particular destination, such as "toward democracy." . . . The analysis thus specifically posits at the outset that the history of income taxation may not indicate democratization in the process of modernization, and therefore can ask, for example, whether the Sixteenth Amendment may have signified not a successful challenge to a less democratic polity, but instead a rejection of fundamental institutional change. . . . The analysis assumes that the history of the organization of wealth and opportunity in the United States is largely characterized by inertia and by structures which tend to perpetuate inertia. Each day that a legislator votes on a measure, each time that a judge renders an opinion, powerful secular conditions constrain the potential outcomes.[49]

The merits of the centrist view are the following: First, it portrays government as an actor in the political arena. This portrayal generally comports with historical reality, for in modern times, government has played an important role in directing the course of economic, social, and political development. Second, the view aptly recognizes that political elites may have their own peculiar objectives, and that these objectives may differ from their constituents'. This distinction makes possible divergent courses of action. For example, while social groups may pursue purely *economic* aims, their representatives may pursue purely *political* aims. Third, the centrist view treats laws and institutions as multidimensional. It acknowledges their legitimating, integrating, and stabilizing functions, thus facilitating sociological analysis. Fourth, the view stresses the element of consensus in government. It suggests, quite correctly, that without such consensus, there would be no government. Last, the centrist view finds support in phenomena that the progressive view simply cannot explain—specifically, that the income tax did not radically redistribute society's wealth, nor did it substantially alter the basic pattern of national wealth distribution. These theoretical strengths add weight to Stanley's central thesis: *that the purpose of the income tax was not to promote meaningful reform, but rather to thwart it.*[50]

Unfortunately, however, the thesis fails for other reasons, the most important of which relate to logical flaws in the centrist vision. First, centrism is founded on a disjointed conception of reality. It presupposes the disunity of state and society—a "divorce," not a "marriage." The state, in the centrist order, stands apart from society and is alien to it. It is an entity unto itself, separate and distinct from the individuals who constitute it. Curiously, once these individuals ascend to public office, they suddenly lose their social identity and abandon their political values. They are free to renege on past promises, because they can deflect public opinion with rhetoric. They fear not social ostracism, because they exist in the ne'erland of government autonomy. Is this really the case? Is government that autonomous? Are public officials that unaccountable? Is the public that naive? The centrist view overlooks the multifarious mechanisms by which members of a democratic society rein in their elected officials. It ignores the element of accountability inherent in public office. Second, the centrist view is built on a conception of the state that is unduly static. In the centrist order of things, the state hovers aimlessly over a turbulent sea of change. It is undisturbed by social transformation, because it effectively manages it. It is uninfected with the virus of change, because it conveniently administers the vaccine. How the state can be so immune in such a contagious environment remains somewhat of a mystery. If social groups are so politicized, how can their representatives be so detached? If society is so dynamic, how can the state be so inert? Third, the centrist view attempts to explain institutional development in terms of a single overriding objective or outcome. In so doing, it underplays the role of diversity, conflict, and compromise in the political process. That government elites pursue a multiplicity of aims is evident to the casual observer. That some of these aims conflict with the goals of other actors is intuitive. Therefore, one is compelled to ask, how can these elites achieve tangible results without surrendering some aims while holding firm to other aims? Indeed, how can government function without compromise? And given this compromise, how can one objective prevail over all others? The centrist view misplaces the element of consensus in U.S. politics. It erroneously presumes that government elites are in consensus over political *ends,* when in fact they are in consensus over political *means.* Furthermore, the view erroneously concludes that the outcome (*laws and institutions)* is consensual, when in fact the process (*legislation* and *adjudication)* is. Fourth, the centrist vision confounds effect with intent. It proceeds upon the faulty premise that what resulted is what was intended. Expressed differently, it mistakenly deduces subjective design from objective outcome. That the income tax had little or no effect on the basic pattern of national wealth distribution does not necessarily mean that its sponsors actually *intended* this result. Indeed, they may have intended something else, but for political reasons (realpolitik) were unable to achieve their subjective aims. Finally, and in light of the foregoing, the centrist view casts doubt on the meaning conveyed by the words and deeds of historical actors. It dismisses these words and deeds as mere rhetoric. It denies their authenticity, that is, that they unequivocally express the actors' true intent. The view then imputes an intent consistent with its own transcendental ideal. This imputation, unfortunately, salvages the theory at the expense of the actors' credibility. And all along, the centrist view treats the meaning ascribed by the historian to the actors' words and deeds as more authoritative than the meaning ascribed by the actors themselves. In effect, it substitutes the judgment of the former for the judgment of the latter and elevates teleological interpretation over subjectively valid facts.

More recent theories of income tax development tend to revive the progressive view—or at least important aspects of it. One such theory, articulated by W. Elliot Brownlee, is "democratic institutionalism." Democratic institutionalism emphasizes the critical role played by social forces in the development of the modern income tax.[51] It is founded on a conception of order similar to the progressive view's. However, it differs from the progressive view in two key respects. First, in accounting for political action, it attaches paramount importance to ideas. Second, in explaining institutional development, it stresses the instrumentality of crisis and contingency.

In the democratic institutional scheme, although society is *structured* along class lines, it is *organized* along ideological lines. To be sure, ideas transcend social structure and order society politically. They unite diverse social classes in a common undertaking. Propounding, if not manipulating, these ideas are the major political parties.[52] They invoke principles of public policy to rally voters to their side and thus align (or realign) themselves along class or sectional lines. Tax politics is rife with struggle and conflict. This conflict, however, is more ideological than classist in character.[53] In the words of Brownlee:

> In its "democratic" dimension, this approach recognizes the power of democratic forces outside the federal government. These were forces that contributed, for example, to the progressively distributional cast of the twentieth-century tax regimes. At the same time, the interpretation stresses the potency of ideas as independent creative forces. Thus concepts of progressive equity, often expressed as the criterion of the "ability to pay" taxes, shaped and gave intention to democratic pressures. In recognizing the power of democratic forces and ideas of equity, this approach has much in common with older progressive histories.[54]

Thus, in the democratic institutional scheme, nineteenth-century political parties invoked philosophical principles to broaden or solidify their base of support.[55] The Democrats, following the lead of the Populists, endorsed "ability to pay" to strengthen their appeal among southerners and westerners. Republicans advocated protectionism to enhance their standing among northerners and easterners. Base broadening enabled these parties to align or realign themselves along new or existing social lines. It allowed the Republicans to align themselves along capitalist lines. It allowed the Democrats to realign themselves along agrarian and working-class lines. Brownlee offers this illustration of the critical role of ideas in tax politics:

> In fact, during the 1880s and 1890s, the two competing political parties came to base their economic appeals on sharply conflicting ideological views of the tariff and of taxation in general. . . . The Republicans' invocation of high tariffs and the Democrats' response had sharply polarized the parties on issues of taxation. These tax issues would exacerbate class conflict for nearly a century. . . .
>
> Central to the appeal of a highly progressive income tax during the 1890s was the claim that the tax would both reallocate fiscal burdens according to "ability to pay" and help restore a virtuous republic free of concentrations of economic power. The rhetoric was, in a sense, conservative; it directed attention to the values of the early republic.[56]

At the center of the democratic institutional order is the state. It draws on ideas to formulate public policy. It exploits national crises to advance institutional reforms. It implements these reforms as a matter of contingency, not some millennial drive to realize a virtuous idea. Within the state, political elites are artful, persuasive, and opportunistic. They are artful in the sense that they meticulously craft government policy. They are persuasive in that they implement this policy by convincing the public to accept personal sacrifice.[57] They are opportunistic in that in doing all of the foregoing, they constantly seek out opportunities to enhance their political power.[58] Their actions have the effect of strengthening the hand of government and centralizing state authority. They expand the federal taxing apparatus at the expense of local institutions. They augment tax administration at the expense of civil society. "Within the economic and social turbulence of each crisis," Brownlee tells us,

> the political leaders in the executive and legislative branches of government struggled to establish coherent tax policies. On the whole, crisis conditions strengthened the power of these leaders, and the tax systems they implemented further enhanced their influence. . . .
>
> Within the conflicted politics of each of the emergencies, the leaders of the federal government worked to persuade Americans to accept new taxes. During wartime, the architects of national mobilization made taxation part of larger strategies of persuading Americans to accept sacrifice. In the Civil War and each of the two world wars, they crafted new tax programs designed both to implement sacrifice and to convince the mass of taxpayers that their sacrifices were fair.[59]

Accordingly, populist Democrats and progressive Republicans institute an income tax to solidify their popular support and augment their political clout. They design the tax to appeal to southerners and westerners. They seize the moment of crisis to enact the requisite legislation. They coax Americans to accept this legislation as a necessary, but fair, expedient. These moves have the effect of transferring fiscal authority from state governments to the federal government. As the federal tax base expands, the scope and power of the federal government likewise expand. As the local tax base contracts, the scope and power of local governments likewise contract.

> Each new tax regime drew political strength from the fact that it not only increased the size of the federal government but also increased the centralization of government. . . . To some extent, the expansion of federal taxing undercut the tax base of state government. But the federal government offset this and won state and local support for its tax regimes by assuming part of the burden of financing public services from states and localities after the crisis, and by finding ways to expedite the levying and collecting of state and local taxes.[60]

Laws and institutions, in the democratic institutional scheme, are largely symbolic. They express the goals and priorities of the federal government. They reflect the ideals and aspirations of a democratic society. They embody the values and virtues of the day. These laws and institutions are stratified in character. Each has a design and purpose peculiar to a historical epoch. Subsequent modifications not only leave this design intact and preserve this purpose, but also add to them. The additions have a design and purpose of their own. Democratic laws and institutions acquire a legitimacy and cultural force that survive long after the circumstances that gave rise to their formation have changed.[61] Their development necessarily leads to their entrenchment. Once established, they are difficult, if not impossible, to dismantle. Explains Brownlee: "[T]he tax regime imposed in each emergency changed economic, political, and intellectual conditions in ways that made it difficult or even impossible for the federal government to return to the tax regime in force before the emergency. Consequently, today's tax system has a stratified quality. Each layer of tax institutions, almost like a layer of the earth's crust, represents the legacy of an earlier epoch, or fiscal regime."[62]

Consistent with this view, the income tax symbolizes "democratic statism"—the use of government power to create a more democratic social order. The tariff represents economic protectionism—a commitment to a strong national market and to capitalists and workers within this market. Both acquire a force and legitimacy that extend well beyond their original enactment. With time, Congress modifies the tax, first to steepen its progressivity, then to carve out exceptions for special-interest groups.[63] The modifications evince a purpose and logic of their own. They, however, preserve the purpose and logic of preexisting provisions. In the words of Brownlee:

> The survival of each emergency-born tax system in the postcrisis era lent the nation's tax system an increasingly layered, or diversified, quality. Each new regime preserved important elements of its predecessor—elements that had survived earlier postcrisis political tests. Thus, the World War II system contained not only the features that lent it distinction but also features that it inherited from the Civil War, World War I, and Great Depression regimes.[64]

History, in the democratic institutional vision, is "path dependent." It is steered by the steady course of institutional development. It is compelled by the changed economic, political, and intellectual circumstances brought about by the establishment of new laws and institutions. It is guided by the direction of previous change. Historical action, in this view, is contextually restricted. It is limited by the structures shaped by economic transformation. It is constrained by constitutional rules, administrative capacities, and technological capabilities. It is inspired by organizational options and institutional possibilities. Catalyzing the movement of history are national emergencies. They influence the manner in which ideas, democratic forces, and policy experts interact to forge new laws and institutions. They give elites an opportunity to implement radical reform and at the same time augment their political power.[65] History, in the democratic institutional model, is spurred by contingency, not incessant drive. It is turbulent, conflict ridden, institutionally saddled, and, above all, uncertain. Hence, we are told, "[I]deas configure fiscal policy in a highly contingent fashion. In other words, the intentionality that has given tax policy its shape has done so in the context of historical contingency and, more specifically, great national emergencies. . . . [B]ecause new fiscal regimes materialized through contingent chains of events—chains embedded in significant national emergencies—the prediction of the components of new regimes lies well beyond the reach of behavioral models."[66]

Accordingly, the income tax is born in the economic depression of 1893. The crisis stimulates national debate over political values and fiscal policy. It accentuates ideological divisions over the tariff and taxation in general. It gives western Populists a historic opportunity to advance their reformist agenda. Fearful of this advance, congressional Democrats seize the moment of crisis to introduce income tax legislation. They see the tax as a means of appealing to farmers and workers and thus broadening their base of support in the West and South. They see it as a symbol of social equality, the very embodiment of their goals and aspirations. Nor could they have acted in more propitious circumstances. By the 1890s, industrialization had created the social and political infrastructure necessary for the institutional expression of democratic ideals. It had created the administrative underpinnings of a fiscal regime designed to redistribute the tax burden according to ability to pay.[67] The Democrats ultimately succeed in their endeavor thanks to the skill and ingenuity of their party leaders. They create a tax system imbued with egalitarian ideals that shapes the course of U.S. institutional development in the years to come.

The merits of the democratic institutional view are several. First, it correctly posits that social transformation alone cannot account for the design and implementation of laws and institutions. It accurately depicts ideas as building blocks in institutional construction. Second, it addresses the critical issue of *timing.* It argues, quite convincingly, that sweeping institutional change occurs *when precipitated by crisis,* and furthermore that political elites implement radical reform *when confronted with a national emergency.* Third, the view cogently explains the growth of representative government. It attributes such growth to human thought and behavior, thus demystifying the process by which public laws and institutions are established. Fourth, the view places political action in broad historical context. It confers upon the words and deeds of historical actors a contextual meaning, which reinforces a textual one. Fifth, the view acknowledges the critical role played by economic transformation in the development of laws and institutions. Yet it is not so deterministic as to attribute this development *solely* to such change. Finally—and perhaps as an aside—the democratic institutional view presents a sound and useful theory of statutory construction. It proposes, quite compellingly, that each modification, each addition, each "stratified layer" of the law must be examined separately to ascertain its peculiar meaning. By implication, frequently amended statutes may have a multiplicity of meanings, each specific to a different historical epoch.

The principal weaknesses of this view are three. First, notwithstanding its adequacy in explaining the timing of institutional development, it often gives the impression that the force of ideas is independent of the actors who espouse them. This result leads one to ask: Are the actors creating the ideas, or are the ideas creating the actors? If the latter, then democratic institutionalism takes on a transcendental quality seemingly at odds with its materialistic roots. If the former, then the view misattributes power and creativity to object, not subject. The problem, of course, can be resolved with the presumption that the allusion to the independence of ideas is more metaphorical than real. Yet the presumption is troublesome because the metaphor is inapt. It goes against the democratic institutional grain that *individuals* act in contingencies to realize reformist ideas. Second, the democratic institutional view depicts ideas as a tool, not the inspiration, of political elites. By implication, it casts doubt on the sincerity of their conviction; it creates government by ruse and manipulation—seemingly at odds with its democratic theme. More important, it raises these perplexing questions: If elites conveniently mobilize ideas to broaden their popular base or reconfigure their political alliances, why are their ideological battles so intense and uncompromising? Indeed, just as these elites would have no qualms about invoking ideas to broaden their base of support, so too would they have no qualms about abandoning these ideas to force a realignment? Third, in emphasizing the roles of ideas, elites, and contingency in the creation of laws and institutions, democratic institutionalism underplays the roles of interest, class, and society in their solidification. Expressed differently, by focusing on the circumstantial variables that give rise to laws and institutions, the view ignores the structural factors that give them longevity. Democratic institutionalism pays scant attention to the *social basis* of U.S. laws and institutions. Yet without this basis, arguably, these laws and institutions would be transitory in character—fleeting images, just as contingent as the critical acts that contribute to their formation. What gives these laws and institutions their stability and vitality? What sustains them over the long haul—the power of ideas alone? the persuasiveness of elites alone? social acquiescence in government action? Democratic institutionalism intimates that the answer lies in the path-driven course of history. Yet it fails to explain what underlies this path. It fails to explain why society chooses to follow it.

The foregoing criticisms in mind, I propose an alternative view of U.S. income tax development (hereinafter referred to as the "socioinstitutional view"). This view is at once institutional, sociohistorical, Weberian, and materialistic in nature. It is institutional in the sense that it regards the income tax as an *institution,* not merely an amalgamation of precepts. The contours of this institution determine the manner in which private wealth is appropriated to meet the exigencies of government. It is sociohistorical in the sense that it explains the development of this institution *historically* in terms of the *social forces* that emerged in the course of U.S. industrialization. These forces not only shaped the structure of the modern income tax, but also imbued it with a purpose. It is Weberian in the sense that it relies on the *subjective orientations of historical actors* to convey meaning.[68] This subjective meaning generally reinforces a contextual meaning inferable from the social and political circumstances surrounding the enactment of the tax. Finally, the view is materialistic in the sense that it explains contextual change in terms of a *social dialectic.* Propelling this dialectic forward is the transformation of the U.S. economy.

In articulating the socioinstitutional view—and without necessarily endorsing the progressive perspective—I shall address several controversial claims regarding the nature and course of U.S. income tax development. Specifically, I shall argue the following: First, that this development evinces no single overriding purpose, but rather a multitude of purposes, some political, some social, some economic, some personal. Second, that seen in light of the institution that preceded it, the income tax was allocative in terms of tax incidence—if not at the onset, then over the course of decades. Third, that what mattered most to income tax opponents was not its *actual* but rather its *potential* allocative effects. Fourth, that pressure to institute the tax came primarily from society, not government. Fifth, that the public clamored for an income tax only sporadically because tariff taxation *unbearably* burdened the public only sporadically. Sixth, that the Civil War schemes should be viewed in terms of their own sociohistorical context and no other. Seventh, that the early income tax did not change the basic pattern of national wealth distribution because it never was intended to do so. And finally, that the original aim of the income tax was to redistribute not *social wealth,* but rather the *tax burden.*

1

A Nation in Transition

No one can entertain a reasonable doubt that there has been an accumulation of wealth in a few individual hands in the United States during the last twenty-five years vastly in excess of any which has taken place in other parts of the world. In no other country have railroad managers, manufacturers, oil refiners, mine owners, bankers, and land speculators accumulated fortunes so rapidly as they have in this. In no other country . . . has the burden of taxation been cast so exclusively upon the working class or the machinery of public taxation been used so unscrupulously for private profit.

—Economist Thomas G. Shearman,
September 1889

The thirty years following the Civil War saw a dramatic transformation of the U.S. economy.[1] Agriculture grew more mechanized and commercialized. Industry grew more capital intensive. U.S. manufactories proliferated in the burgeoning cities of Pittsburgh, Cleveland, and Chicago.[2] Trade was given impetus by the inexorable drive of the railroads toward the natural resources of the West. Fueling this metamorphosis were the great financial centers of New York, Boston, and Philadelphia, as lending activity grew national in scope. Eastern bankers capitalized on lucrative opportunities in the oil fields of Pennsylvania, the wheat farms of Kansas, and the silver mines of Nevada. Agriculture, industry, and commerce grew increasingly dependent on eastern capital.

As the economy expanded, so did the supply of credit.[3] Bankers tapped their ever increasing deposit base to finance the construction of railroads, factories, and steel mills. They provided generous lines of discount to the captains of industry. Manufacturers utilized these lines to augment their stock of inventory, finance trade receivables, and pay wages to workers. They extended liberal credit terms to jobbers, who offered them to retailers, who in turn passed them on to consumers.[4] In the rural heartland, middlemen advanced cash to farmers to purchase fodder, fuel, and seeds. They typically secured these advances with a lien on the season's crop. Bankers lent money for the erection of barns and the acquisition of machinery.[5] They normally took in return a mortgage on farmland and buildings.[6] Commented one observer in 1894:

> Nearly all business had been done on credit. . . . The factories . . . sold goods to every firm and person of whom orders could be secured, and almost without exception, on time. Full credit at the bank had been used by the factories and large obligations had been assumed in the purchase of material and machinery. Jobbers had stocked to the extent of their credit and means and had sold goods to retail dealers on very liberal terms. Many retail dealers had trusted out the bulk of their stock, and, with many, the greater part of their capital was on their books, by credit being extended to their customers.[7]

With the transformation of the economy came the metamorphosis of U.S. business. Nearly every state in the Union had enacted corporation laws.[8] These laws imbued the corporation with limited liability and continuity of life. Industrialists used the corporate enterprise to accumulate capital and hold assets. Tradesmen used it as a means to pool labor, skills, and tools. By the mid-1890s, the corporation had supplanted the partnership as the nation's principal form of business association.[9] Most of the big banks and railroad companies had been organized along corporate lines. So had many of the trading, manufacturing, and processing firms that were sprouting up all over the country. "In my State it is the almost universal practice, and it is a practice which has grown up in England under what they call corporations or associations of limited liability, to go into a joint stock company," remarked a Massachusetts official in June 1894.

> Two or three youngsters just out of their apprenticeship go into partnership together and do some little portion of the work of a machine shop. . . . And so it is in business of all sorts and kinds, partly, I suppose, because it involves legal safeguards, but the chief reason is that when one of the partners dies or goes out of the company for any reason, the survivors in the corporation do not have to liquidate the concern, and wait a year or two and go through a process of law before they can go on with the business.[10]

With the rise of the corporation came the proliferation of stocks, bonds, and annuities.[11] Railroads issued debentures to finance their expansionary drive toward the Pacific. Bankers issued stock to raise capital for loans to the heartland. On Wall Street, trading activity flourished, as a financial market emerged. On Main Street, personal fortunes swelled, as the stock market surged. The infusion of bank capital into the corporate enterprise consummated the marriage of industry and finance. Fortifying this relationship was the interlocking directorate. Railroad, manufacturing, and mining companies appointed bank officials to their boards of directors. Banking corporations appointed railroad, manufacturing, and mining officials to theirs.[12] Collusion and price-fixing were rampant, as were other forms of business abuse. The unscrupulous hid behind the corporate veil. The unprincipled shrouded themselves in the cloak of bankruptcy. The official continued:

> [T]he power of incorporation has created great hardship and in many cases has been accessory to great wrong. Men go in and make up a corporation in order to escape individual liability. Under the laws of my State they can create a corporation, and if there should be a judgment for damages against it, if it should become bankrupt, so long as the stock has been fully paid up the stockholders are not individually liable. In many instances this fact is made avail of by persons in order to escape the individual liability which would otherwise be put on them.[13]

The transformation of society moved in tandem with the transformation of the economy. In the cities emerged a new generation of merchants, bankers, and industrialists, whose prosperity drew the envy of the rest of the nation. In urban areas also emerged an army of workers, whose efforts galvanized the motion of the steel mills, the coal mines, and the textile factories.[14] The ranks of independent artisans dwindled, as the corporation came to dominate the commercial and industrial landscape. Those craftsmen with a modicum of savings formed joint stock companies. Artisans without either resorted to lucrative trades or else sold their labor to the capitalist. In the rural heartland, farmers saw their fortunes decline, as mechanization led to enhanced productivity, falling commodity prices, and shrinking land values.[15] The more affluent managed to consolidate their holdings with the aid of the moneylender. The less fortunate, saddled with debt, either moved to the towns or became the tenants of others.[16] Commented one observer: "The middle classes of society, consisting of farmers, mechanics, and small tradesmen, are rapidly disappearing. Under the present order of things the end will not come until the American farmer is on a level with the Irish tenant, and mechanics and tradesmen are made the servants of the rich."[17]

For the privileged few, the postbellum period was a time of rising fortunes and consolidating power.[18] It was the age of the capitalist: the great oil baron John Rockefeller, the invincible steel magnate Andrew Carnegie, the railroad kings Jay Gould and Cornelius Vanderbilt, the retail giants Marshall Field and John Wannamaker, the legendary financiers Anthony Drexel and J. P. Morgan. It was the age of the big corporation: the Standard Oil Company, the Pennsylvania Railroad Company, the Bethlehem Steel Corporation, the First National Bank of Chicago. It was the age of monopoly and cartel: the oil trust, the iron trust, the sugar trust, more than 160 trusts in all. It was the age of the Cuban cigar, stretch suspenders, pinstriped suits, and the financial prowess of Wall Street.

For millions of Americans, it was also an age of hardship and privation. Confronted with a secular decline in commodity prices, farmers struggled to make ends meet. Overwhelmed by the rising tide of capital, artisans faced the dismal prospect of proletarianization. Though relatively better off than the artisan, the worker found himself precariously at the whim of the manufacturer. Labor turned to Samuel Gompers, as strikes, walkouts, and boycotts became a menace to the existing social order. Farmers looked to the National Grange in a futile attempt to prop up prices, hold down freight charges, and turn back the hands of time.

The Distribution of Wealth

As fortunes rose, so did the disparity between rich and poor.[19] Several studies conducted around 1890 attempted to measure the extent of this disparity. One undertaken by Brooklyn lawyer-economist Thomas G. Shearman drew national attention.[20] Shearman attempted to construct a pyramid of national wealth distribution. Toward forming the apex, he identified seventy individuals whose net worth exceeded $20 million. Among them were John Jacob Astor, whose net worth Shearman estimated at $150 million; Cornelius Vanderbilt, John D. Rockefeller, Jay Gould, and Leland Stanford, each whose net worth he estimated at $100 million; and Anthony Drexel, J. P. Morgan, and Marshall Field, each whose net worth he estimated at $25 million. Shearman

Table 1

Business Trusts in 1894

The Ax Trust
The Barbed-Wire Trust
The Biscuit and Cracker Trust
The Boiler Trust
The Bolt and Nut Trust
The Boot and Shoe Trust
The Borax Trust
The Broom Trust
The Brush Trust
The Button Trust
The Carbon Candle Trust
The Cartridge Trust
The Casket and Burial Goods Trust
The Castor-Oil Trust
The Celluloid Trust
The Cigarette Trust
The Coal Trust
The Condensed-Milk Trust
The Copper-Ingot Trust
The Copper-Sheet Trust
The Cordage Trust
The Cotton-Duck Trust
The Cotton-Seed Oil Trust
The Cotton-Thread Trust
The Crockery Trust
The Electric-Supply Trust
The Envelope Trust
The Flint-Glass Trust
The Fork and Hoe Trust
The Fruit-Jar Trust
The Galvanized Iron and Steel Trust
The Glove Trust
The Harrow Trust
The Harvester Trust
The Hinge Trust
The Indurated Fiber Trust
The Iron and Steel Trust
The Lead Trust
The Leather Board Trust
The Lime Trust
The Linseed Oil Trust
The Lithograph Trust
The Locomotive Tire Trust
The Marble Trust
The Match Trust
The Merchant-Steel Trust
The Morocco Leather Trust
The Oatmeal Trust
The Oilcloth Trust
The Paper Bag Trust
The Pitch Trust
The Plate-Glass Trust
The Pocket-Cutlery Trust
The Powder Trust
The Preserves Trust
The Pulp Trust
The Rice Trust
The Rubber General Trust
The Rubber Gossamer Trust
The Safe Trust
The Salt Trust
The Sandpaper Trust
The Sandstone Trust
The Sanitary Ware Trust
The Sash, Door, and Blind Trust
The Saw Trust
The School-Book Trust
The School Furniture Trust
The Sewer-Pipe Trust
The Shot and Lead Trust
The Skewer Trust
The Smelters Trust
The Snath Trust
The Soap Trust
The Soda-Water Machinery Trust
The Sponge Trust
The Spool, Bobbin and Shuttle Trust
The Starch Trust
The Steel-Rail Trust
The Store-Board Trust
The Straw Board Trust
The Structural Steel Trust
The Sugar Trust
The Teazel Trust
The Tinned Plate Trust
The Tombstone Trust
The Trunk Trust
The Tube Trust
The Type Trust
The Umbrella Trust
The Vapor Stove Trust
The Wall Paper Trust
The Watch Trust
The Wheel Trust
The Whip Trust
The Window Glass Trust
The Wire Trust
The Wood-Screw Trust
The Wool Hat Trust
The Wrapping Paper Trust
The Yellow Pine Trust

Source: Cong. Rec., 53d Cong., 2d sess., 1894, 26, pt. 2:1669 (incorporated in statement of Maddox).

calculated the total wealth of all seventy individuals to be $2.7 billion. Toward structuring the base, Shearman consulted the 1888 property tax statistics for the city of Boston. From these statistics, he extrapolated data for the nation as a whole.

In this extrapolation, Shearman made five adjustments. First, he doubled the figure for tangible asset values. This adjustment was necessary, he reasoned, to correct valuation errors and to account for intangible wealth, which was rarely reported. Second, he grossed up by one-half values greater than $400,000. One-half represents Shearman's estimate of the degree to which property assessors understate the land values of the wealthy. Third, he multiplied the product by forty-five. Forty-five represents the ratio in 1888 of total national wealth to total Boston wealth. Fourth, he multiplied the number of Boston residents by 130. That figure represents the ratio in 1888 of the nation's population to Boston's population. Finally, he recast the resulting figures as "family" wealth. Each individual taxpayer, he surmised, supports a single family. Shearman published the findings of his study in the November 1889 issue of *Forum*. These findings are summarized in tables 2 and 3.

After analyzing these figures, Shearman came up with a startling revelation: about one-seventieth of the nation's families owned more than two-thirds of the nation's wealth, while roughly 40,000 of these families owned more than one-half of the nation's wealth.[21]

A more empirical study was conducted in 1893 by George K. Holmes, a statistician for the U.S. Census Bureau.[22] Like Shearman, Holmes attempted to construct a pyramid of national wealth distribution. Unlike Shearman, however, Holmes started from the base and worked his way up to the apex. He first reviewed data from the Eleventh Census. These data indicate that in 1890, the value of the nation's assets was $60 billion; families in the United States numbered 12,690,152. Of these families, Holmes figured, 11,593,887 were worth $17,356,837,343, or roughly 29 percent of the nation's wealth (see table 4). The remaining 1,096,265 families, he deduced, were worth $42,643,163,657, or roughly 71 percent of the nation's wealth.

Toward disaggregating the latter figures, Holmes consulted a *New York Tribune* survey of American millionaires. This survey revealed that in 1893, 4,047 families owned assets valued at $12 billion. This told Holmes that the remaining 1,092,218 families held approximately $30.6 billion in assets. Hence, 8.6 percent of the population owned 51 percent of the nation's wealth,

Table 2
Distribution of American Wealth in 1888 on the Basis of Boston Tax Returns

Number of Families	Wealth in Thousands *Over*	Wealth in Thousands *Under*	Average Wealth in Thousands	Aggregate Wealth in Millions
70	$20,000	$150,000	$37,500	$2,625
90	10,000	20,000	11,500	1,025
180	7,500	10,000	8,000	1,440
135	5,625	7,500	6,800	968
360	3,750	5,625	4,600	1,656
1,755	1,875	3,750	2,300	4,036
6,000	937	1,875	1,250	7,500
7,000	500	937	650	4,550
11,000	300	500	375	4,125
14,000	200	300	230	3,220
16,500	150	200	165	2,722
50,000	75	150	100	5,000
75,000	50	75	60	4,500
200,000	15	50	20	4,000
1,000,000	3	15	3.5	3,500
2,000,000	1.5	3	2	4,000
9,620,000	—	—	0.75	7,215
13,002,090	—	—	—	$62,082

Source: Thomas G. Shearman, "The Owners of the United States," *Forum* (November 1889): 270–71.

while an additional .03 percent owned another 20 percent. Holmes concluded his study as follows:

> We are now prepared to characterize the concentration of the wealth in the United States by stating that 20 per cent of it is owned by three-hundredths of 1 per cent of the families; 51 per cent by 9 per cent of the families (not including millionaires); 71 per cent, by 9 per cent of the families (including millionaires), and 29 per cent by 91 per cent of the families.
>
> Only 9 per cent of the wealth is owned by tenant families and the poorer class of those that own their farms or homes under incumbrance, and these

Table 3
Class Distribution of American Wealth in 1888

	Number of Families	Wealth in Millions	Average Wealth per Family
Rich	182,090	$43,367	$238,135
Middle	1,200,000	7,500	6,250
Working	11,620,000	11,215	968

Source: Thomas G. Shearman, "The Owners of the United States," *Forum* (November 1889): 271.

together constitute 64 per cent of all the families. As little as 5 per cent of the nation's wealth is owned by 52 per cent of the families, that is, by the tenants alone. Finally, 4,047 families possess about seven-tenths as much as do 11,593,887 families.[23]

Joseph Pulitzer's *New York World* publicized Holmes's conclusion. "The 4,047 multi-millionaires have 50 per cent more wealth than the 55,000,000 members of the 12,010,000 families belonging to the wage-working class," it brazenly announced in early 1894. Going a step further, the *World* popularized the belief that the disparities in wealth were not only gaping, but also growing. These disparities, it decried, were inextricably linked to the absolute impoverishment of the masses:

In 1860 the wealth of this country was very evenly distributed. There were no multi-millionaires, very few millionaires, few large fortunes. . . . [T]he census of 1860 shows half the wealth in possession of half the people. There were no bonanza farms and no tenant farmers. One-half the male workers were on farms they owned, and the average land value of each farm was $3,251, while few went much over or under. Poverty was confined to the cities, and to small sections of them. It is perfectly safe to assert that 91 per cent of the people held in fair and even measure 91 per cent of the wealth, while 4 percent of the people owned the remaining 9 per cent, leaving not more than 5 per cent practically paupers. . . .

The census of 1890 shows that the conditions of 1860 have been reversed; that 91 per cent of the people of the United States are to-day practically paupers, living from hand to mouth, dependent upon their daily labor

Table 4
Wealth Distribution by Classes

1,440,000 farm-hiring families, worth $150 above debts of indefinite amount	$216,000,000
752,760 families owning encumbered farms worth less than $5,000, deducting incumbrance and other debts of indefinite amount, and allowing $500 for additional wealth	1,359,741,600
1,756,440 families owning free farms worth less than $5,000, allowing $1,000 for additional wealth above debts of indefinite amount	5,309,589,600
5,159,796 home-hiring families, worth $500 above debts of indefinite amount	2,579,898,000
720,618 families owning encumbered homes worth less than $5,000, deducting incumbrance and other debts of indefinite amount, and allowing $500 for additional wealth	1,142,531,550
1,764,273 families owning free homes worth less than $5,000, allowing $2,000 for additional wealth above debts of indefinite amount	6,749,076,593
11,593,887 families worth	$17,356,837,343

Source: George K. Holmes, "The Concentration of Wealth," *Political Science Quarterly* (December 1893): 591–92. Also quoted in *Cong. Rec.*, 53d Cong., 2d sess., 1894, 26, pt. 7:6687 (statement of Kyle).

> for their daily bread, while 9 per cent are capitalistic employers, owning 84 per cent of the wealth.[24]

Holmes's and Shearman's findings jolted public opinion. They reinforced the notion, prevalent in Populist circles, that the working poor were being dispossessed, and furthermore that this dispossession was leading to the demise of the existing capitalist order.[25] Despite their flawed methodologies and questionable results, these studies were regarded as authoritative by members of Congress.[26] Their significance, as we shall see, lies less in the veracity of their conclusions than in the force of their political impact.

The Tax Regime

Adding to the hardship of the working poor were taxes. In the nineteenth century, state and local governments raised revenues primarily through property taxes. The federal government raised revenues primarily through import duties.[27] As U.S. industry expanded, pressure mounted on Congress to boost the level of these duties. Congress responded by enacting a series of protective tariff measures, culminating in the McKinley Tariff of 1890.[28] This act imposed specific duties on a long list of consumer and durable items. Its effect was to increase the price of these items by roughly 50 percent.[29]

The price increase affected different segments of U.S. society in different ways. On the one hand, it virtually crippled American farmers and craftsmen. The higher cost of capital goods diminished artisanal and agricultural earnings. Few farmers and craftsmen were in a position either to absorb these costs or to pass them on to others.[30] The higher cost of consumption goods soaked up a greater portion of these earnings. Farmers and artisans could ill-afford a decline in earning power, much less buying power.[31] On the other hand, the price increase generally benefited merchants and manufacturers. Under the tariff regime, trade and manufacturing fortunes were rising. These rising fortunes could readily absorb the higher cost of consumption goods. The national market for domestic manufactures was consolidating. This market, shielded from foreign competition by the tariff, was the very precondition for these rising fortunes. Moreover, merchants and manufacturers *were* in a position to pass on higher capital costs to others in the form of higher prices.[32] The collusive, anticompetitive practices of the business trusts effectively tilted the terms of trade in their favor. The overall result of this scheme was that the burden of taxation fell primarily on the farmer, the artisan, and to some extent the worker. In a sense, the system took from the pockets of the poor to finance the business expansion of the rich.[33] "Federal taxation has increased sixfold since 1860, and the whole of this increase has been taken out of the relatively poorer classes," remarked economist Shearman in November 1889.

> At the same time the profit which is secured to the wealthier classes by the adjustment of indirect taxation in their interest has been increased not less than tenfold. The wealthy classes, collectively, have made a clear profit out of

> the indirect efforts of taxation to an amount far exceeding all that they have paid in taxes, although this profit has been absorbed by a minority of even the rich. But, apart from this, the whole system of taxation is and has been such as to take from the rich only from 3 to 10 per cent of their annual savings while taking from the poor 75 to 90 per cent.[34]

By contrast, state and local taxation achieved a certain degree of equity to the extent that wealth was held in *tangible* form. As tangible wealth increased, so did state and local property taxes. As tangible wealth decreased, property taxes decreased accordingly. The ultimate effect of this scheme was to ease the burden on farmers and artisans and increase it on merchants and manufacturers. The former experienced a secular decline in land, building, and tool values.[35] The latter added to their stock of warehouses, factories, and equipment. On the other hand, to the extent that wealth was held in *intangible* form, state and local taxation achieved no degree of equity. Intangible assets were excluded from the tax base. Neither their value nor income derived from their corpus was reachable by the tax authorities. For all practical purposes, this meant that *interest, dividends, annuities,* and *investment gains* escaped state and local taxation. What is more, given the very nature of customs duties, they also escaped federal taxation.

Not surprisingly, the principal beneficiaries of the nontaxability of intangibles were the business classes.[36] Not only did they earn more than everyone else, but they also saved more than everyone else. Not only did they invest more than everyone else, but they also increasingly shifted their investments from taxable realty to nontaxable stocks, bonds, and insurance contracts. Not content with merely reducing their tax liability, some sought to eliminate it altogether. They did so by acquiring estates beyond the city limits and by investing in ventures overseas. Some even moved overseas to enjoy the fruits of their capital without the headache of the tax man. Remarked George Walsh, a senator from Georgia: "The rich escape their just measure of taxation under the existing law. The steadily increasing number of wealthy Americans who live abroad furnishes a large absentee class who pay nothing at all to support the Government under whose favorable laws their fortunes have been accumulated, and their rights protected."[37] Noted University of Wisconsin economist Richard Ely: "There is a considerable and increasing class living in great comfort on incomes of large proportions, say five, ten, twenty, thirty, or forty, or even fifty thousand dollars, who by insurance and various devices, protect themselves and their families for the future, and yet pay no taxes."[38] Uriel Hall, a congressman from Missouri, referred to these citizens generally as "that class of men who live in the nontaxpayers paradise, outside of the cities. They generally have their property invested in choses in action which are not taxable under the laws of most of the States, or at least are not reached. They remove outside of the city limits and thereby escape municipal taxation."[39]

The tax avoidance schemes of the 1890s were indicative less of the evasive propensities of the wealthy than of *institutional obsolescence*. In a sense, the tax system had become obsolete as a result of U.S. industrialization. It had become ill-suited for a modern society that valued the equitable distribution of the tax burden. Its strict territoriality encouraged the flight of capital beyond the nation's borders. Its protectionist orientation subverted the principle of distributional equality. Its limited scope created an escape hatch for those individuals most able to bear the burden. Its anticonsumption bias worked to the detriment to the poor. By the mid-1890s, U.S. economic development had engendered a certain disconsonance between traditional political values and modern social reality. This disconsonance would become a driving force behind the revolutionary changes that lay ahead. It was symptomatic of a nation in transition. "Great changes have occurred . . . in the body politic," lamented one observer in 1894.

> Population has greatly increased, the methods of doing business have greatly changed, protective tariffs have increased the number of poor people and decreased the number of rich people. Wealth has been transferred from the hands of the many to the pockets of the few, and the exemptions from wealthy holding have increased; it being true that wealth has greatly increased during the last twenty-four years, but it is also true, it being under the control of a less number of owners compared to our whole population, it is more difficult to reach these vast fortunes by the ordinary means of taxation.[40]

The failure of the system to achieve an equitable result undermined its legitimacy in the eyes of the farmer, the artisan, and the worker. At the same time, it fueled their resentment toward the opulent business elite.[41] With time, this resentment would find expression in the political ideology of the Populist Party. According to this ideology, each citizen should contribute to the support of government according to his or her ability to pay. In 1892, voters in six western states elected ten Populists to the House of Representatives and three to the Senate.[42] The Democrats gained control of Congress, as well as the presidency. The emergence of a Democratic majority augured well for broad-based tariff reform, but not for radical institutional change. In the 1892 campaign, the Democrats had committed themselves to a modest reduction in import duties, not a fundamental redistribution of the tax burden.[43] This redistribution would have to come another day. In the meantime, the economy expanded, money grew plentiful, popular discontent subsided, and the need for change receded in the minds of the American public. It was only a matter of time, however, before this discontent would rise to the surface like water boiling in a cauldron. It was only a matter of time before this need would swell in the American psyche with a deep and pervasive sense of urgency.

The *socioinstitutional view* accepts the progressive premises regarding the interrelationship of state, society, and law; the economy as a dynamic engine of change; and the dialectical nature of U.S. institutional development. It sees society as structured by relations of production, not transcendental concepts. It sees the history of the income tax as movement, culminating in the realization of political ideas.

The socioinstitutional view, however, differs from the progressive view (or, more precisely, determinist variants of this view) in six principal respects. First, it sees economic and social transformation as creating *context,* not *end result.* It attributes end result to *individuals,* speaking and acting within peculiar socioeconomic contexts. Second, the view attaches primary importance to human thought, judgment, and reason in the creation of laws and institutions. It recognizes that although one's place in the production process may condition one's receptivity to certain ideas, thinking individuals, guided by the faculties of judgment and reason, actually formulate these ideas. Third, the view posits that political action may be driven by a myriad of objectives—some economic, some social, some personal. These objectives may be devoid of class content. They may be purely ideological in character. Fourth, the view treats government as an actor in the political arena, not just an instrument of political action. In its role as actor, government regulates the conduct of other actors; it impacts the very social basis upon which it is founded. Fifth, the view questions the proposition that ideas realized in the course of history are necessarily virtuous. It postulates that depending upon the subjective aims of historical actors, these ideas may be virtuous, mundane, or even perverse. Finally, the socioinstitutional view rejects the progressive conclusion that the income tax has led to greater social equality. On the other hand, it qualifies this rejection with the assertion that the original aim of the income tax was to redistribute the *tax burden,* not *social wealth.*

Like pluralism, the socioinstitutional view sees society as a driving force in institutional change. It recognizes that social forces play a prominent role in the legislative process. It acknowledges the functionality of political organization and the instrumentality of political elites in this process.

Unlike pluralism, however, the socioinstitutional view stresses the role of individuals, not groups, in U.S. institutional development. It posits that individuals, inspired by political ideals, collectively act to implement change. Although the group embodies these ideals and symbolizes this action, its individual members actually realize these ideals and take this action. What binds these individuals together, what gives them collective identity, is a commonality of purpose. This commonality stems from numerous factors, including race, religion, family, culture, socioeconomic status, geography, and experience.

The socioinstitutional view is similar to democratic institutionalism in three principal respects. First, in explaining institutional development, it attaches paramount importance to ideas. Second, it posits that economic change creates context, not end result. Third, it acknowledges the catalytic role played by crisis and contingency in institutional reform.

The socioinstitutional view, however, differs from democratic institutionalism in three ways: First, it rejects the democratic institutional insinuation that ideas are somehow independent of the actors who espouse them. It contends that just as ideas are the product of mind, so too they are dependent upon mind; just as these ideas derive their meaning from thinking individuals, so too they are meaningless without these individuals. Second, the socioinstitutional view postulates that elites act *primarily* out of personal conviction, not opportunism. Although they may invoke ideas to rally the public to their side and augment their political power, they generally reinforce their self-esteem by promoting ideas in which they earnestly believe. Third, the view stresses the *social basis* of U.S. laws and institutions. While acknowledging the roles of elites, ideas, and contingency in their formation, it emphasizes the roles of class, interest, and social movement in their solidification.

The socioinstitutional view accepts the centrist premise that government elites are key players in the political arena, that they often pursue aims quite distinct from the interests of their constituents, and that aspects of their behavior are consensual.

Socioinstitutionalism, however, differs from centrism in the following respects: First, it rejects the centrist notion that the state is somehow autonomous of society. It posits that because the state emanates from society, it is dependent on society; because it is a concept of the collectivity, it is nonexistent without the individuals that constitute this collectivity. Second, the view rejects the centrist intimation that the state transcends social change. It contends that because state and society are integrally related, any change in society ultimately impacts the state, and furthermore that the transformation of society leads to the transformation of the state. Third, the socioinstitutional view rejects the centrist presumption that historical action is explainable in terms of a single overriding objective. It contends that because such human deeds are oriented toward a multiplicity of objectives, historical action is more adequately explained in terms of a confluence of factors. Fourth, the view distinguishes between objective result and subjective intent. It asserts that what ultimately resulted may never have been intended; indeed, the objective outcome of historical action may be contrary to the actors' subjective intent. Finally, the socioinstitutional view accepts as authentic the meaning conveyed by the words and deeds of historical actors. It presumes that unless controverted by other compelling evidence, the actors' words and deeds faithfully convey the meaning that the actors intended.

According to the socioinstitutional view, nineteenth-century U.S. society was structured along socioeconomic lines (farmers, workers, merchants, industrialists) but organized along ideological lines (Populists, Democrats, Republicans). Its ideological divisions generally coincided with its class divisions. Class and ideology, however, were not mutually dependent. From a *political cultural* perspective, little in the socioinstitutional order portended of conflict. Social classes were integrated through shared symbols of state and nation. Political groups were bound together by common conceptions of law and order. From a *political economic* perspective, however, conflict was endemic to the system. The tariff regime engendered conflicting, if not incompatible, interests. Social classes rationalized the pursuit of these interests through distinctly different ideologies. Political elites, for their part, embraced, articulated, and reformulated these ideologies. They incorporated normative ideas in their party platforms, on the basis of which they vied for elective office.

Thus, contrary to centrist claims, the impetus for the income tax came from "below," not "above." In 1878, for example, the Knights of Labor demanded a graduated income tax. Eleven years later the Northern Alliance, and twelve years later the Southern Alliance, followed suit. Successively in 1877, 1879, and 1880 the Greenback Party endorsed the income tax. Its lead was followed in 1884 by the Anti-Monopoly Party, in 1892 by the People's Party, and also in 1892 by the Socialist Party.[44] These moves can hardly be described as "state initiatives" or elitist attempts to palliate the masses with rhetoric. They reflect a grassroots effort to forge a new fiscal order, a broad-based drive to realize a political idea.

At the heart of this drive were socioeconomic groups adversely affected by tariff taxation. At its forefront were political parties animated by a vision of a new social order. These parties both deified the "common man" and demonized the "capitalist." Some, such as the Populists, saw the income tax as a means of shifting the burden from the working poor to the investing rich. Others, such as the Socialists, saw it as a device for reducing the rich to the level of the poor. Either way, the rich felt threatened.

For the most part, they materially benefited from tariff taxation—or else believed that they did. Thus, out of a sense of self-interest, they stood in defense of the existing fiscal order, which they came to identify with their personal well-being. Through the political parties that they dominated, they vowed resistance to an income tax, even if it were limited in scope. It was not the nominal assessment that mattered, but rather the *principle* of assessment. What was this principle? The "sanctity" of laissez-faire, as well as an individual's absolute "right" to private property. Tax advocates countered with an opposing principle: *the duty of each person to contribute to the support of government according to his or her ability to pay.*

On an ideological plane, the emergence of the modern income tax would involve a struggle over these principles. He who should prevail would determine not only the manner in which the tax burden was to be distributed, but also the laws, the institutions, even the political ethos of an entire era. In the backdrop of this struggle would be the vast social changes that had swept the nation since the Civil War. At its forefront would be dynamic leaders, committed to the creation of a new, more equitable fiscal order. They were men and women of deep-seated conviction, animated by an ardent desire to bring a discordant reality in line with a subjective ideal. Although they promoted class and sectional interests, perhaps unwittingly, and generally adhered to the party line, they ultimately decided critical issues according to the dictates of their conscience. They can hardly be described as "instruments" of some blind dialectic or the "trustees" of dominant social groups. To be sure, they were catalysts of change, of independent mind and character, constrained by the institutional context in which they acted and the society in which they lived.

2

The Impetus to Change

Every mill and every factory was running at its fullest capacity; every vehicle of transportation, whether by rail or water, had all and more than it could carry . . . every blast furnace and every mine was running day and night, and could not then fill its orders . . . every manufacturer and builder had all and more than he could do; every workingman, whether the ordinary laborer or the skilled artisan, who wanted work, had all and more than he could do, and received therefore the highest wages ever paid for labor since the creation of man. . . . [O]ur credit was good and we had the confidence of the whole world; in short, there never was a nation or a people that realized such wonderful prosperity.

—Jacob Gallinger, Republican senator
from New Hampshire, May 19, 1894

The economic cyclone was swift, unexpected, and devastating. It pulverized everything in its path—interest rates, stock prices, business profits, land values. Its genesis lay in industrial overexpansion, fueled by easy money.[1] At the peak of the business cycle in January 1893, U.S. bank deposits had soared to a record $4 billion.[2] Bank loans had reached an unprecedented $4.3 billion.[3] Most of these loans had been made to creditworthy borrowers. A few, however, had been made to bank officers, or their affiliates, whose financial condition was shaky. A great number of the latter loans, used to speculate in the stock market, were undercollateralized. Some became totally worthless. In May, depositors withdrew sizable amounts for the Chicago World Exposition. Several Boston and Philadelphia banks, unable to meet the demand for cash, closed their doors.[4]

The failure of the eastern banks sent ripples throughout the economy. It aggravated an even broader malaise, highlighted by the Philadelphia and Reading Railroad bankruptcy three months earlier.[5] In little time, news of bank insolvency made the headlines of nearly every newspaper in the country. Initially, Americans received the news with calm. Gradually, however, the calm became concern. Then suddenly, the concern turned into alarm. In the major money centers, depositors rushed to retrieve whatever funds they could from their savings accounts. Scores of banks, debilitated by the cash hemorrhage, started to turn customers away.[6] The closure of the urban banks eventually led to a shutdown of rural banks. Soon, there was widespread panic, a national run on deposits, and more bank failures. The crisis continued well into the summer months, virtually paralyzing the financial sector. By the end of June, nearly $400 million in cash had been withdrawn from the banking system.[7] More than four hundred financial institutions had closed their doors.[8]

Their deposit base shrinking, those banks still standing took defensive measures to preserve their liquidity. Most declined to make additional loans and refused to discount even the choicest of paper.[9] Many called existing loans and beefed up reserves for bad debts. Some intensified their collection efforts. Nearly all raised their lending rates. The result was a general contraction of credit that jolted the nation and sent debtors scurrying for cover.[10] The first to feel its impact was U.S. business. Unable to obtain discount at reasonable rates, manufacturers tightened credit with jobbers, who curtailed it with retailers, who cut it off to customers. The ensuing decline in credit sales forced a sharp reduction in inventories. Lower inventories, in turn, led to a further decline in sales. In the words of one observer: "Agents of factories would call upon jobbers and dealers for orders, but merchants dared not stock up. At best, they would but sort up, buying no more than they were obliged to have. They not only gave light orders but often canceled orders previously given for future delivery, well knowing that under no circumstances would it be possible to tide over a difficulty by getting discount at the banks on the choicest paper."[11] As operating activity approached the breakeven point, vendors drastically slashed prices to stimulate sales. Lower prices cut deeper into profit margins, without conferring the added benefit of increased volume.

In July, the crisis deepened. Businesses sharply trimmed overhead as operating losses started to mount. Employers laid off workers in a desperate attempt to get back in the black. The financially resilient reduced hourly wages. The hard-pressed cut back work time. Still others trimmed the workweek from six to three days.[12] On a grand scale, however, these measures proved counterproductive. Lower wages further depressed prices. Lower prices steepened operating losses. Higher operating losses forced more layoffs. Businesses began to fold, as the velocity of the cyclone accelerated. Reported the *Manufacturer's Record* in late July:

> Industrial plants are ceasing operations entirely or working on "short time." The situation has reached this stage. All over the country, mines, factories and furnaces are cutting down expenses and curtailing the output. Every plate-glass factory in the country has closed. Out of 500 silver mines, 325 are idle. The weekly product of 221 iron furnaces July 1, was 155,262 tons, the lowest for two years, with two exceptions. The Maryland Steel Company, employing 3500 men, has banked one of its furnaces. The Otis Steel Company, of Cleveland, has reduced its force from 1,000 to 200 men and reduced wages ten to twenty per cent. These are only samples of the economic policy being enforced throughout the country.[13]

The storm was quick to move to the interior. The number of passengers traveling from the coasts to the heartland dwindled, as did the volume of freight carried from the mines to the steel mills. On July 17, the Erie Railway filed for bankruptcy. Scores of other railroads followed suit.[14] At the end of the line, the farmer was caught between a rock and a hard place as commodity prices plunged and interest rates soared.[15] The middleman refused to advance cash for the season's crop. The banker came knocking at the farmer's door.

By year-end, the crisis had taken its toll. National wealth had shrunk by nearly $9 billion.[16] Import values had fallen by more than $65 million.[17] Business failures stood at 15,560, 51 percent more than in the previous year.[18] Bank suspensions numbered 491, a 514 percent jump from 1892.[19] Income and labor statistics were dismal. Although average farm earnings were off by only 3 percent, nonfarm earnings were down more than 14 percent.[20] *Bradstreet's* reported that in 119 cities, 801,000 workers, supporting 1,953,000 dependents, had been laid off.[21] Samuel Gompers put the national figure at 3 million, including individuals working half-time or less.[22] According to one reliable source:

> What will doubtless be known as the "panic year of 1893" has brought with it, as was to be expected, the largest number of business failures ever recorded in the United States since records of the same have been kept the total . . . amounting to 15,560, in which are included only commercial, in-

> dustrial and financial business failures in which estimated assets are smaller than reported liabilities. . . .
>
> The grand total of estimated liabilities of individuals, firms and corporations in business, including banks which reported liabilities in excess of their actual assets, amounts to $403,000,000 in round numbers, or nearly four times the corresponding total of 1892, when the total number of failures was two-thirds as large as this year.[23]

The cyclone appears to have hit the West and Midwest harder than the South and East. In the first nine months of the year, business failures in New York, Pennsylvania, New Jersey, and Delaware rose by 18 percent, while aggregate liabilities nearly quadrupled.[24] Failures in the South swelled by 25 percent, while liabilities increased only threefold. By contrast, business failures in Ohio, Indiana, Illinois, Missouri, Michigan, Kansas, Kentucky, and Colorado rose by 130 percent, while liabilities practically quintupled. Failures in Wisconsin, Minnesota, Iowa, Nebraska, North Dakota, Montana, and Wyoming grew by 100 percent, while liabilities increased eightfold.[25]

The economic slump affected the body politic in two significant ways. First, it precipitated a major fiscal crisis. Federal receipts were down by $31 million, an 8 percent drop from the previous year. Federal expenditures were up by $14 million, a 4 percent jump from 1892. For the first time in decades, the government faced a massive budget deficit. This deficit stood at $40 million in December 1893.[26] For fiscal year 1894, it was projected to climb to $78 million.[27] Second, the economic downturn exacerbated disparities in wealth.[28] Extensive layoffs added to the ranks of the urban poor. While workers' earnings declined, their consumption of basic commodities remained relatively steady. The tariff kept the price of these commodities artificially high. Duties, being specific, absorbed a greater portion of these earnings.

How was the deficit to be funded? This question put Democrats in a quandary. On the one hand, in the 1892 campaign, they had promised the nation a modest reduction in import duties. On the other hand, they feared that such a reduction would aggravate the burgeoning budget deficit. In his December address to Congress, President Cleveland had proposed a modest tax on corporate investment income.[29] Such a tax, the president believed, would make up for the shortfall that tariff reform would leave. For the Populists, on the other hand, the answer was perfectly clear: fund the deficit with an income tax. In their 1892 platform, the Populists had advocated a broad-based tax on income. Unlike the Democrats, they were committed to a fundamental redistribution of the tax burden.[30]

Action in the House of Representatives

In the latter part of 1893, the issue of tax reform moved from the panic-stricken streets of the nation to the lofty chambers of Congress. In October, House Ways and Means Committee chairman James Wilson commenced hearings on revising the McKinley Tariff. In the course of the hearings, the committee drafted legislation that would, first, change the nature of import duties from specific to ad valorem and, second, lower the average rate on all dutiable merchandise from 50 to roughly 35 percent.[31] The "Wilson Bill," as the legislation became known, was projected to raise $40 million in federal revenues. House Populists proposed funding the shortfall with an income tax, which the chairman adamantly opposed.[32] Wilson reasoned that an income tax would be rejected by Democratic congressmen from the industrial East; any attempt to enact it would jeopardize efforts toward tariff reform.[33] The West Virginia Democrat was essentially correct in his assessment. The income tax *would* be opposed by Democrats from districts east of the Allegheny Mountains and north of the Potomac River.

Wilson appointed a special subcommittee to explore ways to fund the shortfall.[34] He named three Democrats and two Republicans as members, with Tennessee Democrat Benton McMillin as its chair.[35] The subcommittee met throughout the fall. Among the options it considered were the issuance of bonds and an excise tax on whiskey.[36] It ultimately settled for the excise tax on whiskey, projected to raise additional revenues of $8 million. This amount, however, left a gap of $30 million. Toward closing it, the subcommittee turned its attention to an income tax. (For McMillin, this move might have been a way of "getting even" with the Democratic leadership. Months earlier, it had passed him over in its appointment of the Ways and Means Committee chair.)[37]

On October 16, the subcommittee heard testimony from Thomas G. Shearman, the reputed authority on national wealth distribution. The Brooklyn lawyer-economist outlined a proposal for taxing income at the source.[38] He also presented the findings of his economic research. The subcommittee considered, in addition to these findings, the conclusions of statistician

Holmes. Following its deliberations, the subcommittee released both Shearman's and Holmes's statistical results to the full Congress.[39]

Two items weighed heavily on the minds of subcommittee members. The first was the income tax in Europe.[40] In May 1893, Nebraska Democrat William Jennings Bryan had asked the State Department to distribute an income tax questionnaire to its consulates abroad. The questionnaire dealt with the structure of each host country's income tax, including exemptions, inclusions, deductions, and rates. The department complied with Bryan's request, and by December had received replies from the consulates in England, the German states, Austria, Switzerland, and Italy.[41] Because of their significance for U.S. income tax development, these replies are summarized below.

England

England had levied an income tax intermittently since the days of George III. The first tax law was enacted in 1798. It was repealed in 1816, then reenacted in 1842.[42] By the act of 1799, Parliament mandated income tax reporting. Four years later, it instituted "collection at the source." Under this practice, the income payer, not the recipient, is responsible for collecting and remitting the tax to the government. Though initially applicable to rents and interest, the practice was extended to dividends in 1806. Under the British scheme, taxable income included, in addition to rents, interest, and dividends, the following items: annuities, salaries, business profits, and property gains. It, however, excluded income earned by charities, hospitals, and universities. Under the law in effect in 1893, the first £150 (approximately $750) was exempt from taxation. Incomes greater than this amount were taxed at a rate of 2 percent. Earnings greater than £150 but less than £400 were allowed an abatement, that is, a reduction, of £120.[43]

The German States

Prussia had instituted an income tax in 1851.[44] This tax remained in force throughout the second half of the century. Under the law in effect in 1893, the first 900 marks (approximately $214) was exempt from taxation. Incomes greater than this amount were taxed at rates ranging from 0.66 percent to 4 percent.[45] Taxpayers earning 3,000 marks or less were allowed an abatement for each dependent child. They were also allowed special abatements for sickness, injury, and indebtedness. Württemberg's tax originated in 1820, Bavaria's and Bremen's in 1848, Baden's in 1884. The Württemberg scheme taxed salaries and business profits at graduated rates, investment earnings at a flat rate. The Bavarian scheme taxed earnings greater than 350 marks (about $85) at rates ranging from 0.33 percent to nearly 1 percent. In Bremen, incomes greater than 600 marks (roughly $145) were assessed at a flat rate of 4 percent. In Baden, earnings greater than 500 marks (about $125) were taxed at a rate of 2.5 percent.[46]

Austria, Switzerland, and Italy

Austria had levied an income tax at intervals between 1743 and 1893 (the date of the survey). The tax of 1849 remained in effect throughout the second half of the nineteenth century. Under the law in force in 1893, the first 314 florins (about $113) was exempt from taxation. Incomes greater than this amount were taxed at rates ranging from 8.5 percent to 20 percent.[47]

The 1889 law in Zurich exempted the first 500 francs (about $100). Incomes greater than this amount were taxed at rates ranging from 0.10 percent to nearly 8 percent.[48]

In Italy, the 1877 law provided for a "minimum subsistence" exemption of 400 lire (about $77). Earnings above this exemption were taxed at a flat rate of 12 percent.[49]

The second item that weighed heavily on the minds of subcommittee members was the Civil War tax in the United States.[50] In 1862, the Union government had instituted an income tax in the Northern states. This tax had been enacted in the throes of war. Its enactment had drawn little opposition and scant debate.[51] The statutory basis for the Civil War tax was the Revenue Act of 1862. Succeeding this act was a series of legislative measures that expanded or modified preexisting provisions.

The Revenue Act of 1862

This act levied an income tax on two classes of individuals: first, residents of the United States, and second, U.S. citizens residing abroad. The first were taxed on their worldwide income, the second only on income derived from property located in the United States. The taxable income of U.S. residents included rents, salaries, business profits, personal property gains, interest on government and railroad bonds, and dividends on railroad and financial stocks. It excluded interest and dividends on all other types of corporate investments. The first $600 in earnings was exempt from taxation. Incomes greater than $600 but less than $10,000 were taxed at a rate of 3 percent, incomes greater than $10,000 at 5 percent. Excluded from the general rate scheme were interest on U.S. government obligations, the income of U.S. citizens residing abroad, and corporate interest and dividends. U.S. government-bond interest was taxed at a rate of 1.5 percent, the income of nonresident citizens at 5 percent (1.5 percent in the case of U.S. government bond interest earned by these citizens), and corporate interest and dividends at 3 percent. Individuals were allowed two deductions: one for local, state, and other federal taxes, the other for income received from corporations that had already paid the tax.[52] The tax on interest and dividends was collectible at the source.

The 1862 act also levied a tax on corporations. The tax bases for different types of corporations, however, varied. For financial institutions (banks, trust companies, and savings institutions), the base consisted of undistributed corporate profits. For railroad, steamboat, toll, and publishing companies, the base was gross receipts. For insurance companies, the base was both undistributed profits and gross receipts. Likewise, tax rates varied. For most corporations, the rate stood at a flat 3 percent. For companies owning railroads driven by power other than steam, it was 1.5 percent. The gross receipts of insurance companies were taxed at a rate of 1 percent. Finally, the act established the Office of Internal Revenue, with which all taxpayers, individual and corporate, were to file tax returns.[53]

The Revenue Act of 1864

In June 1864, Congress amended the 1862 law. It broadened taxable income to include gains from the sale of realty purchased within the year, as well as the taxpayer's distributive share of corporate and partnership profits. The 1864 law subjected the worldwide income of U.S. citizens residing abroad to U.S. taxing authority. It raised the lowest marginal rate to 5 percent, created an intermediate rate of 7.5 percent, and increased the highest marginal rate to 10 percent. In addition, it applied the intermediate rate to incomes greater than $5,000 but less than $10,000. The 1864 law subjected the income of U.S. citizens residing abroad, as well as U.S. government bond interest, to the general rate scheme. It increased the tax on corporate interest and dividends to 5 percent and expanded the list of deductions to include real estate losses, home rents and rental values, and the business-related expenses of labor, interest, rents, and repairs. The law added the undistributed profits of transportation companies to the corporate tax base. It raised the general rate from 3 to 5 percent and broadened the gross receipts tax to encompass the revenues of telegraph, express, lottery, and entertainment companies.[54]

The Revenue Acts of 1865, 1866, 1867, and 1870

Between 1864 and 1870, Congress modified the income tax four times. In 1865, it eliminated the intermediate rate and lowered the 10 percent income threshold to $5,000. In 1866, it subjected the U.S.-source interest, dividends, and business profits of nonresident aliens to U.S. taxation. In 1867, it raised the exemption amount to $1,000. Also in 1867, Congress abandoned the graduated rate scheme in favor of a flat tax of 5 percent. It created three new deductions: one for casualty losses, another for worthless debts, and a third for business losses. Finally, in 1870, Congress increased the exemption amount to $2,000, lowered the flat rate to 2.5 percent, and subjected the U.S.-source rents of nonresident aliens to U.S. taxing authority.[55] Considered no longer necessary, the tax expired by operation of law at the end of 1872.

Treasury officials regarded the tax as successful. In 1865, President Grant created a special commission to formulate the future revenue policy of the United States.[56] He appointed then commissioner of Internal Revenue John Wells as its head. The Wells Commission convened throughout the summer. As a result of its deliberations, it defined this policy in terms of two objectives: first, to eliminate taxes that impede economic development, and second, to retain taxes that fall on realized wealth. The commission singled out the income tax as eminently meeting these objectives. In so doing, it inextricably bound the tax to the future revenue policy of the United States.[57]

Toward the end of 1893, McMillin's subcommittee reviewed the report of the Wells Commission. By this time, all the evidence at hand seemed to support the creation of a modern U.S. scheme. How did this evidence impact the thinking of subcommittee members? Shearman's and Holmes's findings undoubtedly drove home the point that something urgently had to be done about the growing disparities in wealth. The consular reports demonstrated that there was contemporaneous European precedent for an income tax. The Civil War schemes pointed to the existence of national precedent. Consequently, the subcommittee had no difficulty in recommending to the full committee that an income tax be adopted. Committee Democrats hesitated to follow this recommendation—until politics forced their hand.[58]

As the hearings progressed, it became increasingly evident to the Democratic leadership that the Wilson Bill would not pass without the support of the Populists. The proposed reduction in import duties threatened to undermine the competitive position of domestic industries. Many such industries operated in districts from which Democratic congressmen had been elected. These congressmen feared that heightened foreign competition would jeopardize the livelihood of their principal constituents. Several such congressmen declined to support the Wilson Bill. Some openly opposed it.[59]

The Populists, by contrast, had no problem with the measure—or so it seemed. The vast majority of their supporters derived their livelihood from agriculture. Rather than jeopardize this livelihood, most Populists believed, heightened foreign competition would actually improve it. This posture raised the possibility that any loss in Democratic votes could easily be offset with Populist votes. When the Democratic leadership came to this realization, it began to court the Populist members of Congress.

The Populists, for their part, were determined to have their income tax, regardless of what the Democrats decided to do.[60] The only problem was that if their income tax proposal were packaged as separate legislation, it was almost certain to be defeated on the floor. On the other hand, if the proposal were incorporated in the Wilson Bill, in return for a Populist pledge to support the entire measure, the income tax, along with tariff reform, was virtually ensured of success.[61] When the Populists came to this realization, they began to respond to Democratic overtures.

In January 1894, there was a "meeting of the minds." At the commencement of the second congressional session, House Populists refused to vote for a quorum unless an income tax rider were attached to the Wilson Bill.[62] In this refusal, they were joined by several eastern Democrats, who opposed lowering duties on coal, iron ore, and manufactures, and by the overwhelming majority of Republicans, who rejected tariff reform altogether.[63] The lack of a quorum spelled trouble for the Democratic leadership. It not only meant that congressional debate on the Wilson Bill would be endlessly forestalled, but also pointed to the improbability of passage.[64] The odds, however, could be reversed with a little math and some political maneuvering. The number of votes necessary to achieve a quorum (hence, to pass the Wilson Bill) was seven.[65] The number of Populist votes "up for grabs" was ten.[66] Savvy in math, Representatives McMillin and Bryan convened a party caucus. There, over Chairman Wilson's objections, a majority of Democrats, primarily from the South and West, voted to attach an income tax rider to the Wilson Bill.[67]

This vote effectively sealed the fate of the income tax in Congress. At the same time, it left Republicans and eastern Democrats out in the cold. Despite rising sentiment to the contrary, Republicans remained steadfast defenders of protectionism.[68] A handful from the West embraced the income tax. The majority, however, viewed it as antithetical to the interests of their principal constituents. Eastern Democrats, for their part, faced two unsavory alternatives: either support the Populist income tax or oppose Democratic tariff reform.[69] Their choosing the first alternative would draw fire from the chambers of commerce and boards of trade. Their choosing the second would be criticized by the labor unions and farmers' cooperatives.[70]

As the first session of the Fifty-third Congress came to a close, so too did a year of turbulence that had shaken U.S. institutions to their very foundations. The Populist-Democratic alliance promised to place these institutions on a new, more solid footing. It promised to revise a system of tariffs that disproportionately burdened the working poor. It promised to redistribute the tax burden on a more equitable basis. It promised to create a progressive tax regime geared to the social realities of an industrializing nation. It promised to open the doors of Congress to the winds of change that had been stirred up suddenly and unexpectedly by an economic cyclone.

The socioinstitutional view distinguishes between the democratic state and democratic government. The democratic state reflects the political will of members of society. These members share a common conception of citizenship, law, authority, and order. Democratic government, by contrast, reflects the political will of members of society authorized by the state to administer its affairs—effectively, the administrative apparatus of the state. These members share a common conception of process, practice, governance, and procedure. Because the democratic state is founded on a common vision of *right* and *freedom,* it is nonexistent without those individuals who share this vision. Because democratic government is founded on the authority delegated to it by the democratic state, it is nonexistent without this state.

In constituting the state, members of society are unequal in terms of wealth and power. Some are in a better position to propagate their political views and inculcate their social values. Others have greater means at their disposal to realize their subjective aims. Nonetheless, the state exists because its citizens *will* it to be. It is predicated not upon the equality of wealth or power, but rather upon a commonality of *vision.*

Within government, political elites act with a degree of autonomy, although this autonomy is both defined and circumscribed by law. In other words, it is a *limited administrative autonomy,* not an *absolute sovereign power.* It is the autonomy to perform those tasks incidental to one's office. It follows that political elites, however inclined to act on their own, are institutionally constrained in their ability to act. They are not at liberty to impose their will upon society as they see fit. Nor are they free to use the law as an instrument of social control.

The limited autonomy of political elites is implicitly authorized by society. It is an implied authority, not an inherent right. It both emanates from and is contingent on the popular will. Such autonomy derives from the fact that in electing officials to public office, voters implicitly grant them broad authority to perform their duties. It is under this authority that elected officials appoint administrative subordinates. It is also under this authority that they delegate less essential tasks to their appointees. Hence, notwithstanding their wide latitude to act, government officials, as well as their subordinates, are *agents* of society. They are accountable to society for their actions. They are empowered by society to conduct its affairs. They are well aware that if they exceed their institutional bounds, they may be either voted out of office or heralded into a public forum and relieved of their duties. This realization constrains their political behavior. If on occasions government elites have transgressed their authority, if they have breached the public trust, it has been less by institutional design than by individual will or neglect. It is individuals who act within the confines of institutions, not institutions that act within the confines of individuals.

According to this view, government elites are part and parcel of the society in which they live. They are not immune to the virus of change. To be sure, they bring it to bear on government. As a corollary, there is almost as much diversity within government as there is without. This diversity is a source of both conflict and compromise. It transforms government from an inert repository of consensual functionaries into a dynamic forum of dissenting visionaries. Yet despite their diverse backgrounds, government elites are bound by common institutional values. They share a common conception of law, authority, procedure, and administration. They share similar perceptions of *the way things actually are*. They differ, however, in their beliefs as to *the way things ought to be*. These differences provide ideological fodder for debate, maneuvering, alliance, and negotiation.

What is more, political elites pursue a variety of subjective aims—some political, some economic, some personal. They derive satisfaction from seeing their aims realized in the form of law. As a result, they come to see the law not as a rhetorical shield for deflecting public discontent, but rather as the objective embodiment of their subjective aims. If it later turns out that the law's effect was to subvert these aims, this is because *elites are not clairvoyant; they often cannot foresee the long-term consequences of their actions.*

These actions elevate the state to a new level of existence. They elevate it not operationally, but rather ideologically and institutionally. If one focuses on the basic pattern of government operations, one can be deluded into believing that essentially nothing has changed over time. On the other hand, if one focuses on the cases decided, the laws enacted, and the institutions established, one cannot escape the conclusion that *a great deal* has changed over time. Socioinstitutionalism adopts the latter perspective. From this perspective, the state is animated, dynamic, self-transcending. It can aptly be described as "inert" only to the extent that legislators cease to enact laws, judges cease to interpret them, administrators cease to enforce them, and citizens cease to observe them.

Consistent with this view, the nineteenth-century American state reflected the political will of its individual citizens—industrialists, workers, merchants, farmers, all diverse members of an industrializing nation. Nineteenth-century U.S. government embodied the operational ideas of agents of the state—legislators, bureaucrats, judges, and public officials, all authorized by the state to administer its affairs. Despite disparities in power, these citizens shared a common conception of civic duty, governance, authority, and order. Despite their diverse backgrounds, these officials shared a common vision of legislative process, administrative practice, and judicial procedure.

Within Congress, senators and representatives were free to pursue their subjective aims, so long as they acted within reasonable bounds. Defining these bounds were the U.S. Constitution, federal statutes, judicial decisions, and administrative rules, not to mention the expectations of political parties, trade and labor organizations, and home constituents. The subjective aims of these legislators varied. In the 1892 campaign, such aims included broadening one's political base, mollifying the opposition, adhering to the party platform, and being true to one's personal convictions. In the Fifty-third Congress, they included fulfilling past campaign promises, forging new alliances, funding a revenue shortfall, and easing the burden on the working poor. Some of these aims were immediate, tactical, and secondary. Others were more remote, philosophical, and uncompromising. Still others were so general and collective as to define an entire political movement.

The realization of these aims ultimately transformed the American state. It did so not in terms of governmental operations, but rather in terms of *new tax laws and new fiscal regimes.* In the final analysis, the American state emanated from civil society. It was integrally linked to this society through an intricate web of laws and institutions. On an ideological plane, these laws and institutions had been internalized by members of society. They were just as much subjective ideas that animated individual thought and behavior as they were the objective reality of the modern state. Thus, as political elites realized their subjective aims through legislation, administration, and adjudication, they created new and vital laws and institutions. At the same time, they transformed the civic orientation of society and redefined the objective reality that was, in essence, the American state. This notion is key to an understanding of the socioinstitutional view. From social phenomena as they unfold, this view derives the modern state, which it sees as objectified in laws and institutions and idealized in subjective mind.

3

The Legislative Process

"In estimating the gains, profits, and income of any person there shall be included premium on coupons." The eyes of the multimillionaire will pop out at this. The Wall Street shark, not to mention the vulture, will enjoy this thrust. The gargoyle on Trinity church will smile and Chancey Depew's brass monkey will cough its head off with laughter.

—Democratic representative Joseph Hendrix of Brooklyn, January 30, 1894

Benton McMillin took the lead in drafting the income tax provisions.[1] He borrowed language from the 1864 act.[2] He considered technicalities of the European systems.[3] He weighed the manner in which the burden should be allocated among members of society. In actually making this allocation, McMillin sought the assistance of Internal Revenue Commissioner Joseph Miller. He asked Miller how much could be raised by a tax on incomes greater than $4,000. Why $4,000? Treasury officials estimated average U.S. per capita income to be $1,000.[4] Congressional salaries stood at $5,000. According to his detractors, McMillin wanted to shift the burden to the wealthy without subjecting Democratic congressmen to the charge that they were exonerating themselves of the duty to pay taxes.[5] An exemption of $4,000 would serve this aim.

The Committee on Ways and Means accepted McMillin's figure for two reasons. First, it believed that a $4,000 exemption would provide substantial relief for low- to middle-income taxpayers. Specifically, it would exclude from the income of these taxpayers amounts required for "minimum comforts." This approach marked a significant departure from tariff taxation, which effectively charged the latter amounts. For Ways and Means, the purpose of the exemption was to facilitate basic consumption, not diminish it.[6] Explained Democratic representative Elijah Brookshire of Indiana:

> This relieves consumption, and therefore gives relief where it should be given in fact. The committee which has reported this bill to tax individual incomes believes that to tax the excess of incomes over $4,000 is not to tax consumption. A man ought to be able to buy everything which he needs to consume and which is necessary for his comfort for $4,000 a year. In fact, he ought to be able to buy all the necessary and needful comforts of life for himself and family, and to educate his family for a less sum, if he desires to economize.[7]

Second—and what is nearly the same—the committee shared McMillin's belief that a $4,000 exemption would shift the burden from the less wealthy to the wealthy.[8] It clearly realized that about 85,000 Americans earned more than $4,000; hence, to exempt this amount was to target these Americans. On November 23, 1893, Miller had replied to McMillin, "If there were 50,000 persons in 1870 who paid tax on an income of over $4,000, the wealth of the country being about $30,000,000,000, it might reasonably be expected that the number of these taxpayers would now be about 85,000, and that at the rate of 5 per centum on all incomes in excess of $4,000 the revenue derived would be about $40,000,000, or at a rate of about $8,000,000 for each per centum, or of $32,000,000 at 4 per centum." McMillin conveyed this reply to the full committee, which incorporated it in its official report to the House.[9]

By mid-January, the contours of the new system had taken shape.[10] A 2 percent tax would be levied on individual incomes greater than $4,000 and on undistributed corporate profits.[11] Individuals subject to the tax would fall into three categories: first, residents of the United States; second, U.S. citizens residing abroad; and third, nonresident aliens. The first two were to be taxed on their worldwide income, the third only on income derived from a business or property located in the United States. Taxable income was to include salaries, profits, rents, dividends, annuities, property gains, and interest on municipal, state, and corporate obligations. It was to exclude interest on federal obligations that by the terms of their issuance were tax exempt. The 2 percent tax on interest, dividends, and annuities was to be collected at the source. Individuals would be allowed five deductions: business expenses, interest, taxes, casualty losses, and worthless debts.[12]

Corporations subject to the tax were to be organized in the United States, and for profit. They would be allowed deductions for their basic operating expenses. Such expenses would include the normal costs of carrying on a trade or business, but they would exclude amounts paid for interest, dividends, and annuities. The new system was to be equipped with a reporting and compliance mechanism. All taxpayers were to file returns with the Office of Internal Revenue. The commissioner was to have broad powers to inquire, examine, and audit. Substantial penalties were to be imposed for fraud and for willfully failing to file a return.[13]

The proposed system differed from the Civil War schemes in five major respects. First, it purported to reach all domestic corporations organized for profit. The Civil War schemes had reached only such corporations in selected industries. Second, it proposed to tax most types of interest, dividends, and annuities. The Civil War schemes had taxed only interest and dividends paid by financial and transportation companies. Third, the system aimed at subjecting all persons—individuals and corporations, foreign and domestic—to the same rate. The Civil War schemes had subjected these persons to different rates. Fourth, it proposed to tax all sources of income at the same rate. The Civil War schemes had taxed these sources at different rates.[14] Finally, and perhaps most important, the new system was intended to reflect the *permanent revenue policy of the United States.*[15] The Civil War schemes were intended as temporary expedients designed to meet the pressing exigencies of war.[16]

In a sense, this system represented a *liberal* response to the dramatic changes that had swept the nation since the Civil War. It would install new institutional devices designed to appropriate private wealth, all the while leaving the basic structure of society intact. McMillin and his colleagues created a generous exemption to accommodate, not eliminate, the growing disparities in national wealth. They broadened the tax base to shave, not devour, the vast accumulations of individual and corporate property. They included interest, dividends, and annuities in this base to tap income from intangibles, not stifle the generation of such income. And they expanded the tax jurisdiction of the United States to reach foreign earnings, not impede the globalization of U.S. business. By the same token, the new system represented a *radical* response to decades of fiscal nonuniformity. In the past, rates varied, income was schedulized, and the tax base defined sometimes as gross receipts and at other times as net income. Now, rates were to be standardized, income was to be globalized, and the tax base consistently defined as *revenues net of deductions.*

On January 12, the Committee on Ways and Means approved the income tax scheme by a vote of eleven to six.[17] Six days later, House debate on the proposal commenced.

The House Amendments

By caucus agreement, this debate lasted only three days.[18] In its course, several key amendments were introduced. On January 31, Colorado Populist Lafe Pence proposed to substitute graduated rates for the flat tax of 2 percent.[19] Under Pence's plan, the exemption amount would have been lowered to $2,500, and the schedule shown in table 5 would have been instituted. No sooner had Pence offered his amendment than Pennsylvania Democrat Joseph Sibley submitted a substitute.[20] Under Sibley's substitute, the exemption amount would have been raised to $10,000, and the schedule shown in table 6 would have been instituted.

Sibley justified his amendment in terms of distributional equity. Its aim, he openly professed, was to stop individuals from accumulating great fortunes. Missouri Democrat Uriel Hall vigorously disputed this aim. The taxing power of the federal government, Hall argued, should not be used to prevent individuals from amassing wealth. Ultimately, Hall's argument prevailed. The House rejected first Sibley's substitute, then Pence's main amendment.[21]

These actions are significant for two reasons. First, they indicate that early income tax proponents did not regard graduated rates as essential to their scheme. To be sure, they viewed a "flat tax" as sufficient. For these advocates, the progressive nature of income taxation lay not in the tax rate, but rather in the tax base. The very shift from consumption to income marked a dramatic departure from regressivity. Second, the actions reveal that early income tax proponents viewed the accumulation of wealth as a legitimate social goal, and furthermore that they saw the income tax as a means of redistributing not *wealth,* but rather the *tax burden.*[22] Significantly, liberal reformers of the twentieth century would view the tax as a means of reducing, if not eliminating, vast disparities in national wealth. These reformers would transform the tax into a bold new instrument of social policy.

On the same day that Pence offered his amendment, Illinois Democrat William Springer introduced an amendment that would expand taxable income to include cash and property acquired through gift, devise, or inheritance. McMillin pointed out to Springer that Ways and Means had always intended the term to encompass the foregoing items. McMillin, however, urged his colleagues to approve Springer's amendment so as to make this intent perfectly clear. Before the House could proceed to a vote, Indiana Demo-

Table 5
Pence's Proposed Tax Rate Schedule

Taxable Income		Tax Rate
More Than	*But Less Than*	
$2,500	$10,000	1%
10,000	30,000	2
30,000	60,000	3
60,000	100,000	4
100,000	—	5

Source: Cong. Rec., 53d Cong., 2d sess., 1894, 26, pt. 2:1730 (statement of Pence).

crat William Bynum offered a series of substitutes, the last of which would delineate "property" to include notes, bonds, and choses in action. Bynum intended by this delineation to dispel any doubt as to the meaning of the term *property*. After only brief debate, the House approved first Bynum's substitute, then Springer's main amendment.[23]

These measures indicate that early income tax proponents intended the term *income* to be broadly construed—at least, broadly enough to encompass not only wages, profits, and business gains, but also any *accretion to wealth*. Furthermore, they reveal that Congress clearly wanted to reach the vast accumulations of intangible wealth that had previously gone untaxed. Congress sought to do so by appropriating not wealth per se, but rather *surplus wealth*. Finally, the measures indicate that early income tax proponents regarded gift and estate taxation as integral to their fiscal scheme; alternatively, they viewed the taxation of income, gifts, and estates as part of one and the same system. This revelation has profound implications for current tax reform proposals. It suggests that abolishing gift and estate taxation, either alone or in conjunction with the abolition of income taxation, would defeat the original intent of Congress, that is, to reach *total* surplus wealth and *total* ability to pay.

On February 1, the House approved the income tax amendment by a vote of 182 to 48, with 122 abstentions.[24] Voting in favor of the amendment were 167 Democrats, 7 Republicans, 6 Populists, and 2 independents. Of these Democrats, 94 were from the South, 71 from the West, and 2 from the industrial East. All Republicans were from the West.[25] Voting against the amendment were 45 Democrats and 3 Republicans. Of these Democrats, 4 were from the South, 1 from the West, and 40 from the industrial East. All

Table 6
Sibley's Proposed Tax Rate Schedule

Taxable Income		Tax Rate
More Than	*But Less Than*	
$10,000	$50,000	2%
50,000	100,000	3
100,000	200,000	5
200,000	—	10

Source: Cong. Rec., 53d Cong., 2d sess., 1894, 26, pt. 2:1730 (statement of Sibley).

these Republicans were from the industrial East. Not voting were 5 eastern Democrats, 116 Republicans, and 1 Free Silverite. Following this measure, the House approved the Wilson Bill, as amended, by a vote of 204 to 140 with 8 abstentions.[26]

Action in the Senate

On February 2, the Wilson Bill was laid before the Senate, where it was referred to the Finance Committee.[27] Upon its referral, Chairman Daniel Voorhees appointed a special subcommittee to review its various provisions. He named Missouri Democrat George Vest as subcommittee chair, and Democrats Roger Mills of Texas and James Jones of Arkansas as subcommittee members.[28] All favored the income tax, as well as tariff reform.

Like their counterparts on Ways and Means, however, Vest, Mills, and Jones faced an uphill battle in procuring the number of votes necessary for passage. Of eighty-eight senators, forty-four were Democrats. Twenty-three were from the South, fourteen from the West, and seven from the industrial East. Of the seven, one senator—New York's David Hill—openly declared his opposition to the bill. Others such as James Smith of New Jersey endorsed its tariff provisions, but not its income tax feature.[29] Countervailing votes were pledged by Nebraska Populist William Allen and South Dakota independent James Kyle. But this counterweight still left scores of Democrats who were lukewarm toward the measure, not because of its income tax rider, but rather because of its specific schedule of import duties.[30]

As the subcommittee explored ways to broaden support for the Wilson Bill, pressure from the White House mounted. In February and March, Treasury Secretary John Carlisle personally called on the Finance Committee. He spoke of the president's great displeasure over the lack of progress made toward tariff reform. He stressed that the worst possible calamity would befall the nation as a whole (and the Democratic Party in particular) if the McKinley Tariff schedule were not modified.[31] For his part, President Cleveland publicly endorsed tariff reform, but privately scorned the income tax. "You know how much I deprecated the incorporation in the proposed bill of the income-tax feature," he would later chide Ways and Means Committee chairman Wilson.[32]

Toward breaking the impasse, Senate Democrats caucused in early May. After three days' deliberation, they decided, first, to revise the schedule of duties so as to make it more palatable to a majority of Democrats and, second, to preserve the income tax feature so as to retain the support of the Populists.[33] In the weeks that followed, Senator Jones endeavored to carry out these decisions. He canvassed every Democratic senator to ascertain that senator's specific objection to the tariff schedule. He then addressed each objection with a proposed amendment. In all, Jones drafted more than four hundred such amendments. Their overall effect was to raise the average rate on dutiable merchandise by about 3 percent.[34]

The Senate Amendments

On June 21, the Senate turned its attention to the income tax. It considered, first, amendments proposed by the Finance Committee, then amendments proposed from the floor. In its version of the Wilson Bill, the House adopted the following language regarding individuals subject to income taxation: "Every person residing in the United States, or any citizen of the United States residing abroad." The Finance Committee proposed to substitute, in its place, the following language: "Every citizen of the United States, and every person residing therein."[35] Although the substitute was more of form than of substance, it sparked a debate of considerable interest.

Read in isolation, the language of the Finance Committee conveys a fairly straightforward meaning: both U.S. citizens residing in the United States and U.S. citizens residing abroad are to be taxed on their worldwide income. Read in conjunction with proposed Section 58, which would tax nonresident aliens only on U.S.-source income, however, the language appears to be ambiguous.[36] It could mean either that U.S. citizens residing abroad, like U.S. citizens residing in the United States, would be taxed on their worldwide income or that U.S. citizens residing abroad, like nonresident aliens, would be taxed only on property owned and business conducted in the United States. Massachusetts Republican George Hoar favored the first construction:

> So, if an American citizen went abroad and carried the protection of his country, of his citizenship with him, he did not escape its burdens. There are a great many people, I am sorry to say, who go abroad for that very purpose. . . . They lived in luxury, at the same time at less cost, in a foreign capital; they had none of the voluntary obligations which rest upon citizens, of charity, or contributions, or supporting churches, or anything of that sort, and they escaped taxation.
>
> That class of persons, in my judgment, ought to pay taxes on all their property at home or abroad, wherever it may be. If they remain American citizens . . . we have something to do with their property abroad.[37]

So did Democrat Vest, who had taken charge of the income tax debate. Vest offered this interpretation of the language adopted by the committee: "The first classification is 'every citizen of the United States.' No man divests himself of his citizenship by going abroad. Then it says 'and every person residing therein;' that is, in the United States, and that takes in everybody." Toward expressing this intent with greater clarity, Hoar proposed to substitute "whether residing at home or abroad" for the phrase "residing abroad."[38] The provision as modified would thus read, "Every person residing in the United States, or any citizen of the United States, whether residing at home or abroad."

Why is this debate significant? It reveals the rationale behind the taxation of *worldwide* income. The class of individuals at issue was the growing number of Americans residing abroad. Congress clearly wanted to reach the income of these Americans and sought to do so by expanding the tax jurisdiction of the United States. Both Hoar and Vest justified this measure on the basis of *citizenship.* As Hoar points out, citizenship not only confers benefits, but also imposes burdens. Among its benefits is government protection. Among its burdens is the duty to support civil society. Just as citizenship is *extraterritorial,* so too are its incidental benefits. And just as these benefits are extraterritorial, so too are the correlative burdens. This rationale is strikingly different from the basis of tariff taxation. For Democrats, the primary purpose of tariff taxation was to raise government revenues. For Republicans, such purpose was to protect U.S. industry from foreign competition.[39] For both Democrat Vest and Republican Hoar, an important—if not *the most important*—purpose of taxing worldwide incomes was to impose fiscal burdens commensurate with civic benefits. By all indications, the Senate concurred in this rationale. On June 21, it approved, first, Hoar's substitute, then the committee's main amendment.[40]

Traditionally, legal scholars have invoked the benefit principle to justify source-based taxation. The state, they argue, confers upon persons and things within its territory tangible and intangible benefits, which enable such persons and things to generate income; therefore, it is only proper that a portion of this income be contributed for the support of government. Scholars have historically invoked ability to pay to justify residence-based taxation. Ability to pay, they contend, is most adequately measured by worldwide income; the country in which the taxpayer resides is best positioned to assess this income. Finally, scholars have justified nationality-based taxation on grounds of sovereignty. The competence of a state to tax its citizens inheres in sovereignty; this competence extends to wherever the citizens may be found.[41] Curiously, both Hoar and Vest justify nationality-based taxation not on the basis of sovereignty, but rather on the basis of benefit. This posture is most likely owing to the senators' consideration of the preeminent position of the United States in the emerging world order. By virtue of this position, Hoar and Vest were convinced, the United States provided benefits, principally in the form of protection, to its expatriates. Therefore, they reasoned, it was only just for these expatriates to contribute to the support of their government.

A more controversial amendment concerned the corporate tax collection scheme. Under the House version of the bill, the revenues generated by a corporation would be taxed at three incidents: First, at the gross profit level, as interest accruing to debt holders. Although this interest would be taxed to the debt holders, the corporation would be responsible for withholding the tax. Second, at the net income level, as dividends distributed to stockholders. Although these dividends would be taxed to the stockholders, the corporation again would be responsible for withholding the tax. Third, once more at the net income level, as earnings retained in the enterprise. These earnings would be taxed only to the corporation, which would be responsible for remitting the tax. This collection scheme resembled the Civil War schemes. It embodied the British principle of collection at the source.

In the course of the debate, Senator Hill raised four objections to this arrangement. First, it would tax gross earnings at the first level, without allowing an offsetting deduction for interest expense. The result would be that the same stream of earnings would be taxed twice: first, as gross profits distributed to debt holders, then as net income either distributed to stockholders or retained in the enterprise. Second, it would tax gross earnings at the first level, without allowing an offsetting deduction for nonoperating (for example, property) losses. Thus, these earnings would be taxed *unconditionally,* even when such losses exceeded corporate revenues. Third, the scheme would tax gross earnings at the first level, before the corporation had had an opportunity to deduct its operating expenses. Thus again, these earnings would be taxed *unconditionally,* even when the corporation generated an operating loss.[42] Finally, the scheme would tax gross earnings distributed to bondholders and net earnings distributed to stockholders, even when the income of a particular bondholder or stockholder fell short of the exemption amount.[43] The result would be that this bondholder or stockholder, taxed in all events, would be deprived of the benefit of his or her exemption.

To address these objections, the Finance Committee put forth three measures: first, a deduction for interest expense; second a deduction for business losses; third, abandonment of the principle of collection at the source.[44] The committee incorporated these measures in new Section 59:

> [T]here shall be assessed, levied, and collected . . . a tax of 2 per cent annually on the net profits or income above actual operating and business expenses, losses, and interest on bonded and other indebtedness of all banks, banking institutions, trust companies, saving institutions, fire, marine, life, and other insurance companies, railroad, canal, turnpike, canal navigation, slack water, telephone, telegraph, express, electric light, gas, water, street railway companies, and all other corporations, companies, or associations doing business for profit in the United States, no matter how created and organized.[45]

From a tax accounting and reporting perspective, the proposed section promised to change little. Each security holder would still be obligated to include interest and dividends in his or her gross income. Individual security holders would still be entitled to the individual exemption. All security holders would still be required to file tax returns with the Office of Internal Revenue. From a tax collection and payment perspective, however, the proposed section promised to change a great deal. Specifically, it would shift responsibility for collecting and remitting the tax from the corporation to its security holders. It would abolish corporate withholding, except in the case of undistributed corporate profits. These proposals reflected the dramatic transformation of the U.S. corporation, in the eyes of Congress, from a "font of income" taxable to its owners to an "economic unit" taxable in its own right. The proposals also reflected a broad trend in U.S. income tax development from the integration of corporate-individual collection and payment functions to their near separation. As these functions would grow more distinct, the contours of the corporate and individual tax schemes would become more clearly delineated. Eventually, two collection and payment systems would emerge, one for individuals, the other for corporations.[46]

At this juncture, Iowa Republican William Allison asked Vest if the term *operating expenses* included the cost of inventory. Vest replied in the affirmative: "I was under the impression that the word 'operating' would cover such expenses as the Senator from Iowa has alluded to. I do not see how a manufacturing establishment could be operated unless it bought its raw materials, or how a business corporation could be run unless it bought goods which it resold." Senator Hill asked Vest if the term also included state and local taxes. If not, declared Hill, he was prepared to offer a amendment. Vest assured Hill that such an amendment would not be necessary. "If there is any doubt in regard to the meaning of the words 'business expenses and operating expenses' I have no objection to such an amendment. My idea was that it would be absolutely necessary for them in order to operate to pay their taxes."[47] Nonetheless, as a concession to both Allison and Hill, Vest consented to two supplemental changes. The first would include the cost of inventory in "business and operating expenses"; the second would include state and local taxes in such expenses.[48]

The Taxation of Stockholders

A deduction for interest expense would solve the problem of double taxation from the standpoint of the corporation. It would not, however, solve it from the standpoint of the stockholder. The stockholder would still have to include distributed corporate earnings in his or her taxable income. The same stream of earnings would have been previously taxed to the corporation. Aware of the problem, Vest proposed an amendment: "[I]n computing the income of any person, corporation, company, or association there shall not be included the amount received from any corporation, company, or association as dividends upon stock of such corporation, company, or association if the tax of 2 per cent has been paid upon its net profits by said corporation, company, or association as required by this act." This amendment would retain the tax at the corporate level, while eliminating it at the stockholder level. The stream of corporate earnings, taxed once to the corporation, would be excluded from the stockholder's income. The Senate no doubt found this approach appealing. On July 26, it approved Vest's amendment without recorded objection.[49]

This measure indicates that although early income tax proponents wanted to separate the corporate-individual *collection-payment* function, they simultaneously wanted to integrate the corporate-individual *accounting* function, and furthermore that they chose as their integrating mechanism an exclusion, as opposed to a deduction (used in the Civil War schemes), a credit, or differential rates on retained and distributed earnings. But why integrate the accounting function while separating the payment-collection function? Why not uniformly integrate, or consistently separate, all functions? The answer probably lay in Congress's changing conception of the corporate enterprise. This metamorphosis justified the separation of collection and payment, but not accounting. On the one hand, the transformation of the U.S. corporation from a "font of income," taxable to its owners, to an "economic unit," taxable in its own right, facilitated the resolution of problematic collection-payment issues. Legislators were impelled to ask, *If both the individual and the economic unit are to be taxed separately, should not each be responsible for its own collection and payment?* On the other hand, this conceptual metamorphosis also highlighted an issue peculiar to accounting: *double taxation.* Legislators were also impelled to ask, *If the income generated by the economic unit is to be taxed when earned, why should the same income also be taxed to its individual owner(s) when distributed?* With time, as the needs of the public fisc would grow, Congress would abandon its efforts to resolve the issue of double taxation. Ultimately, two unintegrated systems of tax accounting would evolve, one for individuals, the other for corporations.

Just when the issue of double taxation seemed to go away, another more pressing issue arose. This issue concerned those stockholders whose earnings fell short of the exemption amount. In principle, these earnings were supposed to be exempt from federal taxation altogether. The withholding on distributed corporate profits effectively tapped these earnings, thus depriving these stockholders of the benefit of their exemption (which was the essence of Hill's fourth objection). Excluding previously taxed corporate profits from individual incomes was of no benefit to these stockholders, because it excluded what should have been exempted in the first place. By the same token, taxing distributed corporate profits unjustly burdened these stockholders, because it taxed what should have been excluded in the first place. Connecticut Republican Orville Platt illustrated the problem in the following example:

> If on one side of a street three persons carry on business as partners, making a joint profit of $6,000, no income tax is to be paid upon such income, or profit unless the partners have other sources of income which, added to their share of the partnership gains, makes their individual income exceed $4,000. If on the opposite side of the street three persons, having formed a corporation, carry on the same kind of business and make the same amount of profit, the $6,000 profit made by the corporation is to pay an income tax of $120. Is this equal taxation?[50]

New York Democrat David Hill offered a similar illustration:

> I have $5,000, and I invest it in a partnership for carrying on a dry goods store. If my profit is $3,000, if I may assume that by an investment of $5,000 I could make a profit of $3,000, of course that profit of $3,000 is not taxed, as the individual is entitled to an exemption of $4,000, but if I place that $5,000 as an investment in a corporation, before a dividend comes to me from that corporation the tax is already taken out in advance. It of course makes no difference to a man whose income exceeds $4,000, for he has to pay the tax on his income in excess of that amount; but this injustice is upon those people who have incomes of less than $4,000.[51]

Platt's and Hill's remarks interjected a new issue into the income tax debate: *taxable entities*. This issue was inextricably linked to the benefit to be derived from the individual exemption. It could be phrased in this manner: If an individual conducted a business as a partnership or as a sole proprietorship, and if that individual earned less than the exemption amount, he or she would derive the full benefit of the individual exemption. On the other hand, if the individual conducted the same business as a corporation, he or she would derive no benefit—the proposition was "all or nothing." In the debate that was about to ensue, the "entities issue" would come to overshadow the "exemption issue." And in attempting to resolve both issues, the Senate would define the taxable nature of the U.S. corporation.[52]

The central focus of the socioinstitutional view is historical process and subjective meaning. It is historical process that sheds light on the development of laws and institutions, whereas it is subjective meaning that reveals their *original intent*. The view conveys this meaning through the words and deeds of historical actors, speaking and acting within a peculiar social, economic, and institutional context. It is they, not the historian, who have imbued the income tax with a purpose. It is they, not the historian, who convey the most original, authoritative, and unadulterated meaning. The view treats this meaning as authentic, acceptable at face value unless explicitly controverted by the facts. It rejects the notion that these words and deeds are pregnant with a latent meaning to be discovered and exposed by the historian. The historian's role it sees as facilitating logical inferences from subjectively valid facts. The historian does so by placing these facts in sociohistorical context.

With this focus in mind, I have let the actors speak for themselves, without intervening teleologically to divulge their "true intentions." I have let them tell their own story, without attempting to second-guess them. The result, in my opinion, is the authenticity of meaning, not necessarily "political correctness" of interpretation. This meaning reflects the actors' true intent, not what I (or anyone else) think it should be. This, of course, is not to say that the historian has no input in what meaning is conveyed. Nor is it to cast him or her in the role of passive bystander or disinterested party. Rather, it is to elevate the actors' subjective meaning above the historian's imputed meaning. It is to prefer factual inference over historical interpretation.

In determining *which* facts are significant, the historian ultimately influences *which* meaning is conveyed. In faithfully relating these facts to others, he or she participates in the historical process. Because of the historian's superior access to data, however, he or she owes these others a duty to act reasonably and responsibly. The historian fulfills this duty by presenting these data as completely, accurately, and objectively as is possible.

Consistent with this view, one can infer the following from the foregoing historical account: First, the founders of the early income tax intended the term *income* to be broadly construed—broadly enough to encompass the value of, and income derived from, intangibles. This inference can be drawn from McMillin's remarks regarding the nonnecessity of Springer's amendment (concerning the inclusion of gifted and inherited property in taxable income), and from the explicit language of Bynum's subamendment (regarding the delineation of "property" to include notes, bonds, and choses in action). Second, a key rationale for the taxation of worldwide income was to impose extraterritorial burdens commensurate with extraterritorial benefits. This proposition draws support from the discourse between Hoar and Vest, which lucidly articulates this rationale. Third, a fundamental purpose of the individual exemption was to shift the tax burden from the working poor to the wealthy, all the while relieving basic consumption. This finding is clear from Brookshire's remarks explicitly setting forth such a purpose, and from the report of the Committee on Ways and Means, which unequivocally endorsed it.[53] Fourth, the original intent of the early income tax was to redistribute the *tax burden,* not society's wealth. This revelation emerges from Hall's repudiation of Sibley's aim to prevent individuals from amassing great fortunes, as well as from the House's rejection of Pence's and Sibley's proposals to institute graduated rates. Finally, the original intent behind the taxation of corporate income was to tap corporate wealth and check corporate abuse. This conclusion will become evident in the passages that follow.

4

What Is a "Corporation"?

What are corporations? They are aggregations of individuals. Who are the officers of corporations? They are your fellow-citizens, your peers, and your equals. Why do corporations exist? Not for the purpose of the intangible, invisible, and artificial being that the law contemplates for certain purposes. They exist for their stockholders, for the men and the women, the widows and the orphans, who have the right to participate in that mode of human enterprise and in that mode of carrying on the business of life. Why should these aggregations of individuals be attached in their property or in their rights by a method of taxation that we do not dare to apply to the individual when separated from these artificial existences?

—George Gray, Democratic senator
from Delaware, June 27, 1894

It all began when Senator William Allison offered a series of amendments aimed at resolving the stockholder exemption issue. By this stage of the debate, Republicans like Allison had resigned themselves to the inevitability of an income tax. The questions now were "What kind of income tax?" and "How could it be structured to serve the interests of major constituencies?" On the question of the individual exemption, Allison believed that taxing distributed corporate profits would work an injustice on low-income stockholders—in the words of one senator, "the poor people of the country, the widows and orphans, and the men of infirm health" who had happened to invest in stocks.[1] Nor was this injustice peculiar to the taxation of corporate earnings, Allison believed. In a sense, the taxing feature was wrong, because the entire system was wrong.

Income tax proponents saw things differently. They believed that incidentally taxing low-income stockholders, though unfortunate and unintended, was both unavoidable and necessary to reach the vast accumulations of corporate wealth. What was more important than giving "widows and orphans" a break was getting at corporate America. It was forcing those companies that had grown fat at the expense of the "little man" to bear their fair share of the tax burden. Besides, contended tax advocates, investing in a corporation was merely a matter of personal prerogative. One might just as well have invested in a partnership. To be sure, the issue was not so much unjustly taxing low-income stockholders as it was justly taxing those stockholders who had "assumed the risk" of investing in a corporation. In the words of Colorado Republican Henry Teller, "I do not know any way by which you can tax the great corporations that are aggregating to themselves the business of the country and the wealth of the country, unless you tax the man who owns $500, or $50, or any other sum in the corporation. It is incidental to the system. Then if the people who have but little money choose to put it in that sort of business they must take their chances and pay their proportion of the tax."[2]

Allison vowed to put an end to this "nonsense." His first amendment would have exempted all corporations other than the ones specifically mentioned in proposed Section 59. The latter corporations consisted exclusively of financial, transportation, communication, and utility companies. All other corporations, the senator presumed, consisted primarily of small concerns owned by men and women of modest means. In the debate that ensued, Maine Republican Eugene Hale disputed Allison's presumption. Among the proposed exempt corporations, Hale pointed out, would be such giants as the sugar trust. These organizations were no more deserving of a special exemption than were large financial, transportation, communication, and utility companies. Brought to this realization, Allison withdrew his original amendment in favor of a second one. This latter amendment would have exempted not *all* corporations, but rather only corporations with paid-in capital less than $100,000. Allison intended by this limitation to exempt the numerous farmers' cooperatives that operated in his home state, Iowa.[3]

Vest adamantly opposed Allison's amendment. To discriminate against corporations on the basis of their capitalization, he charged, is to ignore the fundamental nature of the corporate enterprise. This enterprise is not an aggregation of individuals, but rather an *artificial being.* As such, it is separate and distinct from its individual owners. Furthermore, argued Vest, to tax some corporations and exempt others is to neglect the primary purpose of corporate taxation. This purpose is not to preserve benefits for individual stockholders, but rather to impose fiscal burdens on this artificial being commensurate with the benefits that it derives from the state. "Now, if we undertake to discriminate between the large and the small corporations we enter into a labyrinth out of which I see no escape whatever," Vest told Allison on the morning of June 27. "Senators may talk about citizens, about widows, for instance, who have their all in these corporations. We do not deal with them. We deal with corporations as artificial beings, whether large or small. We deal with the individual, and give him an exemption on account of consumption over $4,000."[4]

Allison retorted brusquely. True, he insisted, in one sense, a corporation is an artificial being separate and distinct from its individual owners. But in another sense, it is also an *aggregation of individuals,* indistinguishable from its owners. It is the latter sense that should prevail in the case of the small company, contended Allison. Otherwise, corporate taxation would disserve the interests of stockholders of modest means. "What is the proposition as to taxing these corporations?" Allison asked of Vest. "They are entities in one sense, but they are composed of individuals who own the shares, and who would be taxed on these shares without this corporate provision, and who are now exempted if their income exceeds $4,000."[5]

At this juncture, President Pro Tem Isham Harris rose with a motion to table Allison's amendment. Toward preempting this motion, Allison withdrew his amendment. Hours later, however, he resubmitted it in modified form. This third amendment was the same as the second, except that the paid-in capital limit was lowered to $80,000. Allison figured that a corporation's investing $80,000 at a 5 percent rate of return would generate the income equivalent of the exemption amount.[6] Upon offering his amendment, Allison turned to Vest:

> Does the Senator believe that it is right to exempt a man who holds property earning an income of $4,000 a year, and in addition to that, exempting all the taxes that he pays, State, county, and municipal, also the interest upon his debts and upon all property which does not yield an income; and then, if another man has property to the extent of $5,000 in a local corporation, that man shall be required to pay 2 per cent upon that investment? If the Senator says that is justice, I shall be glad to hear him say so.[7]

Clearly agitated, the senator from Missouri replied:

> My argument this morning was to show that we treated a corporation as a legal entity, that we had nothing to do with stockholders, that we treated corporations exactly as we treated individuals, except that we give them no exemptions. . . . I do not think any injustice is done to stockholders because they put their money into corporations knowing that they take the chances of whether they may make any money or not.
>
> We have exempted the bonded indebtedness of corporations; we have given them credit for all their losses; we have taken out all their business expenses and operating expenses, and Senators talk to me now about the stockholder being different from a corporation. We know nothing about the stockholder. We deal with the corporation as an entity, and that is the whole of the argument, whether good or bad.[8]

That afternoon, the question was called on Allison's third amendment. It was rejected, thirty-one to twenty-four, with thirty abstentions.[9]

Eastern Republicans now stepped forward with *their* proposed solutions to the stockholder exemption problem. First in line was Massachusetts Senator George Hoar. Hoar's approach was not to exempt a specific class of corporations, but rather to give all corporations a special exemption.[10] The amount of this exemption would be equal to the aggregate amount of exemptions available to all "qualified stockholders" in the corporation. A "qualified stockholder" would be any individual who earned less than the individual exemption amount. Thus, if a corporation had ten individual stockholders, each of whom earned less than the individual exemption amount, the corporation would be entitled to a corporate exemption of ten times $4,000, or $40,000. Likewise, if a corporation had fifteen individual stockholders, five of whom earned less than this amount, the corporation would be entitled to a corporate exemption of five times $4,000, or $20,000. The advantage of this scheme was that it would confer upon the corporation a benefit exactly equal to the sum total of benefits forfeited by its individual stockholders. These stockholders, in effect, would be transferring their exemptions to the corporation, which in turn would apply them en bloc against its stream of earnings. This stream of earnings, shielded from taxation at the net income level, would then be distributed—presumably to the same class of stockholders.

Vest denounced Hoar's scheme as impractical. It would engulf the corporation in a labyrinth of detail. The corporation's accountants would have to dig through its books and records in search of the name of every stockholder who earned less than the exemption amount. How could one be sure that the benefits would accrue exclusively to the intended class of stockholders? Vest further denounced the scheme as contrary to the purpose of the statutory exemption. This purpose was not to protect stockholders from incidental taxation, but rather to exclude amounts required for basic consumption.[11] This purpose serves individuals well, explained Vest, because as human beings, they consume basic commodities. On the other hand, it serves corporations poorly because as artificial beings, they neither eat, nor drink, nor clothe themselves.

> It is complained that small stockholders in these corporations are made to pay. We do not deal with the stockholders. We deal with a corporation as a legal being, doing business, artificially created, receiving protection upon its property from the General Government like citizens receive protection upon theirs. If it consumed clothing and food and paid the internal-revenue tax and the tariff import tax as does the individual, then the exemption should apply. . . .
>
> We treat a corporation as a legal entity, just as we treat the individual. We say to every corporation in the United States, "You pay no tariff tax, as does the individual citizen, but you shall pay the 2 per cent which we put upon the citizen on account of the protection given to his property." We apply the same rule to the corporations, leaving out the exemption, because of course there is no consumption by the corporation as there is by the individual. This is the theory of the bill.[12]

Once again, President Pro Tem Harris rose with a motion to table the pending amendment. Toward preempting such a move, Hoar called the question. The amendment was defeated, thirty to twenty, with thirty-five abstentions.[13]

It was now the turn of eastern Democrats to come to the rescue of investing widows and orphans. Their approach, embodied in four successive amendments, was to create not a corporate exemption, but rather a corporate deduction. The amount of this deduction would be equal to the aggregate amount of "qualified dividends" paid to "qualified stockholders." A "qualified stockholder" would be any stockholder who received no more than a "qualified dividend." A "qualified dividend" would be any dividend in an amount equal to or less than a statutory cap. The size of the cap varied. In Senator James Smith's proposal, the cap would be $4,000. In Senator David Hill's three proposals, it would be $3,000, $2,000, and $1,000, respectively. Thus, under Smith's proposal, if a corporation paid $2,000 each to three stockholders, $4,000 each to five stockholders, and $5,000 each to two stockholders, the corporation would be entitled to a deduction of three times $2,000 plus five times $4,000, or $26,000. Under Hill's first and second proposals, the same corporation would be entitled to a deduction of three times $2,000, or $6,000. Under Hill's third proposal, the corporation would be entitled to no deduction. In submitting his amendments, Hill asked the quintessential question, "What is a corporation?" He offered the following answer: "It is a creature of State government in the main, created by investments furnished by citizens, having certain corporate powers, enabled to perform business like individuals. A corporation does not subsist merely for the benefit of the ideal corporation; it subsists for the benefit of its stockholders."[14]

Vest rejected these proposals for three reasons. First, from a tax reporting perspective, they would have been cumbersome. They would have required the corporation to account for dividends paid to every stockholder. They would have required it to distinguish between "qualified" and "nonqualified" stockholders. Second, from an tax accounting perspective, the proposals would have allowed a deduction for a discretionary nonoperating item. Vest believed that only fixed operating costs should be deductible. Third, from a philosophical perspective, they embodied a notion of the corporate enterprise that was fundamentally different from Vest's. According to this notion, a corporation is not an artificial being, but rather the instrumentality of its stockholders. It has no existence of its own, but rather *subsists* for the benefit of these stockholders. On the afternoon of June 27, the Senate vindicated George Vest. It rejected first Smith's amendment, then each of Hill's three amendments.[15]

Through these successive actions, Congress once and for all defined the taxable nature of the U.S. corporation.[16] Henceforth, a corporation would be an artificial being, separate and distinct from its individual owners. It would not be an aggregation of individuals. Nor would it be the instrumentality of its stockholders. The purpose of corporate taxation, moreover, would be not to preserve benefits for individual owners, but rather to impose fiscal burdens upon this artificial being commensurate with the benefits that it derives from the state. If this purpose somehow disserved the interests of these owners, it was because they had "assumed the risk" of investing in a corporation.

At this historical juncture, the tax treatment of corporations markedly diverged from the tax treatment of partnerships. Previously, the two treatments had been similar. Under the Civil War schemes, the undistributed profits of both partnerships and corporations were attributable to their respective owners.[17] In its version of the Wilson Bill, the House proposed to retain these attribution features.[18] The Finance Committee, however, rejected attribution in the case of the corporation, but accepted it in the case of the partnership. Nor was its decision inadvertent. In the debate over the corporate tax provisions, Allison had asked Vest if the proposed rules would apply to anything other than "associated corporations." Vest replied unequivocally, "That is the meaning of it. I have not had any doubt about it. If I had intended to use the word 'partnerships,' I should have said 'partnerships.' " Hill had pointed out to Vest fundamental inconsistencies in the taxation of corporations and the taxation of partnerships.[19] In declining to address these inconsistencies, Vest implicitly acknowledged them.

So why did Congress want to tax corporations, but not partnerships? This question unnerved Senate Republicans. "There is no more reason why we should tax the income of a corporation because it is a corporation than why we should tax the income of a partnership because it is a partnership," argued Connecticut Republican Orville Platt.

> A few skillful men who have been able to acquire by economy and savings from their wages a little capital come together, joining their capital, or perhaps they get some man with money who is willing to help them along, and they start thereby a little manufacturing or a mercantile business or joint stock corporation. . . . Why should those institutions be taxed . . . any more than men who enter into partnership should be taxed as partners?"
>
> . . . [W]hy tax the corporation as a corporation and not tax a partnership as a partnership? Why tax this business when you do not tax all business?"[20]

Rhode Island senator Nelson Aldrich broadened the scope of Platt's inquiry. Asked Aldrich, "Why tax corporations, but not sole proprietorships?"

> [B]y the provisions of this bill, an individual who carries on a manufacture of any kind is exempted from the burdensome and annoying exactions of the bill in other respects; a partnership that carries on a business of this kind would be exempt from taxation and from these annoyances, while a corporation is subjected to them all.
>
> . . . It is very difficult to understand by the application of any of the

> principles which should be applied to government or to taxation why these discriminations are made. A corporation is certainly no more vicious than an individual or a partnership that is doing the same business and carrying it on in the same way.[21]

An answer can be inferred from the political climate of the day. By 1894, the corporation had become the principal form of business association in the United States. Corporations abounded not only in numbers, but also in size. This size was negatively associated with power over prices, politics, and men. Strengthening this association were monopoly and cartel. Fortifying it were unethical business practices. Solidifying it was the panic of 1893. Buoyed by anticorporate sentiment, the Populists pressed forth their agenda in Congress. An important item on this agenda was ending corporate abuse. "[W]hen corporations undertake to control the entire policy of the States and the nation," declared Nebraska Populist William Allen,

> when they undertake to rob the producers of the country through overcapitalization and methods of that kind, then the Populist party rises up and protests against such conduct and calls upon the corporations and those in charge of them to cease conduct of that kind. That is not undue hostility; it is not undue hostility to the exercise of legitimate corporate powers. It is a hostility to the abuse of this power by corporations which endangers the rights of the people and the permanency of the Government itself.[22]

By contrast, Americans seem to have been less antagonistic toward the partnership. Its joint and several liability usually checked its growth both in numbers and in size. Its unlimited liability precluded any "hiding behind a partnership veil." Limited in size, the partnership was also limited in power. Few, if any, partnerships controlled prices, politics, and labor to the same extent as did corporations. True, partnerships and corporations engaged in virtually the same business practices. Undoubtedly, many corporations and partnerships committed the same business abuses. On the whole, however, partnership abuses seem to have been less numerous than were corporate abuses. If not less numerous, they were infinitely less notorious.

The Populist approach to ending the abuses of *some* corporations was to tax *all* corporations. This approach drew fire from Delaware Republican Anthony Higgins, who protested: "[B]ecause certain overgrown, bloated corporations, which make an unfair and unjust use of the quality of corporate power exist in the country, is that the reason why all the owners in small corporations and all the small owners in large corporations in the country are to be brought under the income tax. . . ?" Equally critical was Democrat Hill, who found no justice in punishing all corporations for the abuses of a few. If a corporation misbehaves itself, admonished Hill, simply dissolve it.[23]

To return to the central question: Why did Congress want to tax corporations, but not partnerships? *Because of the political sentiment of the day.* This sentiment was decidedly anticorporate. It was spawned by the abuses of *some,* though not *all,* corporations. It found expression in the political ideology of the Populist Party. And it proceeded on the premise that by appropriating the wealth of all corporations, society would somehow be compensated for the abuses of a few. "It is the sentiment that in some way or another the Legislature must get at the corporation, which accounts for the tax upon the incomes of corporations in this bill," explained Senator Platt.

> It has been a remark made more than once in the Senate, and so publicly that I may refer to it during the consideration of this tariff bill, that the persons trying to pass it desire to "get at the rich men," and that is why this tax is laid on corporations. They wish some way or other to get at corporations.
>
> . . . I speak only about the Populist party as representing the sentiment or as having crystallized in some way a sentiment which prevails in the country. That sentiment seems to be that if a corporation does anything wrong, strike at all corporations, tax them. Now, why not tax a partnership? This bill does not tax the income of a partnership; and the corporations of this country, when you step outside of those which are continually in the mind of the people and which are exciting the criticism of people, are nothing more than commercial partnerships.[24]

What were the alternatives to taxing the corporation? Senate Republicans proposed taxing only the individual. Individual incomes, they reasoned, already include corporate earnings. That which can be achieved inefficiently through two accounting, reporting, and collection systems can be achieved efficiently through one. Under the Republican scheme, earnings distributed to security holders would have been taxed exclusively to the security holder. Earnings retained in the enterprise would have been tax exempt. Retained earnings, Republicans maintained, were necessary for investment in plant and equipment. Distributed corporate profits, by contrast, were wasted on personal consumption. "What should be the scheme of an income tax?" asked Connecticut's Platt. "It should be to tax the personal incomes of individuals which exceed the amount exempted, and in that way you get all the income of the country. But here you will observe that confusion is created by trying to tax the corporation. There is no necessity for it, because, if you put the income tax upon personal incomes, you reach all the earnings of the corporation in the hands of the individuals whose incomes exceed the exemption."[25] Added New Hampshire Republican William Chandler:

> I see no reason why there should be any special clause taxing the income of corporations. The tax upon individual incomes includes all the receipts of those individuals from the corporations in which they own stock; the tax upon individual incomes includes all the receipts of those individuals from interest upon the bonds of all corporations; and, therefore, unless there is an evasion by the individual of his honest dues under an income tax, everything that is income and the profit of a corporation is taxed by an individual income tax, unless it be such exemption as a corporation may carry to the credit of surplus or to the construction account, or to the account of some other fund.[26]

The Republican scheme had four advantages over its Democratic counterpart. First, it was simple. It would have abolished corporate reporting in favor of individual reporting. It would have eliminated collection at the source in favor of "collection at the destination." Second, the Republican scheme would have been efficient. It would have integrated the corporate and individual accounting systems. It would have taxed the same stream of earnings once and only once. Third, the Republican scheme would have preserved the benefit of the individual exemption. Specifically, it would have reached only earnings in excess of the exemption amount. Finally, in all likelihood, the Republican scheme would have fostered greater capital formation. Excluding retained earnings from the tax base would have encouraged the reinvestment of corporate profits. Such reinvestment, in turn, would have added to the nation's stock of business assets.

On the other hand, the Republican scheme posed three disadvantages. First, from a tax incidence perspective, it would have been cumbersome. It would have required higher rates to raise the same level of revenue. It would have substantially increased the burden on individual taxpayers. Second, from a behavioral perspective, the Republican scheme would have created an incentive for stockholder tax avoidance. Indeed, what would have prevented stockholders from compelling their directors to stop paying dividends so as to enhance share values? Finally, and most important, from a social perspective, the Republican scheme would have aggravated existing disparities in wealth. With time, reducing these disparities would become a principal aim of the income tax.

The essential ideas embodied in the corporate scheme of 1894 would inspire the next generation of senators and representatives. Fifteen years later, in 1909, the Sixty-first Congress would draw on these ideas to structure its "excise tax" on corporate income. Two decades later, in 1913, the Sixty-third Congress would merge this corporate levy into its new scheme for taxing individual income. In this way, the Populist-Democratic view of the U.S. corporation as a taxable entity would be handed down from one generation to the next, the legacy of nineteenth-century statesmen would be permanently enshrined in twentieth-century laws and institutions, and the essential ideas formulated in the debates of 1894 would lay the foundation for our modern system of corporate taxation.

On July 3, the Senate approved the Wilson Bill, as amended, by a vote of thirty-nine to thirty-four, with twelve abstentions. Voting for the measure were thirty-seven Democrats, one Populist, and one independent. Voting against it were thirty-two Republicans, one Democrat, and one Populist. Senators not voting were equally divided between Democrats and Republicans. Because the Senate version of the bill differed from the House version, a conference committee was called to resolve the differences.[27] This committee met in early July. After a month's deliberation, it decided to adopt the Senate version of the bill. On August 13, the House approved this version by a substantial margin.[28] The bill then went to the president for his signature. Here, however, enactment hit a snag. President Cleveland refused to sign the measure because of the hefty duties it imposed on raw materials. Consequently, the Wilson Bill became public law by default. The winds of change that had swept Congress finally moved a nation. The United States, at last, had an income tax.[29]

Laws and institutions, in the socioinstitutional order, serve a multitude of purposes, each specific to a peculiar legislative, political, and historical context. These laws and institutions can be thought of as the subjective aims of their creators, projected, objectified, and universally recognized as legitimate. Alternatively, they can be thought of as *compromises* among these aims, embodied in socially accepted instruments of governance. As Democratic institutionalist W. Elliot Brownlee points out, although these laws and institutions evolve over time, they evince a constant or core structure. And as pluralist John Witte implies, this structure reflects the interests of broad-based constituencies and special-interest groups (or trade-offs among these groups), merged with the subjective aims of their legislative proponents.

History, in the socioinstitutional view, is movement not toward the realization of the virtuous idea, but rather toward the realization of the subjective aims of historical actors. This movement does not necessarily lead to greater democracy, or greater freedom, or greater equality, but rather to a new level of existence consonant with these subjective aims. Given its transcendental quality, the path of history may be said to be neither linear, nor progressive, nor horizontal. Rather, it is multidirectional, guided by the nature of the aims pursued, the political strength of the actors who pursue them, and the force of resistance encountered. Finally, in tracing the path of history, the historian must carefully distinguish between subjective intent and objective effect. Subjective intent refers to the purposive aims of historical actors. Objective effect refers to the ultimate result of their political action.

So it was with the Income Tax of 1894. This act reflected *not* a bureaucratic obsession with preserving the status quo, but rather a Populist drive to redistribute the tax burden merged with a Democratic campaign to reform the tariff. It reflected *not* an elitist consensus over how to stem the tide of revolution, but rather a political alliance among legislators in pursuit of diverse, though not incompatible, aims. It embodied *not* the overriding interests of dominant social groups, but rather compromises among the claims of farmers, industrialists, workers, and businessmen. It reflected *not* the realization of an egalitarian ideal, but rather the political will of congressmen acting on behalf of various constituents. The core structure of the tax was simple. It consisted of income broadly defined, an allowance for business operating expenses, and the exemption of amounts required for "minimum comforts." This structure reflected both the economic interests of the working poor and the operating needs of small businesses, as mediated through the political aims of Democratic and Populist congressmen.

The foregoing historical account addresses how and why members of the Fifty-third Congress structured the income tax in the way in which they did. It does not explain how these legislators rationalized or legitimated this structure. To this inquiry, we now turn.

5

The Rationale

The subjects of every State ought to contribute towards the support of the Government, as nearly as possible, in proportion to their respective abilities; that is, in proportion to the revenue which they respectively enjoy under the protection of the State.

—Adam Smith,
The Wealth of Nations

In a republic like ours, where all men are equal, this attempt to array the rich against the poor or the poor against the rich is socialism, communism, devilism.

—Republican senator John Sherman
of Ohio, June 22, 1894

What was the rationale for the system, and on what grounds was it opposed? Income tax proponents put forth three principal arguments in favor of the tax. The first was based upon ability to pay.[1] According to this argument, equity is achieved when each citizen contributes to the support of government according to his or her ability to pay. Ability to pay is nearly synonymous with revenue. Thus, equity is achieved when each citizen contributes to the support of government according to his or her revenue. This argument was first propounded by the political economist Adam Smith. Tax proponents contended that being a charge on revenue, an income tax compels each citizen to contribute according to his or her ability to pay; thus, it is equitable. Remarked Democratic representative Henry Talbert of Georgia: "[T]he income tax is the most equitable and just way of taxation, putting the burden of taxation upon the shoulders of who are most able to bear it, and takes it from the shoulders of those who are least able to bear it."[2] Declared Democratic representative William Jennings Bryan of Nebraska:

> There is no more just tax upon the statute books than the income tax, nor can any tax be proposed which is more equitable; and the principle is sustained by the most distinguished writers on political economy.
>
> Adam Smith says: "The subjects of every State ought to contribute to the support of the Government, as nearly as possible, in proportion to their respective abilities . . ."
>
> The income tax is the only one which really fulfills this requirement.[3]

For proponents of this argument, the main problem with tariff taxation was that it burdens those citizens with the least ability to pay to a greater extent than it burdens ones with the most. Tariffs raise the prices of basic commodities. These prices absorb a greater portion of the earnings of the poor. Explained Nebraska Populist Omer Kem:

> Under our present system of collecting revenue the wealthier men become, the less tax they pay in proportion to their ability. To illustrate: Revenues are now collected from articles of consumption. The man of moderate income who has a family of ten to support may consume ten times as much as the man who has no family but is worth a million dollars. Since each is taxed in proportion to the amount he consumes, it can readily be seen that this poor man will contribute ten times as much to the support of the Government as this old bachelor millionaire.[4]

Some contemporary scholars have attacked the minor premise by contending that wealth or consumption is a better gauge of ability to pay than is revenue. To this contention, one might retort that abundant assets do not necessarily ensure solvency. Indeed, such assets may be illiquid in form, thus undermining the ability of the asset holder to pay his or her debts as they fall due. As for the charge that consumption is a better gauge of ability to pay, one might retort that consumption can be facilitated through unfettered borrowing. Arguably, the greater the borrowing, the greater the debt burden, and the less the ability of the consumer to pay his or her debts as they fall due. By contrast, and as is implicit in the minor premise, the greater the revenue, the greater the liquidity, and the greater the ability of the revenue generator to liquidate his or her debts as they fall due.

The second major argument advanced by income tax proponents was based on "equality of sacrifice." According to this argument, equity is achieved when the sacrifices made by all citizens in defraying the cost of government are equal. These sacrifices are equal when each citizen feels neither more nor less inconvenienced than the next. This maxim was first articulated by the utilitarian philosopher John Stuart Mill.[5] Tax proponents contended that being proportionate to wealth, an income tax inconveniences the rich to the same extent as it does the poor; thus, it results in equality of sacrifice. "I am in favor of an income tax," declared Representative Hernando Money of Mississippi. "I . . . favor this tax because there is an equality in the sacrifice that is made by the taxpayer. I would have it so that each man in this broad Republic who pays any tax to the Government should feel just the same inconvenience in the payment of it that any other man should feel. That is only right and just."[6] Proclaimed fellow Mississippian John Williams:

> Now, government has a right to such revenues as are necessary in order to answer the ends and aims of government economically administered. This is taxation. That is also a truism, as well as that in collecting the money for this purpose it has the right to demand from each citizen only an equal sacrifice, and nothing more. . . .
>
> Therefore you may lay down as the basis of all taxation this maxim—that equal sacrifice is equal taxation; that unequal sacrifice is unequal taxation. . . .
>
> "[E]quality of taxation is impossible in any community without an income tax."[7]

For proponents of this argument, the key problem with tariff taxation was that it demands sacrifices of the poor greater than the sacrifices that it demands of the rich. Import duties diminish *basic consumption,* they pointed out. By contrast, the income tax diminishes *surplus value.* Continued Representative Williams:

> With this principle of equality of sacrifice before him, let each American citizen institute a comparison between tariff taxation . . . on the one hand, and an income tax upon the other. With the idea of equal sacrifice in your mind, the first thing that strikes you is that all tariff taxation is a tax upon consumption . . . things destroyed in the using. The next thing that strikes you is this: That the measure of taxes upon consumption, like the tariff upon imports, is *things consumed.* . . .
>
> The other measure, the income tax, is *value received.* Take it as a question, not of protection at all, but a question of taxation by tariff for revenue

> only on the one hand and by income tax on the other. Which one of these two systems most nearly demands and secures equality of sacrifice from each citizen in proportion to his ability to support the state?[8]

The third major argument advanced by income tax proponents was based on the benefit principle. According to this argument, equity is achieved when each citizen bears a share of the tax burden according to the degree of benefits that he or she derives from the state. Chief among these benefits is protection. Thus, equity is achieved when each citizen bears a share of the tax burden according to the degree of protection that he or she derives from the state. This argument was first propounded by the contract theorist Thomas Hobbes.[9] Tax proponents contended that the benefits derived from the state are directly proportional to wealth and that only the income tax reaches this wealth. Asked Democratic representative George Cooper of Indiana:

> But to whom do the benefits of government accrue? . . . [I]f you abandon your Government, the Government of this Republic, what becomes of your stocks, of your bonds, of your corporations, and all of these intangible and incorporeal rights the machinations of the mind of man that are built up under the protection of government? They will disappear like the airy fabric of a dream.
>
> Therefore I say the men who have incomes, the men who have property of this character, are the most greatly benefitted.[10]

Asserted Ways and Means Committee member John Tarsney:

> Sir, government is instituted for the protection of the lives, the liberties, and the property of its citizens, and it is but fair and equitable that each citizen should contribute of his means for the support of government in proportion to the protection he receives from the government and in proportion to the cost that his protection entails upon the government. . . . We base it [the income tax] upon the theory that the citizen receives the benefits and enjoys the protection of government in proportion to the wealth he has to be protected, and that it is his duty to contribute by way of taxation in proportion to such protection and the cost which it imposes.[11]

For proponents of this argument, the inequity of tariff taxation lay in its mismatching of burdens and benefits. Tariffs impose burdens on the poor greater than the benefits that the poor derive. By contrast, tariffs confer benefits upon the rich greater than the correlative burdens. Remarked Arkansas Democrat Hugh Dinsmore:

> The poor man spends the whole of his income for the support of himself, his wife, and children in supplying the bare necessities of life. He is taxed upon these things through the custom-houses of the country. . . . He is protected in his life, liberty, and the pursuit of happiness by the Government, and he pays for it. But the rich man is protected in his life, liberty, and pursuit of happiness; and, moreover, he is protected in the great excess which he has been able to acquire for himself through business, through money that is invested, that is protected by the Government, and he is enabled thereby to make himself wealthy.[12]

The benefit principle was invoked to justify not only the taxation of individual incomes, but also the taxation of corporate incomes. The benefits that corporations derive from the state, proponents were quick to point out, include limited liability, perpetuity of life, judicial recourse, and the protection of property. Because of these benefits, they insisted, taxing the corporation is only just.[13] Reported the Committee on Ways and Means: "Corporations are by the law given special privileges and advantages. Their stockholders in the main are freed from personal liability by the laws of their creation. They have almost perpetual life; they may sue or be sued as individuals. Through the courts of the country they are protected and enabled to carry on their operations. It has therefore been deemed by the committee not unjust to place a tax of 2 per cent on their net earnings."[14]

Income tax opponents countered with five major arguments. The first was a variation on the benefit principle. In advancing this argument, opponents accepted the major premise that each citizen should bear a share of the tax burden according to the degree of benefits that he or she derives from the state. They, however, questioned the *degree* of benefits actually derived from the state. Furthermore, to bolster their argument, they substituted "federal government" for "state" and drew a comparison between federal benefits and local benefits. Thus, they contended, the benefits that each citizen derives from the federal government are negligible. By contrast, those benefits that he or she derives from state and local governments are substantial. Consequently, each citizen incurs only a negligible obligation to support the federal government. On the other hand, he or she incurs a substantial obligation to support state and local governments.[15] "Much is said about the General Government 'protecting' property, and that therefore property should pay taxes directly to it," adverted Senator David Hill.

> Such protection is more of a fiction than a reality, more of a theory than a practical result. In truth and in fact the property and personal liberty of the citizen is protected almost exclusively and entirely by his town, county, and State governments. The local governments are those which protect property and personal rights, which supply us with fire and police protection, with sewer privileges, with pure and wholesome water, with gas and electricity for our streets, which maintain our pavements and roads, which arrest and punish our offenders, which support our public schools and sustain our countless charitable institutions, and charter our public conveyances, protect our suffrages, and maintain public order everywhere, and which make life worth living. . . .
>
> The obligation of ourselves and our accumulated property is to the State and local governments and not to the General Government, except in the remotest degree.[16]

Income tax proponents disputed the central claim that individuals and corporations derive *little* protection from the federal government. To the contrary, they asserted, these persons derive *substantial* protection, which is incidental to the federal government's constitutional purpose of safeguarding person and property. If not for this purpose, proponents pointed out, the federal government would have little reason to exist. "[W]hile the powers of the corporation may come from the State," countered Senator Vest,

> it is protected by the strong arm of the General Government, as is every other person. If you ignore the fact that any protection is given by the General Government to the citizens of the United States, you eliminate all the functions of the General Government itself. If the property of the individual is protected under the Constitution by the General Government, the property of the corporation is also protected. . . . What does it pay to the General Government for the protection that is given to it and its franchises and property?[17]

The second major argument advanced by income tax opponents constituted an assault on ability to pay. True, opponents charged, the income tax reaches one's ability to pay. But at the same time, and as an unintended consequence, it also penalizes industry, thrift, and talent. Income is a reward for ingenuity, hard work, and saving, they insisted. To appropriate it, thus, is like snatching the bone from the dancing dog. "It looks very fair to tax large incomes to support the Government," lectured Maine Republican Seth Milliken. "Why not do it? They who have the great incomes are best able to sustain the burden of taxation. Well, why not? There are some very serious reasons why not. In the first place it is a penalty upon the industry, frugality, temperate habits, enterprise, and persistent, tireless effort by which great incomes are achieved, in the course of which, in a vast majority of instances, the community is many fold more benefitted than he who has secured the income."[18] Massachusetts Republican Joseph Walker conjured up a similar argument in a scornful rebuke of the intemperate:

> The income tax takes from the wealth of the thrifty and enterprising and gives it to the thriftless—the sluggards who have equal opportunity and wealth. . . . The sluggard, the thriftless, the inheritor of property who is wasting his fortune in riotous living and in debauchery, under your income tax pays nothing. . . .
>
> Such men, I say, pay nothing; but the thrifty, the men who accumulate fortunes and serve their country and serve their generation by furnishing work for those they employ, they are obliged to pay a penalty, and in proportion to their services to their country, directly into the pockets of their reprobate neighbors. That is what an income tax comes to at last.[19]

For proponents of the "thrift" argument, the wealthy were wealthy for a reason: they were smarter, worked harder, and saved more than everyone else. It naturally followed that social disparities existed for a reason: they reflected the unequal distribution of effort, forbearance, and talent. "[Y]ou may divide the people into tenths," continued Walker.

> You may take the tenth that contribute the most in invention, in restless genius and indomitable perseverance, in direction, in the management of the great affairs of this country, and are the richest and best circumstanced in this country; take the tenth that are the least favorably circumstanced, do the coarsest work, the hewers of wood and drawers of water, and the tenth at the

> top work the most hours, wear out quickest, and contribute tenfold more in proportion to what they can consume . . . than the tenth at the bottom. In fact, but for the modern Christian civilization which develops the class described at the top, the man at the bottom either never would have been born or would have died in infancy.[20]

What is more, argued critics, just as this inequality inheres in nature, so too do these disparities. Thus, any attempt to eliminate them is destined to fail. Predicted Hill:

> [T]his attempt to control the brain, the resources, the exertions, the thrift, the prudence, and the industry of the people will fail, miserably fail. Men are not constituted alike; members of the same family differ from one another. One boy will be strong and vigorous and another will be puny and weak; one boy will be bright, and another boy will be dull; but this new argument is that they must share all their resources alike. . . . One boy will start out in the morning with a pin, and by judicious trading with his playmates, will come back with a jackknife at night; another boy will start out on the same day with a jackknife, and he will come back with a pin. There is no regulating the brains, the industry, the prudence, and the thrift of mankind, and there should not be.[21]

For these critics, the central problem with income taxation is that it ignores this fundamental truth. It purports to eliminate disparities in wealth, despite disparities in talent. It exults ability to pay over "ability to earn."

A third and related argument was that in exempting the poor and burdening the rich, the income tax unfairly discriminates against the wealthy. Or, expressed differently, by shifting the burden from the "have-nots" to the "haves," the income tax is the child of class legislation. Implicit in this argument is the notion that every individual has a duty to contribute to the support of government, *regardless* of his or her ability to pay. Also implicit is the basic premise that this duty inheres in citizenship, not income, status, or wealth. "So large an exemption necessarily creates a numerous class receiving a respectable income, twice as much as is ordinarily necessary to furnish a fair living, who pay no tax whatever," complained Hill. "This necessarily creates a privileged or exempted class on the one hand as against a taxpaying class on the other. . . . The larger the exemption the more emphatically the bill becomes class legislation, utterly indefensible by fair-minded and intelligent men." What rendered this "discrimination" all the more unbearable was the belief that all citizens have an equal opportunity to generate income and to accumulate wealth. Only the industrious and thrifty actually seize this opportunity, asserted tax opponents. The lazy and profligate recklessly squander it. "Does it never occur to the income-taxer that the Government afforded precisely the same facilities to the other man who did not accumulate that wealth?" asked Senator James Smith. "The individual must have had something to do with it. He may have been more thrifty, more honest, more sober, more capable. But it matters not how he attained a position to command an income of more than $4,000. He has the money, and because he has it, and for no other reason under heaven, he must pay another's debt to the Government. Is that 'just and right'? Done by an individual without sanction of law, it would be called highway robbery."[22]

Tax proponents responded with outrage. Men of modest means are just as thrifty as the wealthy, they protested. These men, however, happen to be endowed with fewer privileges, less lucrative opportunities, and milder business acumen than the rich. Thus, to tax wealth is not to tax thrift, proponents insisted. Rather, it is to tax these unequal privileges, opportunities, and abilities. "You say it is a tax upon thrift," remonstrated Arkansas Democrat Clifton Breckinridge.

> Who are the thrifty people? Shall we exclude those who labor, and all the people of moderate means who, under our present system of taxation only upon consumption, are now taxed out of all proportion to the balance of their fellow-citizens? Shall we include only those who, by inheritance or by reason of privilege under State or Federal Government, or by their superior endowment by nature, if you please, are more fortunate and successful than their neighbors? . . .
>
> Is thrift only that thrift in which industry is coupled with opportunity and ability? Is thrift only that thrift in which property is acquired by inheritance or privilege and without labor? . . . Is it not juster, is it not wiser, that we should lay the burdens of taxation, here and now, in accordance with the great principles of equality, for the support of a common government?[23]

The fourth major argument advanced by opponents was that the manner in which the tax is collected is inquisitorial in nature. The thrust of this argument is twofold. First, the income tax demands inquiry into the private affairs of the taxpayer. This inquiry is vexatious because conducted under threat of penalty. Second, the income tax requires an army of government agents to administer. These agents pry into the affairs of the ordinary citizen and otherwise invade his privacy. So complained Brooklyn Democrat Joseph Hendrix: "The law sends a prying, curious lot of officials about with power to invade homes and business houses and to exercise all sorts of tyranny. It must be inquisitorial to the last degree." Added Philadelphia Republican Robert Adams: "The imposition of the tax will corrupt the people. It will bring in its train the spy and the informer. It will necessitate a swarm of officials with inquisitorial powers. It is a direct step towards centralization, of which our Democratic friends profess such horror."[24] Particularly objectionable to these critics were two features of the Wilson Bill. The first was the requirement that taxpayers report, on their tax returns, information relating to their personal and business affairs. This information, critics feared, would be improperly disclosed by government agents. The second feature was the broad authority granted to these agents to inspect taxpayer books and records. This authority, critics charged, would be arbitrarily exercised. Complained Senator Hill:

> This bill compels the taxpayer, under severe pains and penalties, to make a return under oath of his income, whereby he discloses all his private affairs and business to the agents of the Government; and if in the opinion—*the mere belief*—of such agents the return is false, fraudulent, or contains any misstatement, they may arbitrarily summon the citizen before them with all his books and papers, and compel him to submit to examination under oath. They may question, cross-examine, and annoy him to their heart's content. There is no limit fixed anywhere.[25]

All taxes, not just the income tax, are *necessarily* inquisitorial, retorted advocates. Indeed, inquiry is basic to tax administration. It is essential for the assessment of personal property taxes, excise taxes, and customs duties.[26] Besides, reasoned tax proponents, determining the object of taxation is a legitimate government activity. "It seems to me eminently proper that the Government should ascertain the ability of the citizen to support it," declared Nebraska Populist Omer Kem.[27]

The final major argument put forth by opponents was that the income tax invites fraud and evasion. Those citizens subject to the tax, they claimed, will come to resent its discriminatory character. This resentment, in turn, will prompt them to devise ways to defeat the tax.[28] Explained Representative

Milliken: "The natural impulse to evade the payment of taxes is proverbial. They who have accumulated wealth in personal property and are living on its income may in many ways evade the tax collector. They will have no scruples of conscience to prevent their doing it, if the tax appears to be unjust."[29] Argued Senator Smith: "[The income tax] not only provides for additional taxation without representation, but puts a premium upon dishonesty and evasion of the law. . . . Say what we may of the devotion of American citizens to the decrees of their Government, there is not a Senator in this Chamber who does not know that they will feel quite justified in evading by every possible method the payment of a tax which they know to be unnecessary and consider offensive."[30]

Tax advocates proposed a simple solution to the problem: *incarceration.* He who attempts to evade the tax, they preached, should be sent, like other "rascals," to the penitentiary. One who looks for the opportunity to lie, they moralized, is by very nature a liar.[31] That criminals are apt to break just laws, they abjured, should not deter Congress from enacting just laws. Indeed, the justice of legislation has nothing to do with the propensity of the unscrupulous to defeat it. In the words of Ways and Means Committee member Tarsney:

> There are undoubtedly individuals who would evade this measure if it were law, just as there are individuals who evade every other law, whether divine or human. There are men who violate the provisions of the laws against homicide. There are violators of the laws against theft. There are violators of the laws against perjury; but because these laws against homicide, against larceny, and against perjury are by some violated, do we cease to enact laws, denouncing penalties against such crimes, and because there will be found individuals who will, by fraud and perjury, evade or seek to evade the provisions of any revenue law? Shall we therefore for that reason omit to provide a proper system of revenues to meet the wants of the Government?[32]

Still, there were other arguments. Some claimed that an income tax is a "direct tax" and that, unapportioned, it violates the Constitution. Others alleged that the income tax is aimed at the industrial East; thus, it is sectional in character. Still others contended that it was designed to meet the exigencies of war; hence, it is unnecessary in a time of peace.[33] The first of these arguments augured a constitutional challenge. Advocates believed that the tax would survive such a challenge. They based their belief on *Springer v. United States.*[34]

In *Springer,* the United States Supreme Court was asked to decide the constitutionality of the Income Tax of 1864. The defendant, an Illinois lawyer, argued that the tax was "direct," and that not having been apportioned among the several states, it violated Article 1, Section 2 of the Constitution. The U.S. Government, as plaintiff, contended that the tax was of the nature of a "duty" or "excise"; as such, the tax conformed to Article 1, Section 8. The Supreme Court took up the case and ultimately sided with the government. The Court ruled that only capitation and real estate taxes are "direct" within the meaning of the Constitution, and that the tax in question was of the nature of an excise or duty.

Senator Hill cautioned tax proponents not to rely on *Springer.* The Court as presently constituted, he warned, could always reverse an earlier decision. Populist William Allen took Hill's remarks to mean that tax opponents would take their battle directly to the Supreme Court. These opponents, Allen swore, would stop at virtually nothing. "[T]he remark has significance. . . . It shows that the power which is dominating legislation to-day, the power which shows its hand in the Senate every once in a while and in the other branch of Congress, is not satisfied with reaching out its long bony fingers through the legislation of congress, but that it is seeking to fasten itself upon the supreme tribunal of the land."[35]

In the end, arguments in favor of the tax carried the day, as much for their cogency as for the power of the men who propounded them. These arguments would both outlive these men and outweigh their power. They would provide an enduring rationale for the income tax in the next two centuries.[36]

Significantly, Hill singularly defended a tax on consumption.[37] His defense is noteworthy, less for its legislative impact than for the perspicuity of its author. Hill postulated a fundamental relationship between consumption and production. It is to consume that we produce. It is to produce that we consume. Each activity is the correlative of the other. The more we produce today, Hill reasoned, the less we will consume today. By the same token, the more we produce today, the more we *will be able* to consume tomorrow. Accordingly, the central question for tax policy, argued Hill, is not whether we should tax wealth but, rather, where along the "economic pipeline" we should tap it to raise government revenues. If at the point of present consumption, present production will be encouraged, and future consumption will be facilitated. If at the point of present production, present consumption will be encouraged, and future consumption will be inhibited.

> Whereabouts in the eternal round shall we tap for taxation?
>
> How plain it is now, when a mere phrase no longer shuts off vision, that for purposes of taxation toward the public expense and general welfare, consumption should be tapped and not production. Increased production of whatever is good and necessary for consumption is palpably everybody's interest. Other things being equal, price falls as production increases, making consumption less costly. Wants are satisfied by production, and nobody can contract himself out of everybody's similar interest in its increase.
>
> But there is no such universal and similar interest of everybody in anybody's consumption. That is the individual's affair, and his consumption offers the least injurious point of taxation for him in every individual case.[38]

Hill regarded a consumption tax as equitable for two reasons. First, its burden is proportionate to use, that is, the more one consumes, the more one pays in taxes. Second, its incidence falls on rich and poor alike. Thus, no one escapes its burden. In addition to being equitable, Hill believed, a consumption tax is readily assessable. It is payable at the will of the consumer with the least possible inconvenience.[39]

The Committee on Ways and Means thought differently. "Where along the 'economic pipeline' should wealth be tapped to fund the exigencies of government?" the committee also asked. At the point of present consumption or at the point of present *accumulation*? The committee ultimately concluded that wealth should be tapped at the point of present accumulation. To tax present consumption, it reasoned, ultimately depresses wages. "Burdening consumption restricts production. Restricting production diminishes the demand for labor. Diminution of demand for labor necessarily forces down the price of labor." The committee viewed a consumption tax as inequitable because it burdens citizens on the basis of what they need. By contrast, the committee viewed the income tax as equitable because it burdens citizens on the basis of what they have to spare.[40]

On a conceptual level, the Income Tax of 1894 resolved many of the tariff-related problems brought to light by the industrialization of America. It expanded the tax jurisdiction of the United States to encompass the worldwide income of all U.S. citizens. It inaugurated a secular shift in the tax base from consumption to income. It broadened this base to include income derived from intangibles. Last, it exempted amounts required for "minimum comforts." Still, tax advocates faced a major hurdle in the way of institutionalizing the tax: a constitutional challenge. This challenge would be bold enough to delay institutionalization for decades. It would not, however, be so bold as to crush the political forces that propelled the tax forward or stifle the populist ideas that went into its making.

The socioinstitutional view distinguishes among intent, rationale, and effect. Intent reflects the subjective aims of historical actors. Rationale involves justification in terms of ethical norms and policy aims. Effect connotes objective result.

Intent and rationale differ in that the one need not relate to normative standards, while the other necessarily does. Intent coincides with rationale when what is desired can be justified. Rationale and effect differ in that the one depends on ethical understanding, while the other does not. Rationale coincides with effect when the result conforms to the norm. Intent and effect differ in that the one emanates from subjective wants, while the other derives from objective facts. Intent coincides with effect when objective result comports with subjective design.

Thus, to speak of intent, rationale, or effect is not necessarily to speak of all three. What may be intended may not be justifiable; it may be worthless, depraved, or corrupt. What may be justifiable may not be effective; it may be unrealistic, impractical, or inoperative. What may be effective may not be intended; it may be the result of compromise or of forces beyond the realm of foresight.

To illustrate, the intent of legislators in enacting a revenue law may be to grant political concessions to special interest groups. The law's rationale may be to promote distributional equality. Its effect may be to placate popular discontent and forestall radical change. Thus, when John Witte speaks of the tax expenditure system, is he not referring to a structure forged by subjective intent? When Sidney Ratner attempts to justify the tax in terms of an egalitarian ideal, is he not alluding to the law's historical rationale? And when Robert Stanley describes the allocative impact of the tax, is he not attempting to expose its centrist effect? Theoretically, at least, the "intent" proposed by Witte, the "rationale" offered by Ratner, and the "effect" suggested by Stanley may not be entirely inconsistent. Each could embody a different type of concept—the first, subjective; the second, normative; the third, functional—to describe the same historical phenomenon.

In actuality, however, the three views *are* inconsistent, primarily because the latter two historians fail to distinguish among intent, rationale, and effect. Stanley mistakes effect for intent. This error leads him to a conclusion that is not only flawed, but also in conflict with the findings of Ratner and Witte. Ratner confounds rationale with effect. This confusion brings him to an outcome that is ethically appealing, but empirically unsound. Although Witte distinguishes among intent, rationale, and effect, he does so with respect to the tax expenditure system. As a result, he derives a conclusion that is cogent and clear, but not entirely apposite to the *origins* of the U.S. income tax.

In the socioinstitutional view, the legislative intent behind the early income tax was to shift the burden from the less wealthy to the wealthy. The rationale for the tax was threefold: first, to assess citizens according to their ability to pay; second, to promote equality of sacrifice; and third, to impose fiscal burdens commensurate with civic benefits. The effect of the tax was manifold: to console citizens as to the justice of "the system," to present a spectacle of equality in an order of inequality, to prevent social upheaval, and to preserve the existing political order. Such effect can be inferred from the socioinstitutional circumstances surrounding enactment of the tax, as corroborated by subsequent developments. The rationale is evident from the legislative record. The intent is transparent from the words and deeds of historical actors.

Why does this distinction matter? It matters because of the broad implications for political action. If the intent of legislators in enacting the income tax was to placate social discontents and preempt radical change, then their motives are suspect and our government is unrepresentative. No action short of impeachment and institutional overhaul would suffice to remedy the situation. If the effect of the tax was to redistribute national wealth and democratize society, then there is hardly a need for further social reform. At last, we can find comfort in our egalitarian order and bask in the sun of our past political achievements. If the rationale of the tax is consistent with its effect, then we can congratulate our officials for realizing an ethical ideal. If this rationale is consistent with its intent, then we can congratulate ourselves for electing ethical officials!

On the other hand, if the intent, rationale, and effect of the early income tax are distinct and distinguishable, then we have our work cut out for us. If the intent behind the tax was to shift the burden from the less wealthy to the wealthy, then we should evaluate its effect in terms of the degree to which it comports with its professed aim. If the incidence of the tax falls heavily on the less wealthy, then we should either fine-tune the system, abandon it altogether, or reject the original aim in favor of one more realizable. If the effect of the tax has been to present a spectacle of equality in an order of inequality, then for the sake of transparency, we should expose and eliminate the ghastly contradiction. If its inegalitarian effect falls short of its egalitarian ideal, then we should institute policies to bridge the gap, if indeed we value egalitarianism. Finally, if the original intent behind the income tax is premised on an order of inequality, while its rationale speaks to the antithesis, then we should ask ourselves, "Which do we prefer—a tax system shaped by the existing social order, or a social order shaped by the existing tax system?" Indeed, the course of action before us ultimately depends upon how we define the central issue. This definition, in turn, hinges on our distinguishing among the intent, rationale, and effect of the early income tax.

6

Pollock

Great and rich corporations, by hiring the ablest lawyers in the land and fighting against a petty tax upon superfluity as other men have fought for their liberties and their lives, have secured the exemption of wealth from paying its just share towards the support of the Government that protects it.

—Editorial, *New York World*,
May 21, 1895

The millionaires have escaped and the people generally will have to make up the deficit. It is a strange comment both on American democracy and the limits of the American Constitution.

—Editorial, *London Chronicle*,
May 21, 1895

May 20, 1895

The air was electric.[1] The august chamber was thronged to capacity. This chamber was the same one in which Daniel Webster had moved mountains in defense of liberty. Its contours befit so grand an occasion. It was shaped like a half moon. On its flat side, high above the marble dais, was a towering clock. Below it was a golden eagle, straining its neck and spreading its wings. Its talons clutched a long metal bar supporting a scarlet curtain. In front of this curtain, several feet above the ground, was the mahogany bench. It resembled one of those old-fashioned bars found in the grandest and stateliest of hotels. Adorning its facade was a brigade of wooden columns. Behind it were nine huge armchairs generously padded with brown leather.

Along the room's semicircular wall were busts of the former justices, from John Jay to Morrison Waite. They gazed upon the bench with stoic indifference. Vigilantly guarding the main entrance was the statuesque doorman. His bleached shirt and black necktie commended themselves stylishly to his solemn sense of dignity. Paralleling this wall was the spectator's gallery, neatly aligned with red-cushioned benches. In the center of the chamber, directly beneath the dome, was a string of tables and chairs reserved for the bar.

Within this stretch sat Attorney General Richard Olney and his assistant, David Whitney. Near them sat Commissioner of Internal Revenue Joseph Miller and several distinguished congressmen. Behind these dignitaries, notebooks in hand, swarmed an army of eager reporters. Further back, immediately beyond the bar, sat the wives of several justices. At the far end of the gallery, wedged between the red-cushioned benches, stood a hoard of faceless bystanders. They strained their necks in vain to see and hear what was going on.

A few minutes before the hour, a young woman with gray puffed sleeves meticulously arranged blotting paper on the bench. Exactly at noon, someone rapped, the crowd stood up, and the marshall solemnly announced, "The Chief Justice and the Associate Justices of the United States of America." Impulsively, all eyes turned to the low door on the left. Through it marched nine imposing figures in black silk robes. Each was accompanied by a page, a messenger, and a secretary. The justices and their attendants ascended the dais, then stood for an moment. The marshall continued, "Oyez, oyez, oyez, this honorable Supreme Court of the United States is now in session. All persons having business with the Court draw near and give attention, and they shall be heard. God save the United States and this honorable Court." Then, with ceremonious dignity, the justices bowed to the bar, and the bar bowed to the bench. The pages withdrew the brown leather chairs and courteously seated the justices. After a brief pause, Chief Justice Melville Fuller stood up and stepped forward. A hush fell over the courtroom.

The lawsuit had been instigated by William Guthrie at the behest of his New York clients. The cost of the litigation lay somewhere between $500,000 and $1 million. This cost had been borne chiefly by clients of Guthrie's law firm. They had been joined by patrons of correspondent law firms in major cities throughout the country.[2] Who were these clients? The *New York Sun* spoke of "a large body of public-spirited New York merchants and businessmen." The *New York World* alluded to "several large trust companies and other corporations." The *Cincinnati Commercial Gazette* singled out "the Astors and other wealthy New Yorkers."[3] Did these persons embody the power of the "moneyed interests" to which Senator William Allen had so forebodingly alluded?

1. "Hearing the Income Tax Decision by the Supreme Court," reprinted from *New York World,* April 9, 1895, 3.

Guthrie retained, as senior counsel, Joseph H. Choate, a prominent New York attorney. He sought, and found, the nominal defendants in the case, the Farmers' Loan & Trust Company and the Continental Trust Company. These defendants were ideal because they derived most of their income from realty and intangibles. The "controversy," as Guthrie envisioned it, would center around the constitutionality of a tax on rents and municipal bond interest. Guthrie next searched for the plaintiffs in the case—stockholders willing to lend their names to an action for breach of trust.[4] After some difficulty, he found Charles Pollock, a stockholder in Farmers' Loan, and Louis Hyde, a stockholder in Continental. Pollock resided in Massachusetts, and Hyde in New Jersey.

At Guthrie's behest, Pollock and Hyde filed separate lawsuits in the United States District Court for Southern New York. In their lawsuits, the plaintiffs alleged: First, that insofar as the Income Tax of 1894 reached income derived from realty and personalty, it was a "direct tax"; furthermore, not having been apportioned among the several states, it violated Article 1,

2. "They May Decide the Fate of the Income Tax To-Day," reprinted from *New York World,* April 8, 1895, 1.

Section 2 of the Constitution. Second, that if not "direct," the 1894 tax was of the nature of an "excise, duty, or impost"; not being uniform throughout the states, it violated Article 1, Section 8 of the Constitution. Third, that insofar as it charged municipal bond interest, the 1894 tax burdened the instrumentalities of the states; under Article 10 of the Constitution, the states are not the proper subjects of the federal government's taxing power. Fourth, that the corporations' paying the tax would subject the corporations to a multiplicity of lawsuits; these lawsuits, in turn, would diminish share values. In light of these allegations, the plaintiffs prayed the Court to restrain the corporations from paying the tax. They urged the Court to declare the Income Tax of 1894 unconstitutional.[5]

The Court joined the lawsuits in a single action, *Pollock v. Farmers' Loan & Trust Company and Hyde v. Continental Trust Company.* About the same time, the government filed a brief as amicus curiae. Because both Guthrie and Solicitor General Lawrence Maxwell wanted to proceed expeditiously to the appellate level, they agreed that the government would file a demurrer.[6] The government did so, and, as expected, the demurrer was sustained. The case involving a constitutional question, appeal was made directly to the Supreme Court.[7]

. . .

Chief Justice Fuller bent forward to unravel the roll of manuscript in his hand. As he did so, a great shock of white hair parted in the middle and cascaded gracefully down his mustached face. Then, in a voice so low, so pleasant, and so distinct that it captivated its audience, he began what everyone, in almost breathless silence, had long been waiting for. "Whenever this court is required to pass upon the validity of an act of congress, as tested by the fundamental law enacted by the people, the duty imposed demands, in its discharge, the utmost deliberation and care, and invokes the deepest sense of responsibility."[8] The associate justices settled themselves comfortably in the brown leather chairs. Justice Edward White threw his head back, gazed anxiously at the ceiling, then tightly closed his eyes. Chief Justice Fuller fastened his eyes on the typeset document before him. He raised them but once or twice throughout the reading of the majority opinion.[9]

The chief justice began: The circumstances surrounding the framing of the Constitution indicate that the framers intended taxes on realty and personalty to be "direct." Just as these taxes are "direct," so too are taxes on the income from such property. Earlier cases touching on the issue should be construed narrowly, Justice Fuller advised, thus sidestepping the rule of stare decisis. That there had ever been a practical construction of the Constitution based on the legislative acts of Congress, he resolutely denied. This instrument, Fuller intimated, had been the result of a bargained-for exchange. In this exchange, the thirteen original states had granted taxing power to the federal government. They had received in return a solid assurance that this power would not be abused. What form did this assurance take? In the case of direct taxes, apportionment; in the case of indirect taxes, uniformity. Under the latter standard, the income tax had been most deficient. It had exempted a host of individuals and institutions on a basis that was questionable, if not unjustified.[10]

The chief justice continued: An income tax is not a "duty." To assert the contrary is to ignore the views of legal scholars and the framers. The latter have maintained that an income tax is "direct." The former have equated duties with customs and imposts. Nor is it an assessment on the taxpayer on account of his money-spending power. To declare otherwise flies in the face of the Court's reasoning relating to the exemption of municipal bond interest. According to this reasoning, to tax such interest is indirectly to tax the instrumentalities of the states. By implication, to tax income is indirectly to tax its underlying source. If apportioning the tax would result in inequalities, reasoned the chief justice, then these inequalities must have been stipulated. If it would impair the government in national emergencies—well, this was just not the concern of the judiciary. Besides, consoled Fuller, the Constitution could always be amended to accommodate more practical aims.[11]

But what was so difficult about apportionment? the Chief Justice went on to ask. Could not Congress demand of each state an amount calculated on the basis of census data? Could it not proceed to collect this amount directly, a state failing to fill its quota?[12] To be sure, the prohibition was not against an income tax per se, but rather against an *unapportioned* income tax. To tax income was perfectly legitimate, so long as such a levy conformed to the requirements of the Constitution.

The chief justice then turned to the critical question: Did the unconstitutional provisions of the act invalidate the income tax as a whole? Fuller prefaced his remarks by saying that the income tax provisions were so interdependent that not to enforce them in their entirety would be to defeat the intent of Congress. What was this intent? To raise a certain amount of revenue by taxing capital, not a fraction of this amount by taxing labor.[13] Thus, affirmed the chief justice, the unconstitutional provisions of the act *did* invalidate the system as a whole. The Income Tax of 1894, in its entirety, was unconstitutional.

Chief Justice Fuller concluded his remarks at eight minutes past the hour. As he returned to his seat, applause burst out spontaneously in the gallery.[14]

The Income Tax of 1894 was dead. What had been conceived in a political movement shaped by the economic and social realities of the day, what had been made flesh by the haggling of politicians and the rhetoric of statesmen, what had been breathed life by the lofty ideals of the most sagacious of political economists, was now dealt a fatal blow by the implacable authority of the U.S. judiciary. The Populists, at long last, had been defeated. The winds of change that had so turbulently swept through the streets of the nation and the halls of Congress had finally been laid to rest. The egalitarian revolution was over. Yet the same egalitarian spirit that filled the hearts and minds of millions of Americans had once invaded the very forum that denied its realization. What accounts for this seemingly strange and undemocratic result?

3. "Handed Down," reprinted from *New York World,* May 21, 1895, 1.

Some legal scholars might say, on a positivistic note, that the act itself was inherently flawed, that its sponsors disregarded the clear mandates of the Constitution or else were utterly impervious to them. Political analysts might point to the peculiar composition of the Court, to the juridical philosophies of its individual justices and to their socioeconomic backgrounds. Social historians might cite the overwhelming strength of "reactionary forces" in society—their eminent ability to thwart progressive legislation through their tenacious grip on state institutions. In this regard, the scholarly work of Arnold Paul is revealing.

Paul tells us that by the 1890s, the U.S. judiciary had become the principal bulwark of political conservatism against the forces of popular democracy. According to Paul, rapid industrialization, the concomitant concentration of wealth, the rise of the corporate enterprise, and the secular decline in commodity prices fueled discontent among farmers, workers, and small businessmen. Offended by the inequities of the day, these groups vigorously pressed Congress for industrial regulation and social reform. Threatened by these moves, political conservatives turned to the judiciary to uphold their "rights"

STILL ANOTHER BLACK EYE FOR THE POOR OLD DEMOCRATIC DONKEY.
—*New York Herald.*

4. "Still Another Black Eye for the Poor Old Democratic Donkey," reprinted from *New York Herald,* April 11, 1895, 1.

and defend their interests. They hoisted the banner of laissez-faire to subvert the regulation of industry. They invoked the sanctity of private property to thwart social reform. They denounced progressive legislation as a device used by the democratic majority to tyrannize the wealthy minority. Committed to stability and order, the judiciary ultimately took up the cause of the right. It set up the Constitution as the main line of defense against the "onslaught of numbers" and abandoned traditional doctrine in favor of political creed.[15]

Robert Stanley presents a somewhat different view. He tells us that the decision in *Pollock* represents an attempt on the part of the U.S. judiciary to scale down congressional power. According to Stanley, the growth of statist capitalism strengthened the "economic and legal nexus" in Congress and concentrated power in the legislative branch of the federal government. This outcome was disturbing to elements of the political center, which included a majority of justices on the United States Supreme Court. These "decentralists" sought to fragment this nexus and disperse this power. How did they do so? By interjecting the states into the process of income taxation, thereby diverting primary responsibility for bridging the class gap from Congress to the

5. "Niobe," reprinted from *Washington Post,* May 23, 1895, 1.

states. Like Congress, says Stanley, the Supreme Court accepted the centrist goals of preserving the political status quo, maintaining institutional inertia, and forestalling radical change. But unlike Congress, Stanley asserts, the Court rejected the traditional course of centrism toward the concentration of economic and legal power.[16]

An intriguing view of the constitutional crisis, seemingly heretical in its implications, is proffered by the editors of the *New York World.* They allege that the Constitution itself was inherently flawed, that the framers could hardly foresee the problems of an industrializing nation, and furthermore that in

6. "A Story Without Words," reprinted from *Washington Post,* April 26, 1895, 1.

promoting the interests of invested wealth, the Court that decided *Pollock* subverted the true intent of the framers. Thus, in their commentary of April 12, the editors wrote:

> The framers of the Constitution could not foresee our conditions. They knew nothing of multi-millionaires or great corporations. They could not anticipate a time when a single family would own more houses in New York than then existed in any of our cities. They could not foresee that a time would come when nearly all the burdens of taxation would fall upon the poor and the moderately well to do, while the rich paid nothing on their wealth towards the support of the Government. Certainly they did not put any clause into the Constitution with intent to protect invested wealth against the payment of its fair share. Yet that is precisely the use now to be made of the direct-tax clause under the ruling of the Supreme Court.[17]

This view commends itself to comment. Though extremely forward looking, the framers of the Constitution indeed were historical actors constrained by the socioinstitutional circumstances of their day. Their outlook, notion of political order, and constitutional views were to some extent shaped by these circumstances. Even the concepts they used to define this order derived their meaning from the society in which the framers lived. This society was quite different from the United States of the 1890s. It was on the *verge* of industrialization, not in its throes. Thus, when the framers drafted the Constitution, they probably had in mind a different set of institutional possibilities based on a different set of social relationships.

They undoubtedly weighed the manner in which the tax burden would fall upon the wealthy and the less wealthy. But in their assessment, they likely conceived of wealth in a manner fundamentally different from the conception of succeeding generations (that is, in terms of *tangible wealth*), and developed a substantially different notion of how to reach it effectively (that is, through *direct taxes, imposts, excises, and duties*). They could not have fully appreciated the long-term effects of income taxation, because they could not have fully anticipated the long-term defects of tariff taxation. They could not have anticipated the latter defects, because they could not have predicted with accuracy the future course of U.S. industrialization. Thus, what the framers intended in the 1780s may be quite different from what they *would have intended* in the 1890s. And the concepts they used to convey this original intent may have been somewhat inadequate to address the peculiar problems of the later era.

An alternative view, more appealing from a legalistic perspective, emphasizes the foresight of the framers and the vitality of the instrument they created. According to this view, the framers need not have been able to predict with any degree of accuracy the future course of U.S. industrialization to adequately provide for it; indeed, they need have been only perspicacious enough to create a flexible constitutional framework, which through sound judicial construction could accommodate socioeconomic change. By implication, the problem lay not with the concepts used by the framers to convey their original intent, but rather with the Fuller Court's interpretation of these concepts, in light of the Constitution's broad grant of taxing authority to the federal government. The merits of this view are that it properly attributes to the framers, as founders of a modern republic, foresight in the realm of *governmental organization,* not *social transformation,* and that it recognizes the potential for human error in constitutional construction.

The liberal press lambasted the decision. Predicted the editors of the *World:* "The people at large will bow to this decision as they habitually do to all the decrees of their highest courts. But they will not accept law as justice. No dictum or decision of any court can make wrong right." Declared the *Richmond Dispatch:* "We see nothing in the opinion of the court to extinguish the dogma that men of great incomes are men of great influence." Decried the *St. Louis Post-Dispatch:* "To-day's decision shows that the corporations and plutocrats are as securely intrenched in the Supreme Court as in the lower courts which they take such pains to control." Asked the *Syracuse News:* "Viewing the question solely on its merits, does it not imply that there is somewhere a spoke loose in our constitutional wheel when . . . great landed proprietors can shift the burdens of Federal taxation from their own shoulders to the backs of the poor laborer?"[18]

Industrialists, bankers, and businessmen rejoiced. Remarked Samuel Sloan, president of the Delaware, Lackawanna, and Western Railroad: "Every sound-thinking man sympathizes with the judges who upset the Income Tax law. It is a good thing for business." Stated John Stewart, president of the U.S. Trust Company: "The effect of the decision will be felt beyond the boundaries of our own country. It will go to show that this tirade against property which is being raised on all sides by Populists and Socialists may be carried to a certain length, but no further." Commented Thomas Fowler, president of the New-York, Ontario, and Western Railroad: "All I can say is that I am delighted with the Supreme Court decision. If it had been otherwise it would have opened the gates for oppressive legislation, and would seriously have affected the financial standing of our railroad corporations." Noted J. Edward Simmons, president of the Fourth National Bank of New York: "The decision of the Supreme Court declaring the income tax unconstitutional can have only a beneficial effect. It insures the frugal and industrious against the depredations of the profligate and the idle, and it demonstrates that the communistic and Populist element that has been conspicuous of late in Congress legislation cannot override the Constitution of the United States."[19] Also rejoicing was Senator David Hill:

> The judgment is "a robe and a diadem." It will be "eyes to the blind" and "feet to the lame."

> It is a victory of law over socialism. It is a triumph of decent and intelligent men over demagogues and adventurers. It is a vindication of the Constitution as the best lawyers of the country understood it; it is a defeat for political blatherskites who were clamoring without reason or justice for new schemes of taxation. The decision today announced will do more for our country, will be of more lasting benefit to our free institutions, will clear the political atmosphere better than anything which has occurred in this decade.
>
> . . . Undoubtedly in some sections of the country there will arise a demand for an amendment of the Constitution, so as to enable an income tax law to be passed, but it will be unavailing, spasmodic, and silly.[20]

For nearly two decades, the decision in *Pollock* would set up the direct tax clause of the Constitution as the principal barrier to taxing invested wealth according to ability to pay. It would consecrate an order of inequality probably never fathomed by the founding fathers. It would leave the populist forces that had pushed for radical institutional change in broad disarray. By the same token, it would give U.S. business heartwarming solace that the accumulation and investment of capital would not be impeded by the state. For this outcome, the "moneyed interests" of the nation were profoundly grateful. No better was this gratitude expressed than by the editors of the *New York Sun:*

> There is life left in the institutions which the founders of this republic devised and constructed. The wave of socialistic revolution has gone far, but it breaks at the foot of the ultimate bulwark set up for the protection of our liberties. Five to four, the Court stands like a rock. . . .
>
> The promoters of those revolutionary ideas concerning the repression of wealth and the shackling of individual energy and thrift, which are the essence of socialism, will not recover for years the ground they had gained and held up to yesterday. . . .
>
> The income tax is dead. The few are not to be taxed for the benefit of the many. Systematic robbery of one part of the country by another is not to be a feature of our national system. The theories of socialism are not to be put into practice. . . .
>
> For all of this let us be profoundly grateful. The magnitude of our deliverance will be the more apparent as years go by.[21]

Epilogue

The Vitality of Ideas

> *The Congress shall have power to lay and collect taxes on incomes, from whatever source derived, without apportionment among the several states, and without regard to any census of enumeration.*
>
> —Sixteenth Amendment to the United States Constitution

> *The sixteenth amendment to the Constitution was proposed and adopted to authorize Congress to impose a tax like that of 1894, after which this is modeled, and which is proposed to be enacted under that power, in so far as it taxes incomes arising from real and personal property.*
>
> —Democratic senator John K. Shields of Tennessee, May 1913

By 1913, the men and women who had shaped the course of U.S. income tax development had either died or retired. Their legacy, however, lived on. This legacy would be taken up by a new generation of American legislators who were firmly committed to institutional change. One such legislator was a Democratic congressman from Tennessee named Cordell Hull.

Hull was a protégé of Benton McMillin. He had closely followed the 1894 debates and had meticulously studied the *Pollock* decision.[1] Early in his career, he championed the cause of the income tax. Like populist statesmen before him, Hull believed that a tax on consumption unjustly burdened the working poor. Like his political mentor, he aspired to create an institutional structure that would shift the burden from those citizens with the least ability to pay to the ones with the most. And like his legislative predecessors, he endorsed the Hobbesian rationale that each citizen should bear a share of the tax burden according to the degree of benefits that he or she derives from the state.[2] Thus, on the floor of the Sixty-first Congress, citing the lessons to be learned from legislative history, Hull offered this testimonial:

> I have no disposition to tax wealth unnecessarily or unjustly, but I do believe that the wealth of the country should bear its just share of the burden of taxation and that it should not be permitted to shirk that duty. Anyone at all familiar with the legislative history of the nation must admit that the chief burdens of government have long been borne by those least able to bear them, while accumulated wealth has enjoyed the protection and other blessings of the Government and thus far escaped most of its accompanying burdens.[3]

Cordell Hull was the principal architect of the Income Tax of 1913.[4] In structuring this tax, he used as his prototype the Income Tax of 1894.[5] The Sixty-third Congress adopted Hull's scheme, based on many of the same arguments that had been propounded in 1894.[6] Thus, in both word and deed, this legislative body accepted the act of the Fifty-third Congress and endorsed its rationale.

The 1913 tax and its institutional predecessor, however, were not identical. The 1913 tax expanded the list of deductions, introduced graduated rates, and reinstated collection at the source.[7] The 1894 tax was narrower in scope and less progressive in character. In terms of basic structure, however, the two schemes were so similar as to evince a common or core purpose. *This purpose was to shift the burden from the less wealthy to the wealthy, all the while exempting amounts required for "minimum comforts."*

The socioinstitutional circumstances surrounding enactment of the 1913 tax, *as perceived and understood by members of the Sixty-third Congress,* reinforce this conclusion. By 1913, the disparities between rich and poor had grown progressively worse, as illustrated by a member of the 63d Congress: "And the great problem remains—the increasing accumulations of the rich. In spite of all our laws in regard to taxation, in spite of all the tariff theories we have, of this variety and that, . . .the very rich of this country succeed in doing one thing. They continue to grow richer. In different degrees and among all of us the supreme quandary of our hour is the vast increasing accumulation of wealth in the hands of the few."[8] Tariff taxation continued to weigh heavily on the working poor.

> The amount each citizen contributes is governed, not by his ability to pay tax, but by his consumption of the articles taxed. It requires as many yards of

> cloth to clothe, and as many ounces of food to sustain, the day laborer, as the largest holder of invested wealth; yet each pays into the Federal Treasury a like amount of taxes upon the food he eats, while the former at present pays a larger rate of tax upon his cheap suit of woolen clothing than the latter upon his costly suit. The result is that the poorer classes bear the chief burden of our customhouse taxation.[9]

And the wealthy continued to avoid the tax. "Under the fiscal systems in vogue in most of the States the wealthy and powerful classes find ways to evade taxation, and are constantly succeeding, in one way or another, in shifting the chief weight of taxation from those most able to bear it to the shoulders of those weaker, poorer, and less able to protect themselves."[10] Acutely aware of these conditions, the Sixty-third Congress, like its nineteenth-century predecessor, set out to institute a tax system that would shift the burden from those individuals with the least ability to pay to the citizens with the most. In the words of the Finance Committee chair, such a system reflected Congress's intent "to provide a revenue, and in addition to that, to a large extent to relieve the backs and the stomachs of people of burdens under the present system and to place those burdens, as far as may be, upon the backs of those who are able to stand them, to begin a system at any rate, of taxing people according to their ability to pay and not according to their necessities."[11] Such may be said to be the *original intent* of the modern U.S. income tax.

What had happened in the interim? By the turn of the century, income tax proponents had managed to regroup. In 1909, Senate Democrats introduced legislation that would have established an individual-corporate scheme substantially similar to the Income Tax of 1894. Through this move, they purported to revive the constitutional issues addressed in *Pollock,* with the hope that a newly constituted Supreme Court would reverse the earlier decision of the Fuller Court.[12] Toward preempting passage of a comprehensive tax package, Senate Republicans put forth a more limited plan to tax corporate, but not individual, incomes.[13] They modeled their plan after the corporate scheme of 1894, but labeled their levy an "excise tax" to skirt the constitutional prohibition on an unapportioned tax on incomes.[14] Through adroit political maneuvering, the Republicans pushed their plan through Congress at the expense of the more progressive Democratic proposal.[15]

Notwithstanding this setback, tax advocates grew more intent on tearing down the institutional wall created by *Pollock*. In the aftermath of the decision, congressional Populists and Democrats demanded a constitutional amendment that would allow for the taxation of incomes without apportionment. With time, conservative Republicans would accede to this demand, partly to appease public opinion, partly to facilitate implementation of their agenda, and partly because they viewed ratification by a majority of states as unlikely.[16] In June 1909, Republican president William Howard Taft formally proposed the Sixteenth Amendment. By February 1913, two-thirds of the states had ratified the amendment. In October of the same year, the Sixty-third Congress instituted a new tax on individual incomes and merged this tax with the Corporations Tax of 1909.[17]

The introduction of income tax legislation in 1913 sparked relatively little debate—at least, not on the scale of the 1894 debates.[18] Subdued by ratification of the Sixteenth Amendment, congressional conservatives resigned themselves to the thought that a tax on individual incomes was virtually inevitable. Emboldened by widespread popular support, unfettered by constitutional constraints, and no longer confronted by potent political opposition, congressional Democrats and Progressives could now focus on ancillary issues, such as the schedule of rates, the list of deductions, and the mechanics of withholding. Significantly, the principal controversy in 1913 was not *whether* to tax incomes, but rather *when* and *how much* to tax. The shift to a new tax base ensured progressivity. The adoption of graduated rates enhanced progressivity.

Robert Stanley argues that the meager revenue raised by the 1894 tax—its nominal rate and narrow base—evinces a subliminal, almost invidious purpose. This purpose, according to Stanley, is to maximize the rhetorical effect of the tax all the while minimizing its allocative content. I beg to differ with Stanley. The meager revenue raised by the tax reflects *residual* budgetary requirements, the entrenchment of existing fiscal structures, and the Democratic leadership's assessment of what was both politically feasible and fiscally necessary. There was no need to fund the *major part* of the deficit when a preexisting institution already did so. This institution, the tariff, was backed by both the eastern business establishment and the Democratic and Republican mainstream. Abandoning it in favor of a broad-based income tax was considered politically impractical. Thus, the only issue remaining in light of the shortfall generated by tariff taxation was how to fund the *minor part* of the deficit. This issue was resolved in favor of an income tax, which the Fifty-third Congress viewed as *supplemental* to import duties. (Of course, subsequent Congresses came to view the tax as the government's main source of revenue.)

Moreover, Benton McMillin and the Subcommittee on Internal Revenue deliberately chose a narrow base and nominal rate for political and fiscal reasons. Further broadening the base, they feared, would provoke greater, more widespread political opposition. Further raising the rate, they calculated, would generate revenues far in excess of projected fiscal needs. To claim, as Stanley does, that the essential purpose of the tax was to maximize rhetorical effect while minimizing allocative content is erroneously to infer subjective design from objective effect. On the other hand, to claim, as I do, that the essential purpose of the tax was to redistribute the tax burden, if only on a limited scale, is to admit subjective design *notwithstanding* objective effect.

So why all the commotion over a trifling 2 percent tax rate? Because it was the *principle,* not the nominal rate, that mattered. This principle touched on the self-proclaimed "right" of a wealthy minority not to be fiscally burdened by the democratic majority—the "right" of the more affluent to be free from dispossession by the less affluent. Tax opponents rightly asked, "If a less wealthy majority can succeed in 'soaking' the rich with a 2 percent tax, where will it all end—at 25 percent? at 50 percent? at 100 percent?" The line had to be drawn somewhere, and the obvious place was here and now. In the words of Ohio Republican John Sherman, a prominent tax critic in the Senate: "The idea of seeking out a comparatively few because you can reach them, and because they live mainly in the large cities, is an act of agrarianism and injustice. It is not the amount that is involved, but it is the principle that is involved. If you can legislate for classes in this country, then our system will break down of its own weight."[19] Corroborating Sherman's view was New York Democrat Bourke Cockran, the leading tax opponent in the House:

> But, it is said, this being a very small tax, nobody ought to object to it. So far as the extent of the burden imposed by it is concerned, I concede that it is a small tax, but the principle involved in it is just as vicious though the rate be 2 per cent as if it were 20 per cent. . . .

> The burdens of 85,000 persons subject to this tax are then to be increased with the passage of time, until finally the main support of the Government will be exacted from a very small fraction of the population. Does any sane man believe that Democratic institutions could live under such a system, that government entirely supported by a class would not ultimately be controlled by a class?[20]

These words reflect not a desire to placate the wealthy with rhetoric, but rather a genuine concern over political precedent. To dismiss them as mere rhetoric is to ignore not only the real, but also the *potential* distributive impact of income taxation.

So why did the public press Congress for an income tax only sporadically? Because tariff taxation *unbearably* burdened the public only sporadically. Because during upswings in the business cycle, farmers, artisans, and workers could better absorb the artificially high costs of raw materials, clothes, and implements than they could during downturns. Not surprisingly, it was in times of economic contraction—particularly, in 1878 and in 1893—that the drive for an income tax gained the most momentum. During such periods, wages and agricultural profits declined relative to the cost of dutiable merchandise.[21]

As for Stanley's contentions regarding the Civil War schemes, suffice it to say that not all proponents of the progressive view (nor do I) attempt to explain these schemes in terms of a broad-based democratic movement. Roy and Gladys Blakey clearly state on page 1 of *The Federal Income Tax* that the Income Tax of 1894 "had only a loose causal connection with the Civil War income taxes." Only Sidney Ratner suggests the contrary.[22] In my opinion, the Civil War schemes should be viewed in terms of their own sociohistorical context and no other. This context was war and the financial exigencies arising therefrom. Furthermore, that a historical approach to the study of one phenomenon (for example, the Income Tax of 1894) fails to account for the occurrence of another (for instance, the Civil War schemes or the aborted tax of 1878) does not necessarily destroy its specific validity. This validity depends *not* on the degree to which it can adequately explain *all* historical phenomena, but rather on the degree to which it can adequately explain *at least one* historical phenomenon.

Stanley is correct when he says that the income tax did not significantly alter the basic pattern of national wealth distribution. But he is incorrect as to why. It is not because its sponsors wanted to deflect public opinion from an order of inequality, but rather because they wanted to achieve a particular objective, *given this order.* In other words, it is not because they wanted to preserve an essential social condition, but rather because they premised the structure of their institution on this condition.

To some extent, this premise reflects the political realities of the day. In the early 1890s, the United States was in the throes of industrialization. The captains of trade, industry, and banking were financially strong and politically powerful. Labor was weak, farmers were disorganized, the crafts were on the decline. Republicans opposed any type of legislation that smacked of "socialism." Mainstream Democrats paid lip service to institutional reform, all the while trembling at the thought of proletarian revolution. Under these conditions, an income tax aimed at redistributing society's wealth would have been difficult, if not impossible, to achieve. Its sponsors clearly realized this limitation and gauged their expectations accordingly.

This, of course, is not to say that these sponsors failed miserably in their endeavor. Nor is it to imply that the income tax ended up being a symbolic gesture devoid of allocative content. The income tax was profoundly allocative, not in terms of society's wealth, but rather in terms of the *tax burden.* It was substantially redistributive, not in terms of fortune or opportunity, but rather in terms of *tax incidence.* The founders of the modern income tax intended *not* to dismantle an order of inequality, but rather to build a fiscal institution around the contours of this order. In this their limited aim, they were most successful. In the twentieth century, as the tariff increasingly gave way to the income tax, the burden of taxation increasingly shifted from the working poor to the wealthy.[23]

Some scholars do not fully appreciate this outcome because they fail to view the income tax in terms of its institutional predecessor. They fail to ask the quintessential questions: What were the institutional shortcomings of tariff taxation? How did the income tax address these shortcomings? How did the transformation of society affect the manner in which the tax burden was distributed? How did the income tax change this mode of distribution—if not immediately, then in the long run? These questions are crucial to understanding the real allocative impact of income taxation. Without them, one is left to surmise that if the income tax indeed has a purpose, this purpose must be ephemeral—so ephemeral as to be of the order of *symbol.*

But, old-school progressives may ask, is not shifting the tax burden from the less wealthy to the wealthy nearly the same as redistributing national

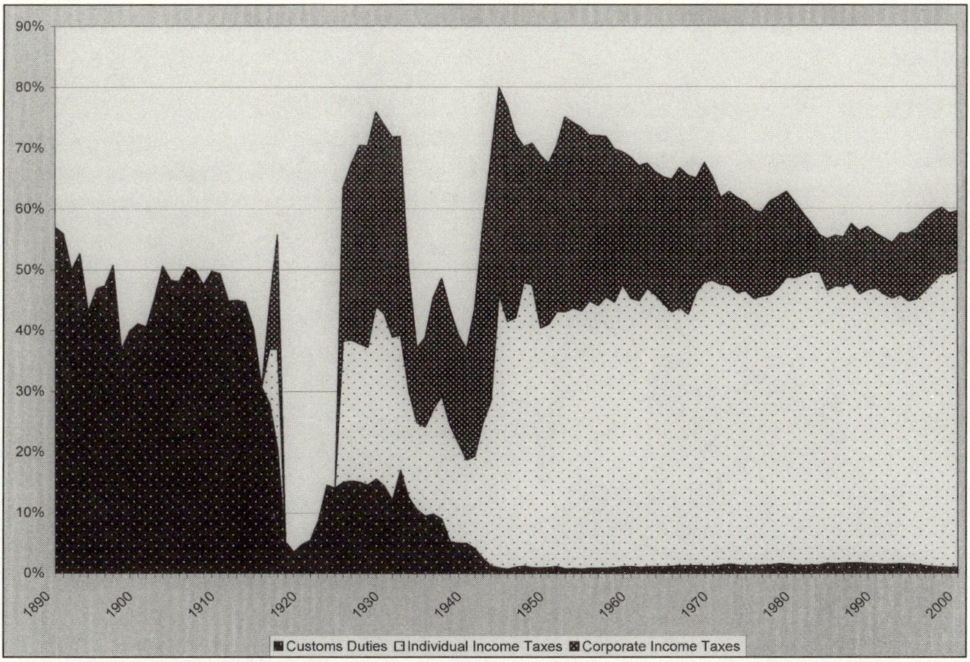

7. Federal Revenues by Source as a Percentage of Total Revenues. *Sources:* 1890–1933: Bureau of the Census, *Historical Statistics of the United States, Colonial Times to 1970,* Series 343–57 (Washington, D.C.: Government Printing Office, 1975); 1934–2000: Historical Tables: Office of Management and Budget, *Budget of the United States Government, FiscalYear 2001,* Tables 2–1, 2–2, 2–5 (Washington, D.C.: Government Printing Office, 2000).

Notes: (1) percentages are based on amounts for the fiscal year ending June 30; (2) individual and corporate income tax data for the years 1918–24 are unavailable; (3) such data for the years 1916–17 and 1925–33 represent internal revenue collections, whether assigned to general revenue or to trust funds; (4) corporate income tax data for the years 1987–2000 include trust fund receipts for the hazardous substance superfund; (5) figures for fiscal year 2000 are based on estimates.

wealth? Or, expressed differently, in setting out to redistribute the tax burden, did not the founders of the modern income tax purport to redistribute total economic benefits among the various social classes? Proceeding on the premise that "benefits" means *specific* benefits in the form of wealth transfers, I argue in the negative for two reasons: First, the American state at the turn of the century was essentially laissez-faire. The revenues that it raised from in-

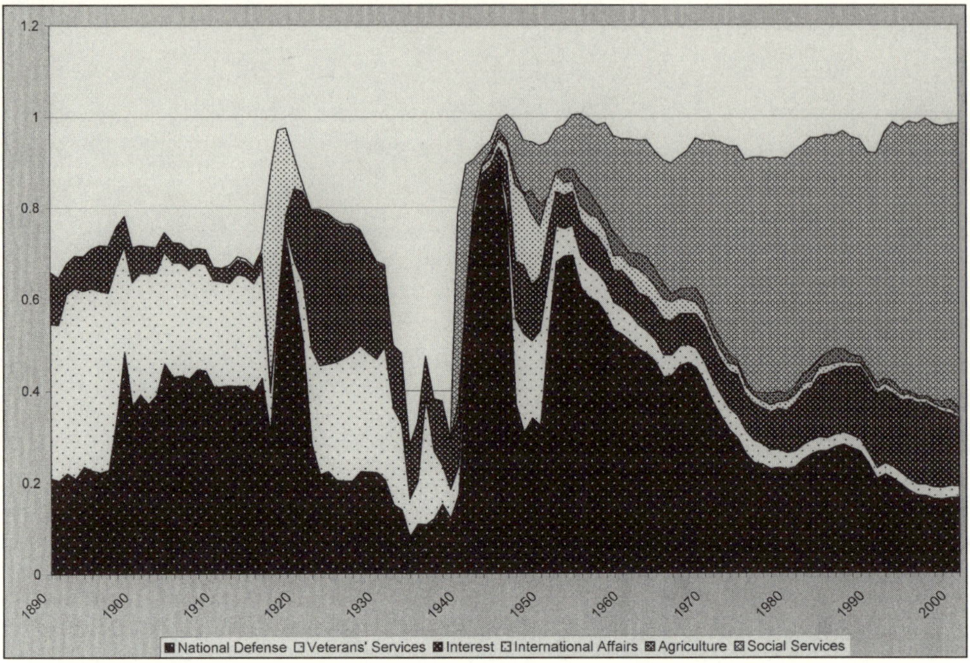

8. Federal Outlays by Function as a Percentage of Total Outlays. *Sources:* 1890–1939: Bureau of the Census, *Historical Statistics of the United States, Colonial Times to 1970,* Series Y 466–71 (Washington, D.C.: Government Printing Office, 1975); 1940–2001: Office of Management and Budget, *Budget of the United States Government, FiscalYear 2002,* Table 3.1 (Washington, D.C.: Government Printing Office, 2001).

Notes: (1) percentages are based on amounts for the fiscal year ending June 30; (2) data for fiscal years 1890–1939 are based on administrative budget figures; data for fiscal years 1940–2001 are based on unified budget figures; (3) "Social Services" represents amounts allocated to education training, employ-ment, income security, social security, community and regional development, and health; (4) "Interest" represents on-budget outlays for interest paid by the U.S. Treasury and by federal government corporations; (5) for fiscal years 1894–1911, "National Defense" represents amounts allocated specifically to the Department of the Army and the Department of the Navy; (6) the residual for fiscal years 1894–1911 consists primarily of amounts allocated for international affairs and finance; (7) the residual for fiscal years 1940–2001 represents amounts allocated for energy, natural resources and environment, commerce and housing credit, transportation, general science, space and technology, the administration of justice, and general government.

come taxation—indeed, from all forms of taxation—were used primarily to expand and modernize the military, fund the army's pension trusts, and pay interest on the national debt (see illustration 8). It was not until the mid-twentieth century that federal revenues were used to confer specific benefits upon farmers, in the form of agricultural subsidies, small businessmen in the form of below-market rate loans, and workers in the form of social security payments, Medicare, and other wealth transfers.

Second, Democratic and Republican members of the Fifty-third and Sixty-third Congresses explicitly rejected the Populist and Socialist creed that the income tax should be used to redistribute society's wealth. In the words of Indiana Democrat Benjamin Shively, a ranking member of the Senate Finance Committee in 1913, "[T]he main purpose [of the income tax] is to provide for the fiscal necessities of the Government, not to provide a system for the redistribution of property or a system with reference particularly to its economic effect. It is with more particular reference to raising the required means with which to pay the expenses of the Government, and on that basis this has been provided in the bill."[24]

As for what has sustained the tax over time, it has not been the tireless efforts of elites to broaden their power base, nor their remarkable ability to persuade the masses to accept personal sacrifice, nor the path-driven course of history, but rather individuals, social classes, business associations, and labor groups that have had an interest in keeping the institution alive. Political elites come and go, but the income tax remains. If its operation were predicated solely on the efforts of elites, then the income tax would have foundered decades ago. Its very existence would have been jeopardized at each congressional election and at each presidential appointment. The fact of the matter is, the changing of the guard has failed to undermine the institution because it is founded on something far more fundamental than the political activity of elites. It is built on agrarian, labor, and middle-class elements that have a vital stake in the equitable distribution of the tax burden.

Let us turn to the question of relevance. How does all this relate to the current debate on abolishing the income tax? Why does it matter today, if at all? It matters because it suggests that abolishing the tax is not just a question of statutory repeal. Nor is it merely a question of tax simplification or postcard reporting. Rather, it is also a question of *deinstitutionalization* and *disallocation*. It is also a question of redistributing the tax burden among members of society. That a consumption or sales tax will have the same allocative impact as tariff taxation is by no means certain. That it will shift the burden from the wealthy to the less wealthy is far from clear. But what is most certain and most clear is that such a levy will impact different socioeconomic groups in different ways. Income tax critics should carefully determine and weigh this impact before embarking upon their project of tax reform.

Conceived in the womb of an industrializing nation, the modern U.S. income tax was born in the politics of a democratic society. Its original intent was to rectify the institutional shortcomings of tariff taxation, all the while leaving the distributional shortfalls of capitalism intact. This limited purpose, articulated by the founders of the modern income tax in 1894, was endorsed by the statesmen of the twentieth century. It was realized in the Income Tax of 1913, which laid the groundwork for our present tax code. This limited purpose is at once the product of mind, politics, and an intense social struggle involving a multiplicity of actors, each pursuing subjective aims in a peculiar sociohistorical context. Through the establishment of the tax, the populist idea of *ability to pay* became the objective reality of the American state, if not immediately, then over the course of time.

Appendixes

Notes

Bibliography

Index

APPENDIX A

Income Tax Provisions

Act of August 28, 1894

An Act to Reduce Taxation, to Provide Revenue for the Government, and for Other Purposes

Section 27

That from and after the first day of January, eighteen hundred and ninety-five, and until the first day of January, nineteen hundred, there shall be assessed, levied, collected, and paid annually upon the gains, profits, and income received in the preceding calendar year by every citizen of the United States, whether residing at home or abroad, and every person residing therein, whether said gains, profits, or income be derived from any kind of property, rents, interest, dividends, or salaries, or from any profession, trade, employment, or vocation carried on in the United States or elsewhere, or from any other source whatever, a tax of two per centum on the amount so derived over and above four thousand dollars, and a like tax shall be levied, collected, and paid annually upon the gains, profits, and income from all property owned and of every business, trade, or profession carried on in the United States by persons residing without the United States. And the tax herein provided for shall be assessed, by the Commissioner of Internal Revenue and collected, and paid upon the gains, profits, and income for the year ending the thirty-first day of December next preceding the time for levying, collecting, and paying said tax.

Section 28

That in estimating the gains, profits and income of any person there shall be included all income derived from interest upon notes, bonds, and other securities, except such bonds of the United States the principal and interest of which are by the law of their issuance exempt from all Federal taxation; profits realized within the year from sales of real estate purchased within two years previous to the close of the year for which income is estimated; interest received or accrued upon all notes, bonds, mortgages, or other forms of indebtedness bearing interest, whether paid or not, if good and collectible, less the interest which has become due from said person or which has been paid by him during the year; the amount of all premium on bonds, notes, or coupons; the amount of sales of live stock, sugar, cotton, wool, butter, cheese, pork, beef, mutton, or other meats, hay, and grain, or other vegetable or other productions, being the growth or produce of the estate of such person, less the amount expended in the purchase or production of said stock or produce, and not including any part thereof consumed directly by the family; money and the value of all personal property acquired by gift or inheritance; all other gains, profits, and income derived from any source whatever except that portion of the salary, compensation, or pay received for services in the civil, military, naval, or other service of the United States, including Senators, Representatives, and Delegates in Congress, from which the tax has been deducted, and except that portion of any salary upon which the employer is required by law to withhold, and does withhold the tax and pays the same to the officer authorized to receive it. In computing incomes the necessary expenses actually incurred in carrying on any business, occupation, or profession shall be deducted, and also all interest due or paid within the year by such person on existing indebtedness. And all national, State, county, school, and municipal taxes, not including those assessed against local benefits, paid within the year shall be deducted from the gains, profits, or income of the person who has actually paid the same, whether such person be owner, tenant, or mortgagor; also losses actually sustained during the year, incurred in trade or arising from fires, storms, or shipwreck, and not compensated for by insurance or otherwise, and debts ascertained to be worthless, but excluding all estimated depreciation of values and losses within the year on sales of real estate purchased within two years previous to the year for which income is estimated: *Provided,* That no deduction shall be made for any amount paid out for new buildings, permanent improvements, or betterments, made to increase the value of any property or estate: *Provided further,* That only one deduction of four thousand dollars shall be made from the aggregate income of all the members of any family, composed of one or both parents, and one or more minor children, or husband and wife; that guardians shall be allowed to make a deduction in favor of each and every ward, except that in case where two or more wards are comprised in one family, and have joint property interests, the aggregate deduction in their favor shall not exceed four thousand dollars: *And provided further,* That in cases where the salary or other compensation paid to any person in the employment or service of the United States shall not exceed the rate of four thousand dollars per annum, or shall be by fees, or uncertain or irregular in the amount or in the time during which the same shall have accrued or been earned, such salary or other compensation shall be included in estimating the annual gains, profits, or income of the person to whom the same shall have been paid, and shall include that portion of any income or salary upon which a tax has not been paid by the employer, where the employer is required by law to pay on the excess over four thousand dollars: *Provided also,* That in computing the income of any person, corporation, company, or association there shall not be included the amount received from any corporation, company, or association as dividends upon the stock of such corporation, company, or association if the tax of two per centum has been paid upon its net profits by said corporation, company, or association as required by this Act.

Section 29

That it shall be the duty of all persons of lawful age having an income of more than three thousand five hundred dollars for the taxable year, computed on the basis herein prescribed, to make and render a list or return, on or before the day provided by law, in such form and manner as may be directed by the Commissioner of Internal Revenue, with the approval of the Secretary of the Treasury, to the collector or a deputy collector of the district in which they reside, of the amount of their income, gains, and profits, as aforesaid; and all guardians and trustees, executors, administrators, agents, receivers, and all persons or corporations acting in a fiduciary capacity, shall make and render a list or return, as aforesaid, to the collector or a deputy collector of the district in which such person or corporation acting in any fiduciary capacity resides or does business, of the amount of income, gains, and profits of any minor person for whom they act, but persons having less than three thousand five hundred dollars income are not required to make such report; and the collector or deputy collector, shall require every list or return to be verified by the oath or affirmation of the party rendering it, and may increase the amount of any list or return if he has reason to believe that the same is understated; and in case any such person having a taxable income shall neglect or refuse to make and render such list and return, or shall render a willfully false or fraudulent list or return, it shall be the duty of the collector or deputy collector, to make such list, according to the best information he can obtain, by the examination of such person, or any other evidence, and to add fifty per centum as a penalty to the amount of the tax due on such list in all cases of willful neglect or refusal to make and render a list or return; and in all cases of a willfully false or fraudulent list or return having been rendered to add one hundred per centum as a penalty to the amount of tax ascertained to be due, the tax and the additions thereto as a penalty to be assessed and collected in the manner provided for in other cases of willful neglect or refusal to render a list or return, or of rendering a false or fraudulent return: *Provided,* That any person, or corporation in his, her, or its own behalf, or as such fiduciary, shall be permitted to declare, under oath or affirmation, the form and manner of which shall be prescribed by the Commissioner of Internal Revenue, with the approval of the Secretary of the Treasury, that he, she, or his or her, or its ward or beneficiary, was not possessed of an income of four thousand dollars, liable to be assessed according to the provisions of this

Act; or may declare that he, she, or it, or his, her, or its ward or beneficiary has been assessed and has paid an income tax elsewhere in the same year, under authority of the United States, upon all his, her or its income, gains, or profits, and upon all the income, gains, or profits for which he, she, or it is liable as such fiduciary, as prescribed by law; and if the collector or deputy collector shall be satisfied of the truth of the declaration, such person or corporation shall thereupon be exempt from income tax in the said district for that year; or if the list or return of any person or corporation, company, or association shall have been increased by the collector or deputy collector, such person or corporation, company, or association may be permitted to prove the amount of income liable to be assessed; but such proof shall not be considered as conclusive of the facts, and no deductions claimed in such cases shall be made or allowed until approved by the collector or deputy collector. Any person or company, corporation or association feeling aggrieved by the decision of the deputy collector, in such cases may appeal to the collector of the district, and his decision thereon, unless reversed by the Commissioner of Internal Revenue, shall be final. If dissatisfied with the decision of the collector such person or corporation, company, or association may submit the case, with all the papers, to the Commissioner of Internal Revenue for his decision, and may furnish the testimony of witnesses to prove any relevant facts having served notice to that effect upon the Commissioner of Internal Revenue, as herein prescribed.

Such notice shall state the time and place at which, and the officer before whom, the testimony will be taken; the name, age, residence, and business of the proposed witness, with the questions to be propounded to the witness, or a brief statement of the substance of the testimony he is expected to give: *Provided,* That the Government may at the same time and place take testimony upon like notice to rebut the testimony of the witnesses examined by the person taxed.

The notice shall be delivered or mailed to the Commissioner of Internal Revenue a sufficient number of days previous to the day fixed for taking the testimony, to allow him, after its receipt, at least five days, exclusive of the period required for mail communication with the place at which the testimony is to be taken, in which to give, should he so desire, instructions as to the cross-examination of the proposed witness.

Whenever practicable, the affidavit or deposition shall be taken before a collector or deputy collector of internal revenue, in which case reasonable notice shall be given to the collector or deputy collector of the time fixed for taking the deposition or affidavit:

Provided further, That no penalty shall be assessed upon any person or corporation, company or association for such neglect or refusal or for making or rendering a willfully false or fraudulent return, except after reasonable notice of the time and place of hearing to be prescribed by the Commissioner of Internal Revenue, so as to give the person charged an opportunity to be heard.

Section 30

The taxes on incomes herein imposed shall be due and payable on or before the first day of July in each year; and to any sum or sums annually due and unpaid after the first day of July as aforesaid, and for ten days after notice and demand thereof by the collector, there shall be levied, in addition thereto, the sum of five per centum on the amount of taxes unpaid, and interest at the rate of one per centum per month upon said tax from the time the same becomes due, as a penalty, except from the estates of deceased, insane, or insolvent persons.

Section 31

Any nonresident may receive the benefit of the exemptions hereinbefore provided for by filing with the deputy collector of any district a true list of all of his property and sources of income in the United States and complying with the provisions of section twenty-nine of this Act as if a resident. In computing income he shall include all income from every source, but unless he be a citizen of the United States he shall only pay on that part of the income which is derived from any source in the United States. In case such nonresident fails to file such statement, the collector of each district shall collect the tax on the income derived from property situated in his district, subject to income tax, making no allowance for exemptions, and all property belonging to such nonresident shall be liable to distraint for tax: *Provided,* That nonresident corporations shall be subject to the same laws as to tax as resident corporations, and the collection of the tax shall be made in the same manner as provided for collections of taxes against nonresident persons.

Section 32

That there shall be assessed, levied, and collected, except as herein otherwise provided, a tax of two per centum annually on the net profits or income above actual operating and business expenses, including expenses for materials purchased for manufacture or bought for resale, losses, and interest on bonded and other indebtedness of all banks, banking institutions, trust companies, savings institutions, fire, marine, life, and other insurance companies, railroad, canal, turnpike, canal navigation, slack water, telephone, telegraph, express, electric light, gas, water, street railway companies, and all other corporations, companies, or associations doing business for profit in the United States, no matter how created and organized, but not including partnerships.

That said tax shall be paid on or before the first day of July in each year; and if the president or other chief officer of any corporation, company, or association, or in the case of any foreign corporation, company, or association, the resident manager or agent shall neglect or refuse to file with the collector of the internal-revenue district in which said corporation, company, or association shall be located or be engaged in business, a statement verified by his oath or affirmation, in such form as shall be prescribed by the Commissioner of Internal Revenue, with the approval of the Secretary of the Treasury, showing the amount of net profits or income received by said corporation, company or association during the whole calendar year last preceding the date of filing said statement as hereinafter required, the corporation, company, or association making default shall forfeit as a penalty the sum of one thousand dollars and two per centum on the amount of taxes due, for each month until the same is paid, the payment of said penalty to be enforced as provided in other cases of neglect and refusal to make return of taxes under the internal-revenue laws.

The net profits or income of all corporations, companies or associations shall include the amounts paid to shareholders, or carried to the account of any fund, or used for construction, enlargement of plant, or any other expenditure or investment paid from the net annual profits made or acquired by said corporations, companies, or associations.

That nothing herein contained shall apply to States, counties, or municipalities; nor to corporations, companies, or associations organized and conducted solely for charitable, religious, or educational purposes, including fraternal beneficiary societies, orders, or associations operating upon the lodge system and providing for the payment of life, sick, accident, and other benefits to the members of such societies, orders, or associations and dependents of such members; nor to the stocks, shares, funds, or securities held by any fiduciary or trustee for charitable, religious, or educational purposes; nor to building and loan associations or companies which make loans only to their shareholders; nor to such savings banks, saving institutions or societies as shall, first, have no stockholders or members except depositors and no capital except deposits; secondly, shall not receive deposits to an aggregate amount, in any one year, of more than one thousand dollars from the same depositor; thirdly, shall not allow an accumulation or total of deposits, by any one depositor, exceeding ten thousand dollars; fourthly, shall actually divide and distribute to its depositors, ratably to deposits, all the earnings over the necessary and proper expenses of such bank, institution, or society, except such as shall be applied to surplus; fifthly, shall not possess, in any form, a surplus fund exceeding ten per centum of its aggregate deposits; nor to such savings banks, savings institutions, or societies composed of members who do not participate in the profits thereof and which pay interest or dividends only to their depositors; nor to that part of the business of any savings bank, institution, or other similar association having a capital stock, that is conducted on the mutual plan solely for the benefit of its depositors on such plan, and which shall keep its account of its business conducted on such mutual plan separate and apart from its other accounts.

Nor to any insurance company or association which conducts all its business solely upon the mutual plan, and only for the benefit of its policy-holders or members, and having no capital stock and no stock or shareholders, and holding all its property in trust and in reserve for its policy holders or members; nor to that part of the business of any insurance company having a capital stock and stock and shareholders, which is conducted on the mutual plan, separate from its stock plan of insurance, and solely for the benefit of the policy holders and members insured on said mutual plan, and holding all the property belonging to and derived from said mutual part of its business in trust and reserve for the benefit of its policy holders and members insured on said mutual plan.

That all State, county, municipal, and town taxes paid by corporations, companies, or associations shall be included in the operating and business expenses of such corporations, companies, or associations.

Section 33

That there shall be levied, collected, and paid on all salaries of officers, or payments for services to persons in the civil, military, naval, or other employment or service of the United States, including Senators and Representatives and Delegates in Congress, when exceeding the rate of four thousand dollars per annum, a tax of two per centum on the excess above the said four thousand dollars; and it shall be the duty of all paymasters and all disbursing officers under the Government of the United States, or persons in the employ thereof, when making any payment to any officers or persons as aforesaid, whose compensation is determined by a fixed salary, or upon settling or adjusting the accounts of such officers or persons, to deduct and withhold the aforesaid tax of two per centum; and the pay roll, receipts, or account of officers or persons paying such tax as aforesaid shall be made to exhibit the fact of such payment. And it shall be the duty of the accounting officers of the Treasury Department, when auditing the accounts of any paymaster or disbursing officer, or any officer withholding his salary from moneys received by him, or when settling or adjusting the accounts of any such officer, to require evidence that the taxes mentioned in this section have been deducted and paid over to the Treasurer of the United States, or other officer authorized to receive the same. Every corporation which pays to any employee a salary or compensation exceeding four thousand dollars per annum shall report the same to the collector or deputy collector of his district and said employee shall pay thereon, subject to the exemptions herein provided for, the tax of two per centum on the excess of his salary over four thousand dollars: *Provided,* That salaries due to State, county, or municipal officers shall be exempt from the income tax herein levied.

Section 34

That sections thirty-one hundred and sixty-seven, thirty-one hundred and seventy-two, thirty-one hundred and seventy three, and thirty-one hundred and seventy-six of the Revised Statutes of the United States as amended are hereby amended so as to read as follows:

Section 3167

That it shall be unlawful for any collector, deputy collector, agent, clerk, or other officer or employee of the United States to divulge or to make known in any manner whatever not provided by law to any person the operations, style of work or apparatus of any manufacturer or producer visited by him in the discharge of his official duties, or the amount or source of income, profits, losses, expenditures, or any particular thereof, set forth or disclosed in any income return by any person or corporation, or to permit any income return or copy thereof or any book containing any abstract or particulars thereof, to be seen or examined by any person except as provided by law; and it shall be unlawful for any person to print or publish in any manner whatever not provided by law, any income return or any part thereof or the amount or source of income, profits, losses, or expenditures appearing in any income return; and any offense against the aforegoing provision shall be a misdemeanor and be punished by a fine not exceeding one thousand dollars or by imprisonment not exceeding one year, or both, at the discretion of the court; and if the offender be an officer or employee of the United States he shall be dismissed from office and be incapable thereafter of holding any office under the Government.

Section 3172

That every collector shall, from time to time, cause his deputies to proceed through every part of his district and inquire after and concerning all persons therein who are liable to pay any internal revenue tax, and all persons owning or having the care and management of any objects liable to pay any tax, and to make a list of such persons and enumerate said objects.

Section 3173

That it shall be the duty of any person, partnership, firm, association, or corporation, made liable to any duty, special tax, or other tax imposed by law, when not otherwise provided for, in case of a special tax, on or before the thirty-first day of July in each year, in case of income tax on or before the first Monday of March in each year, and in other cases before the day on which the taxes accrue, to make a list or return, verified by oath or affirmation, to the collector or a deputy collector of the district where located, of the articles or objects, including the amount of annual income, charged with a duty or tax, the quantity of goods, wares, and merchandise made or sold, and charged with a tax, the several rates and aggregate amount, according to the forms and regulations to be prescribed by the Commissioner of Internal Revenue, with the approval of the Secretary of the Treasury, for which such person, partnership, firm, association, or corporation is liable: *Provided,* That if any person liable to pay any duty or tax, or owning, possessing, or having the care or management of property, goods, wares, and merchandise, articles or objects liable to pay any duty, tax or license, shall fail to make and exhibit a list or return required by law, but shall consent to disclose the particulars of any and all the property, goods, wares, and merchandise, articles and objects liable to pay any duty or tax, or any business or occupation liable to pay any tax as aforesaid, then, and in that case, it shall be the duty of the collector or deputy collector to make such list or return, which, being distinctly read, consented to, and signed and verified by oath or affirmation by the person so owning, possessing, or having the care and management as aforesaid, may be received as the list of such person: *Provided further,* That in case no annual list or return has been rendered by such person to the collector or deputy collector as required by law, and the person shall be absent from his or her residence or place of business at the time the collector or a deputy collector shall call for the annual list or return, it shall be the duty of such collector or deputy collector to leave at such place of residence or business, with some one of suitable age and discretion, if such be present, otherwise to deposit in the nearest post-office a note or memorandum addressed to such person, requiring him or her to render to such collector or deputy collector the list or return required by law, within ten days from the date of such note or memorandum, verified by oath or affirmation. And if any person on being notified or required as aforesaid shall refuse or neglect to render such list or return within the time required as aforesaid or whenever any person who is required to deliver a monthly or other return of objects subject to tax fails to do so at the time required, or delivers any return which, in the opinion of the collector, is false or fraudulent, or contains any undervaluation or understatement, it shall be lawful for the collector to summon such person, or any other person having possession, custody, or care of books of account containing entries relating to the business of such person, or any other person he may deem proper, to appear before him and produce such books, at a time and place named in the summons, and to give testimony or answer interrogatories, under oath, respecting any objects liable to tax or the returns thereof. The collector may summon any person residing or found within the State in which his district lies; and when the person intended to be summoned does not reside and can not be found within such State, he may enter any collection district where such person may be found, and there make the examination herein authorized. And to this end he may there exercise all the authority which he might lawfully exercise in the district for which he was commissioned.

Section 3176

When any person, corporation, company, or association refuses or neglects to render any return or list required by law, or renders a false or fraudulent return or list, the collector or any deputy collector shall make, according to the best information which he can obtain, including that derived from the evidence elicited by the examination of the collector, and on his own view and information, such list or return, according to the form prescribed, of the income, property, and objects liable to tax owned or possessed or under the care or management of such person, or corporation, company, or association, and the Commissioner of Internal Revenue shall assess all taxes not paid by stamps, including the amount, if any, due for special tax, income, or other tax, and in case of any return of a false or fraudulent list or valuation intentionally he shall add one hundred per centum to such tax; and in case of a refusal or neglect, except in cases of sickness or absence, to make a list or return, or to verify the same as aforesaid, he shall add fifty per centum to such tax. In case of neglect occasioned by sickness or absence as aforesaid the collector may allow such further time for making and delivering such list or return as he may deem necessary, not exceeding thirty days. The amount so added to the tax shall be collected at the same time and in the same manner as the tax unless the neglect or falsity is discovered after the tax has been paid, in which case the amount so added shall be collected in the same manner as the tax; and the list or return so made and subscribed by such collector or deputy collector shall be held prima facie good and sufficient for all legal purposes.

Section 35

That every corporation, company, or association doing business for profit shall make and render to the collector of its collection district, on or before the first Monday of March in every year, beginning with the year eighteen hundred and ninety-five, a full return, verified by oath or affirmation, in such form as the Commissioner of Internal Revenue may prescribe, of all the following matters for the whole calendar year last preceding the date of such return:

First. The gross profits of such corporation, company, or association, from all kinds of business of every name and nature.

Second. The expenses of such corporation, company, or association, exclusive of interest, annuities, and dividends.

Third. The net profits of such corporation, company, or association, without allowance for interest, annuities, or dividends.

Fourth. The amount paid on account of interest, annuities, and dividends, stated separately.

Fifth. The amount paid in salaries of four thousand dollars or less to each person employed.

Sixth. The amount paid in salaries of more than four thousand dollars to each person employed and the name and address of each of such persons and the amount paid to each.

Section 36

That it shall be the duty of every corporation, company, or association doing business for profit to keep full, regular, and accurate books of account, upon which all its transactions shall be entered from day to day, in regular order, and whenever a collector or deputy collector of the district in which any corporation, company, or association is assessable shall believe that a true and correct return of the income of such corporation, company, or association has not been made, he shall make an affidavit of such belief and of the grounds on which it is founded, and file the same with the Commissioner of Internal Revenue, and if said Commissioner shall, on examination thereof, and after full hearing upon notice given to all parties, conclude there is good ground for such belief he shall issue a request in writing to such corporation, company, or association to permit an inspection of the books of such corporation, company, or association to be made; and if such corporation, company, or association shall refuse to comply with such request, then the collector or deputy collector of the district shall make from such information as he can obtain an estimate of the amount of such income and then add fifty per centum thereto, which said assessment so made shall then be the lawful assessment of such income.

Section 37

That it shall be the duty of every collector of internal revenue, to whom any payment of any taxes other than the tax represented by an adhesive stamp or other engraved stamp is made under the provisions of this Act, to give to the person making such payment a full written or printed receipt, expressing the amount paid and the particular account for which such payment was made; and whenever such payment is made such collector shall, if required, give a separate receipt for each tax paid by any debtor, on account of payments made to or to be made by him to separate creditors in such form that such debtor can conveniently produce the same separately to his several creditors in satisfaction of their respective demands to the amounts specified in such receipts; and such receipts shall be sufficient evidence in favor of such debtor, to justify him in withholding the amount therein expressed from his next payment to his creditor; but such creditor may, upon giving to his debtor a full written receipt, acknowledge the payment to him of whatever sum may be actually paid, and accepting the amount of tax paid as aforesaid (specifying the same) as a further satisfaction of the debt to that amount, require the surrender to him of such collector's receipt.

APPENDIX B

Pollock v. Farmers' Loan & Trust Company

158 U.S. 601 (May 20, 1895)

On Rehearing

. . .

MR. CHIEF JUSTICE FULLER delivered the opinion of the court.

Whenever this court is required to pass upon the validity of an act of Congress as tested by the fundamental law enacted by the people, the duty imposed demands in its discharge the utmost deliberation and care, and invokes the deepest sense of responsibility. And this is especially so when the question involves the exercise of a great governmental power, and brings into consideration, as vitally affected by the decision, that complex system of government, so sagaciously framed to secure and perpetuate "an indestructible Union, composed of indestructible States."

We have, therefore, with an anxious desire to omit nothing which might in any degree tend to elucidate the questions submitted, and aided by further able arguments embodying the fruits of elaborate research, carefully reexamined those cases, with the result that, while our former conclusions remain unchanged, their scope must be enlarged by the acceptance of their logical consequences.

The very nature of the Constitution, as observed by Chief Justice Marshall, in one of his greatest judgments, "requires that only its great outlines should be marked, its important objects designated, and the minor ingredients which compose those objects be deduced from the nature of the objects themselves." "In considering this question, then, we must never forget, that it is *a Constitution* that we are expounding." *McCulloch v. Maryland,* 4 Wheat. 316, 407.

As heretofore stated, the Constitution divided Federal taxation into two great classes, the class of direct taxes, and the class of duties, imposts, and excises; and prescribed two rules which qualified the grant of power as to each class.

The power to lay direct taxes apportioned among the several States in proportion to their representation in the popular branch of Congress, a representation based on population as ascertained by the census, was plenary and absolute; but to lay direct taxes without apportionment was forbidden. The power to lay duties, imposts, and excises was subject to the qualification that the imposition must be uniform throughout the United States.

Our previous decision was confined to the consideration of the validity of the tax on the income from real estate, and on the income from municipal bonds. The question thus limited was whether such taxation was direct or not, in the meaning of the Constitution; and the court went no farther, as to the tax on the income from real estate, than to hold that it fell within the same class as the source whence the income was derived, that is, that a tax upon the realty and a tax upon the receipts therefrom were alike direct; while as to the income from municipal bonds, that could not be taxed because of want of power to tax the source, and no reference was made to the nature of the tax as being direct or indirect.

We are now permitted to broaden the field of inquiry, and to determine to which of the two great classes a tax upon a person's entire income, whether derived from rents, or products, or otherwise, of real estate, or from bonds, stocks, or other forms of personal property, belongs; and we are unable to conclude that the enforced subtraction from the yield of all the owner's real or personal property, in the manner prescribed, is so different from a tax upon the property itself, that it is not a direct, but an indirect tax, in the meaning of the Constitution.

The words of the Constitution are to be taken in their obvious sense, and to have a reasonable construction. In *Gibbons v. Ogden,* Mr. Chief Justice Marshall, with his usual felicity, said: "As men, whose intentions require no concealment, generally employ the words which most directly and aptly express the ideas they intend to convey, the enlightened patriots who framed our Constitution, and the people who adopted it must be understood to have employed words in their natural sense, and to have intended what they have said." 9 Wheat. 1, 188. And in *Rhode Island v. Massachusetts,* where the question was whether a controversy between two States over the boundary between them was within the grant of the judicial power, Mr. Justice Baldwin, speaking for the court, observed: "The solution of this question must necessarily depend on the words of the Constitution; the meaning and intention of the convention which framed and proposed it for adoption and ratification to the conventions of the people of and in the several States; together with a reference to such sources of judicial information as are resorted to by all courts in construing statutes, and to which this court has always resorted in construing the Constitution." 12 Pet. 657, 721.

We know of no reason for holding otherwise that the words "direct taxes," on the one hand, and "duties, imposts and excises," on the other, were used in the Constitution in their natural and obvious sense. Nor, in arriving at what those terms embrace, do we perceive any ground for enlarging them beyond, or narrowing them within, their natural and obvious import at the time the Constitution was framed and ratified.

And, passing from the text, we regard the conclusion reached as inevitable, when the circumstances which surrounded the convention and controlled its action and the views of those who framed and those who adopted the Constitution are considered.

We do not care to retravel ground already traversed; but some observations may be added.

In the light of the struggle in the convention as to whether or not the new Nation should be empowered to levy taxes directly on the individual until after the States had failed to respond to requisitions—a struggle which did not terminate until the amendment to that effect, proposed by Massachusetts and concurred in by South Carolina, New Hampshire, New York, and Rhode Island, had been rejected—it would seem beyond reasonable question that direct taxation, taking the place as it did of requisitions, was purposely restrained to apportionment according to representation, in order that the former system as to ratio might be retained, while the mode of collection was changed.

This is forcibly illustrated by a letter of Mr. Madison of January 29, 1789, recently published,[1] written after the ratification of the Constitution, but before the organization of the government and the submission of the proposed amendment to Congress, which, while opposing the amendment as calculated to impair the power, only to be exercised in "extraordinary emergencies," assigns adequate ground for its rejection as substantially unnecessary, since, he says, "every State which chooses to collect its own quota may always prevent a Federal collection, by keeping a little beforehand in its finances, and making its payment at once into the Federal treasury."

The reasons for the clauses of the Constitution in respect of direct taxation are not far to seek. The States, respectively, possessed plenary powers of taxation. They could tax the property of their citizens in such manner and to such extent as they saw fit; they had unrestricted powers to impose duties or imposts on imports from abroad, and excises on manufactures, consumable commodities, or otherwise. They gave up the great sources of revenue derived from commerce; they retained the concurrent power or levying excises, and duties if covering anything other than excises; but in respect of them the range of taxation was narrowed by the power granted over interstate commerce, and by the danger of being put at disadvantage in dealing with excises on manufactures. They retained the power of direct taxation, and to that they looked as their chief resource; but even in respect of that, they granted the concurrent power, and if the tax were placed by both governments on the same subject, the claim of the United States had preference. Therefore, they did not grant the power of direct taxation without regard to their own condition and resources as States; but they granted the power of apportioned direct taxation, a power just as efficacious to serve the needs of the general government, but securing to the States the opportunity to pay the amount apportioned, and to recoup from their own citizens in the most feasible way, and in harmony with their systems of local self-government. If, in the changes of wealth and population in particular States, apportionment produced inequality, it was an inequality stipulated for, just as the equal representation of the States, however small, in the Senate, was stipulated for. The Constitution ordains affirmatively that each State shall have two members of that body, and negatively that no State shall by amendment be deprived of its equal suffrage in the Senate without its consent. The Constitution ordains affirmatively that representatives and direct taxes shall be apportioned among the several States according to numbers, and negatively that no direct tax shall be laid unless in proportion to the enumeration.

The founders anticipated that the expenditures of the States, their counties, cities, and towns, would chiefly be met by direct taxation on accumulated property, while they expected that those of the Federal government would be for the most part met by indirect taxes. And in order that the power of direct taxation by the general government should not be exercised, except on necessity; and, when the necessity arose, should be so exercised as to leave the States at liberty to discharge their respective obligations, and should not be so exercised, unfairly and discriminatingly, as to particular States or otherwise, by a mere majority vote, possibly of those whose constituents were intentionally not subjected to any part of the burden, the qualified grant was made. Those who made it knew that the power to tax involved the power to destroy, and that, in the language of Chief Justice Marshall, in *McCulloch v. Maryland,* "the only security against the abuse of this power is found in the structure of the government itself. In imposing a tax, the legislature acts upon its constituents. This is, in general, a sufficient security against erroneous and oppressive taxation." 4 Wheat. 428. And they retained this security by providing that direct taxation and representation in the lower house of Congress should be adjusted on the same measure.

Moreover, whatever the reasons for the constitutional provisions, there they are, and they appear to us to speak in plain language.

It is said that a tax on the whole income of property is not a direct tax in the meaning of the Constitution, but a duty, and, as a duty, leviable without apportionment, whether direct or indirect. We do not think so. Direct taxation was not restricted in one breath, and the restriction blown to the winds in another.

Cooley (On Taxation, p. 3) says that the word *"duty"* ordinarily "means an indirect tax imposed on the importation, exportation or consumption of goods;" having "a broader meaning than *custom,* which is a duty imposed on imports or exports;" that "the term *impost* also signifies any tax, tribute or duty, but it is seldom applied to any but the indirect taxes. An *excise* duty is an inland impost, levied upon articles of manufacture or sale, and also upon licenses to pursue certain trades or to deal in certain commodities."

In the Constitution, the words "duties, imposts and excises" are put in antithesis to direct taxes. Gouverneur Morris recognized this in his remarks in modifying his celebrated motion, as did Wilson in approving of the motion as modified. 5 Ell. Deb.

(Madison Papers) 302. And Mr. Justice Story, in his Commentaries on the Constitution, (§ 952,) expresses the view that it is not unreasonable to presume that the word "duties" was used as equivalent to "customs" or "imposts" by the framers of the Constitution, since in other clauses it was provided that "No tax or duty shall be laid on articles exported from any State," and that "No State shall, without the consent of Congress, lay any imposts or duties on imports or exports, except what may be absolutely necessary for executing its inspection laws;" and he refers to a letter of Mr. Madison to Mr. Cabell, of September 18, 1828, to that effect. 3 Madison's Writings, 636.

In this connection it may be useful, though at the risk of repetition, to refer to the view of Hamilton and Madison as thrown into relief in the pages of the Federalist, and in respect of the enactment of the carriage tax act, and again to briefly consider the *Hylton case,* 3 Dall. 171, so much dwelt on in argument.

The act of June 5, 1794, c. 45, 1 Stat. 373, laying duties upon carriages for the conveyance of persons, was enacted in a time of threatened war. Bills were then pending in Congress to increase the military force of the United States, and to authorize increased taxation in various directions. It was, therefore, as much a part of a system of taxation in war times, as was the income tax of the war of the rebellion. The bill passed the House on the twenty-ninth of May, apparently after a very short debate. Mr. Madison and Mr. Ames are the only speakers on that day reported in the Annals. "Mr. Madison objected to this tax on carriages as an unconstitutional tax; and, as an unconstitutional measure, he would vote against it." Mr. Ames said: "It was not to be wondered at if he, coming from so different a part of the country, should have a different idea of this tax from the gentleman who spoke last. In Massachusetts, this tax had been long known; and there it was called an excise. It was difficult to define whether a tax is direct or not. He had satisfied himself that this was not so." Annals, 3d Cong. 730.

On the first of June, 1794, Mr. Madison wrote to Mr. Jefferson: "The carriage tax, which only struck at the Constitution, has passed the House of Representatives." 3 Madison's Writings, 18. The bill then went to the Senate, where, on the third day of June, it "was considered and adopted," Annals, 3d Cong. 119, and on the following day it received the signature of President Washington. On the same third day of June the Senate considered "an act laying certain duties upon snuff and refined sugar;" "an act making further provisions for securing and collecting the duties on foreign and domestic distilled spirits, stills, wines, and teas;" "an act for the more effectual protection of the Southwestern frontier;" "an act laying additional duties on goods, wares and merchandise, etc.;" "an act laying duties on licenses for selling wines and foreign distilled spirituous liquors by retail;" and "an act laying duties on property sold at auction."

It appears then that Mr. Madison regarded the carriage tax bill as unconstitutional, and accordingly gave his vote against it, although it was to a large extent, if not altogether, a war measure.

Where did Mr. Hamilton stand? At that time he was Secretary of the Treasury, and it may therefore be assumed, without proof, that he favored the legislation. But upon what ground? He must, of course, have come to the conclusion that it was not a direct tax. Did he agree with Fisher Ames, his personal and political friend, that the tax was an excise? The evidence is overwhelming that he did.

In the thirtieth number of the Federalist, after depicting the helpless and hopeless condition of the country growing out of the inability of the confederation to obtain from the States the moneys assigned to its expenses, he says: "The more intelligent adversaries of the new Constitution admit the force of this reasoning; but they qualify their admission, by a distinction between what they call *internal* and *external* taxations. The former they would reserve to the state governments; the latter, which they explain into commercial imposts, or rather duties on imported articles, they declare themselves willing to concede to the Federal head." In the thirty-sixth number, while still adopting the division of his opponents, he says: "The taxes intended to be comprised under the general denomination of internal taxes, may be subdivided into those of the *direct* and those of the *indirect* kind. . . . As to the latter, *by which must be understood duties and excises on articles of consumption,* one is at a loss to conceive, what can be the nature of the difficulties apprehended." Thus we find Mr. Hamilton, while writing to induce the adoption of the Constitution, *first,* dividing the power of taxation into *external* and *internal,* putting into the former the power of imposing duties on imported articles and into the latter all remaining powers; and, *second,* dividing the latter into *direct* and *indirect,* putting into the latter, duties and excises on articles of consumption.

It seems to us to inevitably follow that in Mr. Hamilton's judgment at that time all internal taxes, except duties and excises on articles of consumption, fell into the category of direct taxes.

Did he, in supporting the carriage tax bill, change his views in this respect? His argument in the *Hylton case* in support of the law enables us to answer this question. It was not reported by Dallas, but was published in 1851 by his son in the edition of all Hamilton's writings except the Federalist. After saying that we shall seek in vain for any legal meaning of the respective terms "direct and indirect taxes," and after forcibly stating the impossibility of collecting the tax if it is to be considered as a direct tax, he says, doubtingly: "The following are presumed to be the only direct taxes. Capitation or poll taxes. Taxes on lands and buildings. General assessments, whether on the whole property of individuals, or on their whole real or personal estate; all else must of necessity be considered as indirect taxes." *"Duties, imposts and excises* appear to be contradistinguished from *taxes."* "If the meaning of the word *excise* is to be sought in the British statutes, it will be found to include the duty on carriages, which is there considered as an *excise.*" "Where so important a distinction in the Constitution is to be realized, it is fair to seek the meaning of terms in the statutory language of that country from which our jurisprudence is derived." 7 Hamilton's Works, 848. Mr. Hamilton therefore clearly supported the law which Mr. Madison opposed, for the same reason that his friend Fisher Ames did, because it was an excise, and as such was specifically comprehended by the Constitution. Any loose expressions in definition of the word "direct," so far as conflicting with his well-considered views in the Federalist, must be regarded as the liberty which the advocate usually thinks himself entitled to take with his subject. He gives, however, it appears to us, a definition which covers the question before us. A tax upon one's whole income is a tax upon the annual receipts from his whole property, and as such falls within the same class as a tax upon that property, and is a direct tax, in the meaning of the Constitution. And Mr. Hamilton in his report on the public credit, in referring to contracts with citizens of a foreign country, said: "This principle, which seems critically correct, would exempt as well the income as the capital of the property. It protects the use, as effectually as the thing. What, in fact, is property, but a fiction, without the beneficial use of it? In many cases, indeed, the *income* or *annuity* is the property itself." 3 Hamilton's Works, 34.

We think there is nothing in the *Hylton case* in conflict with the foregoing. The case is badly reported. The report does not give the names of both the judges before whom the case was argued in the Circuit Court. The record of that court shows that Mr. Justice Wilson was one and District Judge Griffin of Virginia was the other. Judge Tucker in his appendix to the edition of Blackstone published in 1803 (Tucker's Blackstone, vol. 1, part 1, p. 294,) says: "The question was tried in this State, in the case of *United States v. Hylton,* and the court being divided in opinion, was carried to the Supreme Court of the United States by consent. It was there argued by the proposer of it, (the first Secretary of the Treasury,) on behalf of the United States, and by the present Chief Justice of the United States, on behalf of the defendant. Each of those gentlemen was supposed to have defended his own private opinion. That of the Secretary of the Treasury prevailed, and the tax was afterwards submitted to, universally, in Virginia."

We are not informed whether Mr. Marshall participated in the two days' hearing at Richmond, and there is nothing of record to indicate that he appeared in the case in this court; but it is quite probable that Judge Tucker was aware of the opinion which he entertained in regard to the matter.

Mr. Hamilton's argument is left out of the report, and in place of it it is said that the argument turned entirely upon the point whether the tax was a direct tax, while his brief shows that, so far as he was concerned, it turned upon the point whether it was an excise, and therefore not a direct tax.

Mr. Justice Chase thought that the tax was a tax on expense, because a carriage was a consumable commodity, and in that view the tax on it was on the expense of the owner. He expressly declined to give an opinion as to what were the direct taxes contemplated by the Constitution. Mr. Justice Paterson said: "All taxes on expenses or consumption are indirect taxes; a tax on carriages is of this kind." He quoted copiously from Adam Smith in support of his conclusions, although it is now asserted that the justices made small account of that writer. Mr. Justice Iredell said: "There is no necessity, or propriety, in determining what is or is not, a direct, or indirect, tax, in all cases. It is sufficient, on the present occasion, for the court to be satisfied, that this is not a direct tax contemplated by the Constitution."

What was decided in the *Hylton case* was, then, that a tax on carriages was an excise, and, therefore, an indirect tax. The contention of Mr. Madison in the House was only so far disturbed by it, that the court classified it where he himself would have held it constitutional, and he subsequently as President approved a similar act. 3 Stat. 40. The contention of Mr. Hamilton in the Federalist was not disturbed by it in the least. In our judgment, the construction given to the Constitution by the authors of the Federalist (the five numbers contributed by Chief Justice Jay related to the danger from foreign force and influence, and to the treaty-making power) should not and cannot be disregarded.

The Constitution prohibits any direct tax, unless in proportion to numbers as ascertained by the census; and, in the light of the circumstances to which we have referred, is it not an evasion of the prohibition to hold that a general unapportioned tax, imposed upon all property owners as a body for or in respect of their property, is not direct, in the meaning of the Constitution, because confined to the income therefrom?

Whatever the speculative views of political economists or revenue reformers may be, can it be properly held that the Constitution, taken in its plain and obvious sense, and with due regard to the circumstances attending the formation of the government, authorizes a general unapportioned tax on the products of the farm and the rents of real estate, although imposed merely because of ownership and with no possible means of escape from payment, as belonging to a totally different class from that which includes the property from whence the income proceeds?

There can be but one answer, unless the constitutional restriction is to be treated as utterly illusory and futile, and the object of its framers defeated. We find it impossible to hold that a fundamental requisition, deemed so important as to be enforced by two provisions, one affirmative and one negative, can be refined away by forced distinctions between that which gives value to property, and the property itself.

Nor can we perceive any ground why the same reasoning does not apply to capital in personalty held for the purpose of income or ordinarily yielding income, and to the income therefrom. All the real estate of the country, and all its invested personal property, are open to the direct operation of the taxing power if an apportionment be made according to the Constitution. The Constitution does not say that no direct tax shall be laid by apportionment on any other property than land; on the contrary, it forbids all unapportioned direct taxes; and we know of no warrant for excepting personal property from the exercise of the power, or any reason why an apportioned direct tax cannot be laid and assessed, as Mr. Gallatin said in his report when Secretary of the

Treasury in 1812, "upon the same objects of taxation on which the direct taxes levied under the authority of the State are laid and assessed."

Personal property of some kind is of general distribution; and so are incomes, though the taxable range thereof might be narrowed through large exemptions.

The Congress of the Confederation found the limitation of the sources of the contributions of the States to "land, and the buildings and improvements thereon," by the eighth article of July 9, 1778, so objectionable that the article was amended April 28, 1783, so that the taxation should be apportioned in proportion to the whole number of white and other free citizens and inhabitants, including those bound to servitude for a term of years and three-fifths of all other persons, except Indians not paying taxes; and Madison, Ellsworth, and Hamilton in their address, in sending the amendment to the States, said: "This rule, although not free from objections, is liable to fewer than any other that could be devised." 1 Ell. Deb. 93, 95, 98.

Nor are we impressed with the contention that, because in the four instances in which the power of direct taxation has been exercised, Congress did not see fit, for reasons of expediency, to levy a tax upon personalty, this amounts to such a practical construction of the Constitution that the power did not exist, that we must regard ourselves bound by it. We should regret to be compelled to hold the powers of the general government thus restricted, and certainly cannot accede to the idea that the Constitution has become weakened by a particular course of inaction under it.

The stress of the argument is thrown, however, on the assertion that an income tax is not a property tax at all; that it is not a real estate tax, or a crop tax, or a bond tax; that it is an assessment upon the taxpayer on account of his money-spending power as shown by his revenue for the year preceding the assessment; that rents received, crops harvested, interest collected, have lost all connection with their origin, and although once not taxable have become transmuted in their new form into taxable subject-matter; in other words, that income is taxable irrespective of the source from whence it is derived.

This was the view entertained by Mr. Pitt, as expressed in his celebrated speech on introducing his income tax law of 1799, and he did not hesitate to carry it to its logical conclusion. The English loan acts provided that the public dividends should be paid "free of all taxes and charges whatsoever;" but Mr. Pitt successfully contended that the dividends for the purposes of the income tax were to be considered simply in relation to the recipient as so much income, and that the fund holder had no reason to complain. And this, said Mr. Gladstone, fifty-five years after, was the rational construction of the pledge. Financial Statements, 32.

The dissenting justices proceeded in effect upon this ground in *Weston v. Charleston,* 2 Pet. 449, but the court rejected it. That was a state tax, it is true; but the States have power to lay income taxes, and if the source is not open to inquiry, constitutional safeguards might be easily eluded.

We have unanimously held in this case that, so far as this law operates on the receipts from municipal bonds, it cannot be sustained, because it is a tax on the power of the States, and on their instrumentalities to borrow money, and consequently repugnant to the Constitution. But if, as contended, the interest when received has become merely money in the recipient's pocket, and taxable as such without reference to the source from which it came, the question is immaterial whether it could have been originally taxed at all or not. This was admitted by the Attorney General with characteristic candor; and it follows that, if the revenue derived from municipal bonds cannot be taxed because the source cannot be, the same rule applies to revenue from any other source not subject to the tax; and the lack of power to levy any but an apportioned tax on real and personal property equally exists as to the revenue therefrom.

Admitting that this act taxes the income of property irrespective of its source, still we cannot doubt that such a tax is necessarily a direct tax in the meaning of the Constitution.

In England, we do not understand that an income tax has ever been regarded as other than a direct tax. In Dowell's History of Taxation and Taxes in England, admitted to be the leading authority, the evolution of taxation in that country is given, and an income tax is invariably classified as a direct tax. 3 Dowell, (1884,) 103, 126. The author refers to the grant of a fifteenth and tenth and a graduated income tax in 1435, and to many subsequent comparatively ancient statutes as income tax laws. 1 Dowell, 121. It is objected that the taxes imposed by these acts were not, scientifically speaking, income taxes at all, and that although there was a partial income tax in 1758, there was no general income tax until Pitt's of 1799. Nevertheless, the income taxes levied by these modern acts, Pitt's, Addington's, Petty's, Peel's, and by existing laws, are all classified as direct taxes; and, so far as the income tax we are considering is concerned, that view is concurred in by the cyclopædists, the lexicographers, and the political economists, and generally by the classification of European governments wherever an income tax obtains.

In *Attorney General v. Queen Insurance Co.,* 3 App. Cas. 1090, which arose under the British North America act of 1867, (30 and 31 Vict. C 3, § 92,) which provided that the provincial legislatures could only raise revenue for provincial purposes within each province, (in addition to licenses,) by direct taxation, an act of the Quebec legislature laying a stamp duty came under consideration, and the judicial committee of the Privy Council, speaking by Jessel, M.R., held that the words "direct taxation" had "either a technical meaning, or a general, or, as it is sometimes called, a popular meaning. One or the other meaning of the words must have; and in trying to find out their meaning we must have recourse to the usual sources of information, whether regarded as technical words, words of art, or words used in popular language." And considering "their meaning either as words used in the sense of political economy, or as words used in jurisprudence of the courts of law," it was concluded that stamps were not included in the category of direct taxation, and that the imposition was not warranted.

In *Attorney General v. Reed,* 10 App. Cas. 141, 144, Lord Chancellor Selbourne said, in relation to the same act of Parliament: "The question whether it is a direct or an indirect tax cannot depend upon those special events which may vary in particular cases; but the best general rule is to look to the time of payment; and if at the time the ultimate incidence is uncertain, then, as it appears to their lordships, it cannot, in this view, be called direct taxation within the meaning of the second section of the ninety-second clause of the act in question."

In *Bank of Toronto v. Lambe,* 12 App. Cas. 575, 582, the Privy Council, discussing the same subject, in dealing with the argument much pressed at the bar, that a tax to be strictly direct must be general, said that they had no hesitation in rejecting it for legal purposes. "It would deny the character of a direct tax to the income tax of this country, which is always spoken of as such, and is generally looked upon as a direct tax of the most obvious kind; and it would run counter to the common understanding of men on this subject, which is one main clue to the meaning of the legislature."

At the time the Constitution was framed and adopted, under the systems of direct taxation of many of the States, taxes were laid on incomes from professions, business, or employments, as well as from "offices and places of profit;" but if it were the fact that there had then been no income tax law, such as this, it would not be of controlling importance. A direct tax cannot be taken out of the constitutional rule because the particular tax did not exist at the time the rule was prescribed. As Chief Justice Marshall said in the *Dartmouth College case:* "It is not enough to say, that this particular case was not in the mind of the convention, when the article was framed, nor of the American people, when it was adopted. It is necessary to go further, and to say that, had this particular case been suggested, the language would have been so varied, as to exclude it, or it would have been made a special exception. The case being within the words of the rule, must be within its operation likewise, unless there be something in the literal construction so obviously absurd, or mischievous, or repugnant to the general spirit of the instrument, as to justify those who expound the Constitution in making it an exception." 4 Wheat. 518, 644.

Being direct, and therefore to be laid by apportionment, is there any real difficulty in doing so? Cannot Congress, if the necessity exist of raising thirty, forty, or any other number of million dollars for the support of the government, in addition to the revenue from duties, imposts, and excises, apportion the quota of each State upon the basis of the census, and thus advise it of the payment which must be made, and proceed to assess that amount on all the real and personal property and the income of all persons in the State, and collect the same if the State does not in the meantime assume and pay its quota and collect the amount according to its own system and in its own way? Cannot

Congress do this, as respects either or all these subjects of taxation, and deal with each in such manner as might be deemed expedient, as indeed was done in the act of July 14, 1798, c. 75, 1 Stat. 597? Inconveniences might possibly attend the levy of an income tax, notwithstanding the listing of receipts, when adjusted, furnishes its own valuation; but that it is apportionable is hardly denied, although it is asserted that it would operate so unequally as to be undesirable.

In the disposition of the inquiry whether a general unapportioned tax on the income of real and personal property can be sustained, under the Constitution, it is apparent that the suggestion that the result of compliance with the fundamental law would lead to the abandonment of that method of taxation altogether, because of inequalities alleged to necessarily accompany its pursuit, could not be allowed to influence the conclusion; but the suggestion not unnaturally invites attention to the contention of appellants' counsel, that the want of uniformity and equality in this act is such as to invalidate it. Figures drawn from the census are given, showing that enormous assets of mutual insurance companies; of building associations; of mutual savings banks; large productive property of ecclesiastical organizations; are exempted, and it is claimed that the exemptions reach so many hundred millions that the rate of taxation would perhaps have been reduced one-half, if they had not been made. We are not dealing with the act from that point of view; but, assuming the data to be substantially reliable, if the sum desired to be raised had been apportioned, it may be doubted whether any State, which paid its quota and collected the amount by its own methods, would, or could under its constitution, have allowed a large part of the property alluded to to escape taxation. If so, a better measure of equality would have been attained than would be otherwise possible, since, according to the argument for the government, the rule of equality is not prescribed by the Constitution as to Federal taxation, and the observance of such a rule as inherent in all just taxation is purely a matter of legislative discretion.

Elaborate argument is made as to the efficacy and merits of an income tax in general, as on the one hand, equal and just, and on the other, elastic and certain; not that it is not open to abuse by such deductions and exemptions as might make taxation under it so wanting in uniformity and equality as in substance to amount to deprivation of property without due process of law; not that it is not open to fraud and evasion and is inquisitorial in its methods; but because it is preëminently a tax upon the rich, and enables the burden of taxes on consumption and of duties on imports to be sensibly diminished. And it is said that the United States as "the representative of an indivisible nationality, as a political sovereign equal in authority to any other on the face of the globe, adequate to all emergencies, foreign or domestic, and having at its command for offence and defence and for all governmental purposes all the resources of the nation," would be "but a maimed and crippled creation after all," unless it possesses the power to lay a tax on the income of real and personal property throughout the United States without apportionment.

The power to tax real and personal property and the income from both, there being an apportionment, is conceded; that such a tax is a direct tax in the meaning of the Constitution has not been, and, in our judgment, cannot be successfully denied: and yet we are thus invited to hesitate in the enforcement of the mandate of the Constitution, which prohibits Congress from laying a direct tax on the revenue from property of the citizen without regard to state lines, and in such manner that the States cannot intervene by payment in regulation of their own resources, lest a government of delegated powers should be found to be, not less powerful, but less absolute, than the imagination of the advocate had supposed.

We are not here concerned with the question whether an income tax be or be not desirable, nor whether such a tax would enable the government to diminish taxes on consumption and duties on imports, and to enter upon what may be believed to be a reform of its fiscal and commercial system. Questions of that character belong to the controversies of political parties, and cannot be settled by judicial decision. In these cases our province is to determine whether this income tax on the revenue from property does or does not belong to the class of direct taxes. If it does, it is, being unapportioned, in violation of the Constitution, and we must so declare.

Differences have often occurred in this court—differences exist now—but there has never been a time in its history when there has been a difference of opinion as to its duty to announce its deliberate conclusions unaffected by considerations not pertaining to the case in hand.

If it be true that the Constitution should have been so framed that a tax of this kind could be laid, the instrument defines the way for its amendment. In no part of it was greater sagacity displayed. Except that no State, without its consent, can be deprived of its equal suffrage in the Senate, the Constitution may be amended upon the concurrence of two-thirds of both houses, and the ratification of the legislatures or conventions of the several States, or through a Federal convention when applied for by the legislatures of two-thirds of the States, and upon like ratification. The ultimate sovereignty may be thus called into play by a slow and deliberate process, which gives time for mere hypothesis and opinion to exhaust themselves, and for the sober second thought of every part of the country to be asserted.

We have considered the act only in respect of the tax on income derived from real estate, and from invested personal property, and have not commented on so much of it as bears on gains or profits from business, privileges, or employments, in view of the instances in which taxation on business, privileges, or employments has assumed the guise of an excise tax and been sustained as such.

Being of opinion that so much of the sections of this law as lays a tax on income from real and personal property is invalid, we are brought to the question of the effect of that conclusion upon these sections as a whole.

It is elementary that the same statute may be in part constitutional and in part unconstitutional, and if the parts are wholly independent of each other, that which is constitutional may stand while that which is unconstitutional will be rejected. And in the case before us there is no question as to the validity of this act, except sections twenty-seven to thirty-seven, inclusive, which relate to the subject which has been under discussion; and as to them we think the rule laid down by Chief Justice Shaw in *Warren v. Charlestown,* 2 Gray, 84, is applicable, that if the different parts "are so mutually connected with and dependent on each other, as conditions, considerations or compensations for each other, as to warrant a belief that the legislature intended them as a whole, and that, if all could not be carried into effect, the legislature would not pass the residue independently, and some parts are unconstitutional, all the provisions which are thus dependent, conditional or connected, must fall with them." Or, as the point is put by Mr. Justice Matthews in *Poindexter v. Greenhow,* 114 U.S. 270, 304: "It is undoubtedly true that there may be cases where one part of a statute may be enforced as constitutional, and another be declared inoperative and void, because unconstitutional; but these are cases where the parts are so distinctly separable that each can stand alone, and where the court is able to see, and to declare, that the intention of the legislature was that the part pronounced valid should be enforceable, even though the other part should fail. To hold otherwise would be to substitute, for the law intended by the legislature, one they may never have been willing by itself to enact." And again, as stated by the same eminent judge in *Sprague v. Thompson,* 118 U.S. 90, 95, where it was urged that certain illegal exceptions in a section of a statute might be disregarded, but that the rest could stand: "The insuperable difficulty with the application of that principle of construction to the present instance is, that by rejecting the exceptions intended by the legislature of Georgia the statute is made to enact what confessedly the legislature never meant. It confers upon the statute a positive operation beyond the legislative intent, and beyond what any one can say it would have enacted in view of the illegality of the exceptions."

According to the census, the true valuation of real and personal property in the United States in 1890 was $65,037,091,197, of which real estate with improvements thereon made up $39,544,544,333. Of course, from the latter must be deducted, in applying these sections, all unproductive property and all property whose net yield does not exceed four thousand dollars; but, even with such deductions, it is evident that the income from realty formed a vital part of the scheme for taxation embodied therein. If that be stricken out, and also the income from all invested personal property, bonds, stocks, investments of all kinds, it is obvious that by far the largest part of the anticipated revenue would be eliminated, and this would leave the burden of the tax to be borne by professions, trades, employments, or vocations; and in that way what was intended as a tax on capital would remain in substance a tax on occupations and labor. We cannot believe that such was the intention of Congress. We do not mean to say that an act laying by apportionment a direct tax on all real estate and personal property, or the income thereof, might not also lay excise taxes on business, privileges, employments, and vocations. But this is not such an act; and the scheme must be considered as a whole. Being invalid as to the greater part, and falling, as the tax would, if any part were held valid, in a direction which could not have been contemplated except in connection with the taxation considered as an entirety, we are constrained to conclude that sections twenty-seven to thirty-seven, inclusive, of the act, which became a law without the signature of the President on August 28, 1894, are wholly inoperative and void.

Our conclusions may, therefore, be summed up as follows:

First. We adhere to the opinion already announced, that, taxes on real estate being indisputably direct taxes, taxes on the rents or income of real estate are equally direct taxes.

Second. We are of opinion that taxes on personal property, or on the income of personal property, are likewise direct taxes.

Third. The tax imposed by sections twenty-seven to thirty-seven, inclusive, of the act of 1894, so far as it falls on the income of real estate and of personal property, being a direct tax within the meaning of the Constitution, and, therefore, unconstitutional and void because not apportioned according to representation, all those sections, constituting one entire scheme of taxation, are necessarily invalid.

The decrees hereinbefore entered in this court will be vacated; the decrees below will be reversed, and the cases remanded, with instructions to grant the relief prayed.

[Dissenting opinions omitted.]

APPENDIX C

Internal Revenue Form 365

Taxpayer's Return for Assessment of Income Tax for 1894

Form No. 365.—United States Internal Revenue.

TAXPAYER'S RETURN

FOR

ASSESSMENT OF INCOME TAX

FOR 1894.

To..

Of............ ....

In the............*Division*, ...*District*,

State of..........................

NOTICE.

Pursuant to an Act of Congress, in force August 28, 1894, you are required to make out a return according to the forms within, and deliver the same to me, at my office, on or before the first Monday in March, 1895; otherwise, I shall make such return and add fifty per centum to the amount of the tax.

The gross income from any particular source should be given first, and the amount should be entered in the return, in gross, opposite the name of the object or article included in the return.

The exemption and the deductions should be given next, in order named, and the several amounts should be entered opposite the item or items of deduction appearing in the return to which they refer.

In case the income about to be assessed for said year did not exceed $4,000, or in case you have paid the tax on the income for said year elsewhere in the United States, you will be permitted to so declare, under oath or affirmation, in the manner and form prescribed by affidavits Nos. 1 and 2 on this page.

Dated this ....day of........... ..., 189

....

................*Collector*.

Office at..............................

(Form No. 365.)

UNITED STATES INTERNAL REVENUE.

RETURN of Gains, Profits, and Income received by citizens of the United States, whether residing at home or abroad, and by other persons residing therein, having an income of more than three thousand five hundred dollars for the year 1894; and by persons residing without the United States owning property therein, or engaged in any business, trade, or profession carried on in the United States during said year; and by guardians and trustees, executors, administrators, agents, receivers, and all persons or corporations acting in any fiduciary capacity.—Sections 27, 29, and 31, Act of August 28, 1894.

Return to be made to the collector or a deputy collector of the district on or before the first Monday of March, 1895, and the tax to be paid to the collector or deputy on or before the first day of July, 1895.—Sections 29, 30, and 34, Act of August 28, 1894.

Annual Return of Gains, Profits, and Income received by or accrued to ...., of ...., in the County of .... and .... District of the State of ...., from the first day of January, 1894, to the thirty-first day of December, 1894, both days inclusive, pursuant to the provisions of the Internal Revenues Law:

		dollars.	cts
1	Gross receipts, credits, earnings, and gains from any business, or any interest therein, wherever carried on..........		
2	From rents received or accrued during the year..........		
3	From profits realized on sales of real estate purchased since December 31, 1892..........		
4	From farming operations: Proceeds from sales of live stock..........		
	" " " Proceeds from sales of agricultural products..........		
5	Money, and the value of all personal property acquired by gift or inheritance..........		
6	Premium on bonds, stocks, notes, or coupons..........		
7	Income from profession, trade, or other employment, except stated salary or pay..........		
8	From salary, or compensation received for services, and not including salary, or compensation received from the United States		
9	From salary, or compensation received for services in the civil, military, naval, or other service of the United States, including salary of Senator, Representative, or Delegate in Congress..........		
10	From gains and profits, divided or undivided, of any partnership..........		
*11	From interest received or accrued within the year upon all notes, bonds, mortgages, or other forms of indebtedness bearing interest, whether paid or not, if good and collectible..........		
12	From interest or coupons paid or accrued on any bonds, or other evidences of indebtedness, of any corporation, company, or association..........		
13	From dividends or interest paid or accrued on the stock, capital, or deposits of any corporation, company, or association..........		
14	Income of wife or minor children computed on the same basis as this return..........		
15	From all sources not above enumerated, viz.:		
	TOTAL GAINS, PROFITS, AND INCOME..........		

DEDUCTIONS.

		dollars.	cts	dollars.	cts
1	Exempt by law..........	4,000	00		
2	Interest which has become due or which has been paid during the year..........				
3	National, State, county, school, or municipal taxes paid within the year, not including taxes assessed against local benefits..........				
4	Amount expended in the purchase or production of live stock, or produce sold within the year..........				
5	Necessary expenses actually incurred in carrying on any business, occupation, or profession, and not elsewhere deducted in this return..........				
6	Losses actually sustained during the year, incurred in trade or arising from fires, storms, or shipwreck, and not compensated for by insurance or otherwise, and not already deducted in ascertaining profits..........				
7	Actual losses on sales of real estate purchased since December 31, 1892..........				
8	Debts ascertained within the year to be worthless, and not elsewhere deducted in this return..........				
9	Cost price of material purchased for manufacture or resale, not increasing stock on hand December 31, 1893..........				
10	Dividends, heretofore included in the statement of profits, under paragraph 13, received from corporations, companies, or associations, on which the tax of two per centum has once been paid by such corporation..........				
	TOTAL DEDUCTIONS..........				
	Taxable income for the year 1894..........				
	Amount of tax at 2 per cent..........				

* See Instructions Nos. 11 and 16.

FORM No. 365.—UNITED STATES INTERNAL REVENUE—*Continued.*

The person making the foregoing return is required to answer the following questions, namely:

Question 1. Had your wife, or any minor child or children of yours, any income last year?

Answer 1. ....

Question 2. Have you included such income or incomes in this return?

Answer 2. ....

Question 3. Have you kept books of account?

Answer 3. ....

Question 4. Is your income herein estimated, or taken from your books?

Answer 4. ....

Question 5. What are the particular items of "Losses" set forth by you opposite paragraph 6 of "Deductions," and when did each occur?

Answer 5. ....

....

....

Question 6. Are you a citizen of the United States, and what is your occupation?

Answer 6. ....

Question 7.* How did you determine that debts returned by you as "worthless" could not be collected?

Answer 7. ....

Question 8. What were the "necessary expenses," and the amount of each class, included in the amount set opposite paragraph 5 of "Deductions"?

Answer 8. ....

....

State of ____________ }
County of ____________ } *ss:*

____________, being duly sworn, on his oath, (or affirmation), deposes and says that the foregoing return contains a full, true, particular, and correct account of all gains, profits, or income received by or accrued to ____________ from the first day of January, 1894, to the thirty-first day of December, 1894, both days inclusive, and that said return contains a true account of all his income from every source, whether derived from any kind of property, rents, interest, dividends, undivided profits, wages, or salary, or from any trade, profession, employment, or vocation, or from any other source whatever, during said year; and that he has not received from any or all sources of income together, any other sum for the said year besides what is herein set forth in detail; and that each item stated under the head of Deductions is correct, and he is honestly and truly entitled to make all the deductions from his income for said year as specifically stated in detail, and that the written answers to the above questions are true.

Sworn to and subscribed before me this ________ *day of* ________, *1895.*

____

____

____

____

* See Instruction No. 17.

APPENDIX D

Internal Revenue Form 366

Annual Return of Net Profits or Income of a Corporation

(Form No. 366.)

INCOME TAX, 1894.

ANNUAL RETURN

OF

NET PROFITS OR INCOME

OF A CORPORATION,

FOR ASSESSMENT OF TAXES FOR 1894,

By..

of..

President, or (..............................) *of*

....

of..

in the..........................*District, State*

of..

To................. ....

NOTICE.

Pursuant to an Act of Congress of the United States, in effect August 28, 1894, you are required to make out a return for the corporation or association of which you are an officer or agent, according to the forms within, and deliver the same to me, at my office, on or before the first Monday of March, 1895.

Dated this..............*day of*............,

1895, *at my office at*..........................

....

................*Collector.*

(Form No. 366.)

UNITED STATES INTERNAL REVENUE.

Return by Banks, Banking Institutions, Trust Companies, Savings Institutions, Fire, Marine, Life, or other Insurance Companies, Railroad, Canal, Turnpike, Canal Navigation, Slack Water, Telephone, Telegraph, Express, Electric Light, Gas, Water, Street Railway Companies, and all other Corporations, Companies, or Associations doing business for profit in the United States.—Sections 32, 34, and 35, Act of August 28, 1894.

Return to be made to the Collector of the district where the principal office or place of business is located, on or before the first Monday of March, 1895, and the tax to be paid to the Collector on or before the first day of July, 1895.

The .... of .... in the County of ...., and .... District of the State of ...., makes and renders the following return of all gains, profits, or income received by or accrued to said .... from the first day of January, 1894, to the thirty-first day of December, 1894, both days inclusive, pursuant to the provisions of the Internal Revenue Laws:

		$ cts.
1	Gross receipts, credits, earnings, and gains from any business, or any interest therein, wherever carried on..............	....
2	From interest or coupons, due or paid on any bonds, or other evidences of indebtedness of any corporation, company, or association..............	....
3	From dividends or interest on the stock, capital, or deposits of any corporation, company, or association..............	....
4	From undivided profits of any corporation, company, or association..............	....
5	From premium on bonds, stocks, notes, or coupons..............	....
6	From commissions, or percentage..............	....
*7	From interest on notes, bonds, or other securities of the United States, except such bonds of the United States the principal and interest of which are exempt from Federal taxation..............	....
8	From interest received or accrued on all notes, bonds, mortgages, or other forms of indebtedness not included in the foregoing items..............	....
9	From profits realized within the year from sales of real estate purchased since December 31, 1892..............	....
10	From rents received or accrued..............	....
11	From all sources not above enumerated (specifying same), viz.:	
	....	....
	....	....
	....	....
	....	....
	TOTAL RECEIPTS, GAINS, AND INCOME..............	....

		$ cts.	
12	OPERATING AND BUSINESS EXPENSES:		
	1. Interest paid or accrued within the year on bonded or other indebtedness..............	....	
	2. Losses actually sustained during the year..............	....	
	3. State, county, municipal, or town taxes accrued during the year 1894 and actually paid..............	....	
	4. Salaries, compensation, or pay of officers or other persons employed during the year..............	....	
	5. Rents, or necessary repairs, but not including amount used for construction or enlargement of plant..............	....	
	6. Actual losses on sales of real estate purchased since December 31, 1892..............	....	
	7. Cost price of material purchased for manufacture or resale, not increasing stock on hand Dec. 31, 1893..............	....	
	8. Other expenses not above enumerated, viz.:	....	
	....	....	
	....	....	
	TOTAL OPERATING AND BUSINESS EXPENSES..............	....	
13	Net profits or income over operating and business expenses..............		....
14	Dividends and gains heretofore included in the statement of profits under paragraphs 3 and 4, received from corporations, companies, or associations, on which the tax of two per centum has once been paid by such corporation, etc..............		....
	AMOUNT OF NET PROFITS OR INCOME LIABLE TO TAX..............		....
	TAX AT TWO PER CENTUM..............		....
15	Amount paid in salaries, or other compensation, or pay of officers or other persons employed, not including salaries of more than four thousand dollars..............		....
16	Amount paid in salaries, or other compensation, or pay of officers or other persons employed, including only salaries of more than four thousand dollars..............		....
	TOTAL SALARIES, ETC., PAID..............		....

NOTE.—The interest on all bonds of the United States should be returned as income by the person, corporation, company, or association owning or holding such bonds, except the interest on bonds of the funded loan of 1891 continued at two per cent., and the four per cent. funded loan of 1907, and the five per cent. loans of 1904, which is exempt.

FORM NO. 366.—UNITED STATES INTERNAL REVENUE—*Continued.*

*17 Name and address of each person to whom a salary of more than four thousand dollars was paid, and the amount paid, to such person:

NAME OF PERSON.	POST-OFFICE ADDRESS.	$ cts.
....	....	....
....	....	....
....	....	....
....	....	....
....	....	....
....	....	....
....	....	....
TOTAL..........		....

Statement of all Interest, Annuities, and Dividends declared due, or paid to shareholders, stockholders, policy holders, or Depositors by the..........from the first day of January, 1894, to the thirty-first day of December, 1894, both days inclusive, and of all undivided profits of said.......... on hand or added to any fund, and amount of net annual profits, or income, of said.......... used for construction, enlargement of plant, or any other expenditure or investment, paid from the net annual profits of said..........for said year, pursuant to the provisions of the Internal Revenue Laws.

		$ cts.
1	Dividends declared or paid on stock, capital, or deposits, etc..........	....
2	Annuities declared or paid on bonds, stock, capital, or policies..........	....
3	Interest paid on shares, stocks, capital, or deposits..........	....
	TOTAL INTEREST, ANNUITIES, AND DIVIDENDS..........	....
4	Undivided profits, over dividends declared or paid, on hand or carried to the account of surplus or other fund..........	....
5	Amount of net profits or income used for construction..........	....
6	Amount of net profits or income used for enlargement, betterment, or permanent improvement of plant..........	....
7	Amount of net profits or income used for other expenditures, or investment..........	....
	TOTAL NET PROFITS..........	....

Question 1. Has the corporation, company, or association for which this return is made, kept full, regular, and accurate books of accounts, upon which all its transactions were entered from day to day for the full period covered by this return? **Answer**..........

Question 2. Is this return made exclusively from said books? **Answer**..........

Question 3. Have the full amounts set forth in this return as salaries of officers and pay to employés been actually paid within the year covered by this return to bona fide officers and employés of this corporation, company, or association for services actually rendered? **Answer**..........

Question 4. What are the particular items of losses included in the amount set opposite paragraph 2, under "Operating and Business Expenses" on page 2 of this return, and when did each occur?

Answer..........

....

....

....

STATE OF.........., COUNTY OF.........., ss:

I, ..., of the..........

do swear (or affirm), that the foregoing return contains a true, full, regular, and accurate account of all the gains, profits, and income received by or accrued to said.........., from the first day of January, 1894, to the thirty-first day of December, 1894, both days inclusive, and a true and complete statement of the net profits or income of said..........for said year, and the true amount and kind of operating and business expenses thereof; and all dividends, interest, or annuities declared due or paid by said..........; and of all undivided profits thereof; and the amount of net profits or income used for construction, enlargement of plant, or investment, as therein specified; and that the above questions have been fully and truthfully answered.

Sworn to and subscribed before me this..........

day of.........., 1885.

....

....

....

†..........

* In case there is not sufficient space to contain the names of persons under paragraph 17, a supplementary list should be made and securely attached to the return and made a part thereof, under said paragraph, and marked "Exhibit A to paragraph 17."

† "President," "Cashier," "Secretary," as the case may be, of resident corporations, etc. "Resident Manager," or "Resident Agent," as the case may be, of foreign corporations, etc.

In computing income for taxation non-resident corporations shall include in their annual returns the entire profits or income of such corporations derived from all business conducted in the United States, deducting the operating and business expenses incurred in conducting such business.

Notes

Prologue: History and the Income Tax

1. Richard Theodore Ely (Apr. 13, 1854–Oct. 4, 1943), associate professor of political economy, Johns Hopkins University; director, School of Economics, University of Wisconsin; author, *Political Economy* (1883). See *Dictionary of American Biography,* s.v. "Ely, Richard Theodore." Arthur Latham Perry (Feb. 27, 1830–July 9, 1905), professor of political economy and history, Williams College; author, *Principles of Political Economy* (1891). See ibid., s.v. "Perry, Arthur Latham." Francis Amasa Walker (July 2, 1840–Jan. 5, 1897), professor of political economy and history, Sheffield Scientific School, Yale University; president, Massachusetts Institute of Technology; author, *Political Economy* (1883). See ibid., s.v. "Walker, Francis Amasa." William Graham Sumner (Oct. 30, 1840–Apr. 12, 1910), professor of political and social science, Yale University; author, *Science of Society* (1927). See ibid., s.v. "Sumner, William Graham."

2. See Edwin R. A. Seligman, *Double Taxation and International Fiscal Cooperation;* Michael J. Graetz, "The 'Original Intent' of U.S. International Taxation"; and Henry Simons, *Personal Income Taxation.* Seligman, for example, shifted his attention from income tax history to the taxability of dividends, gains, and municipal bonds. See his *Studies in Public Finance,* with particular reference to chaps. 5 and 7.

3. Cf., for example, *Cong. Rec.,* 53d Cong., 2d sess., 1894, 26, pt. 2:1605 (statement of Williams), 1656 (statement of Bryan), and pt. 9:185 (statement of Tarsney) with *Cong. Rec.,* 63d Cong., 1st sess., 1913, 50, pt. 2:1250 (statement of Fowler), pt. 4:3807 (statement of Borah), and 3812 (statement of Works).

4. Representative Cordell Hull, principal author of the 1913 legislation, was a protégé of Representative Benton McMillin, principal author of the 1894 legislation. In structuring the 1913 tax, Hull used as his prototype the Income Tax of 1894. See Hull, *The Memoirs of Cordell Hull,* 48; and U.S. Senate, *Opinion of the Honorable John K. Shields, Senator from Tennessee, Furnished to the Finance Committee at the Request of the Chairman of That Committee,* 63d Cong., 1st sess., 1913, S. Doc. 63–171, 14.

5. Within this tradition are Roy G. Blakey and Gladys C. Blakey, *The Federal Income Tax;* Sidney Ratner, *Taxation and Democracy in America;* and T. S. Adams, "Ideals and Idealism in Taxation."

6. See, for example, Ratner, *Taxation and Democracy,* 13–17; and Adams, "Ideals and Idealism."

7. See Ratner, *Taxation and Democracy,* 13–17, 180–81.

8. A passage from Ratner is illustrative: "A struggle developed against the dominance of the industrialists, merchants, and financiers of the farmer and worker. Attacks were made on corporate privilege and on the inequalities of the taxation system" (ibid., 164).

9. Ibid., 16.

10. See ibid., 15.

11. Ibid.

12. See ibid., 16, 145; Blakey and Blakey, *The Federal Income Tax,* 1, 8–12; and Adams, "Ideals and Idealism."

13. Adams, "Ideals and Idealism."

14. See Ratner, *Taxation and Democracy,* 13–16.

15. Ibid., 13–14.

16. See ibid.; and Blakey and Blakey, *The Federal Income Tax,* 1.

17. See Ratner, *Taxation and Democracy,* 145–46.

18. See Blakey and Blakey, *The Federal Income Tax,* 8–12.

19. Ibid., 1.

20. John Witte, *The Politics and Development of the Federal Income Tax,* 8–9, 16.

21. Ibid., 285.

22. See ibid., 87.

23. Ibid., 71.

24. See ibid., 21, 226, 324, 365, 372–73, 376, 378.

25. Ibid., 376.

26. See ibid., 78.

27. Ibid.

28. See ibid., 20, 23–24, 245, 248, 275, 283, 285, 290, 297, 310, 369.

29. Ibid., 369–70.

30. Ibid., 375.

31. See ibid., 20, 30, 244–46, 365–66, 374, 376.

32. Ibid., 247.

33. See ibid., 78–79, 87, 244–45.

34. Ibid., 78–79.

35. See ibid., 108, 366.

36. See Robert Stanley, *Dimensions of Law in the Service of Order,* 6–7, 134, 233, 325.

37. See ibid., 12–13, 134.

38. See ibid., 10, 13, 244, 247.

39. Ibid., 244.

40. See ibid., 10–13, 20, 239–41, 244, 261.

41. See ibid., 13–14, 134–45, 244–45, 256–57.

42. Ibid., 244.

43. Ibid., 135.

44. See ibid., 11–12, 134, 240, 245–46.

45. See ibid., 13–14, 134, 239, 241, 243–45.

46. Ibid., 14.

47. See ibid., 11, 236, 244–45, 257.

48. See ibid., 7, 134.

49. Ibid., 11.

50. See ibid., 13–14, 241.

51. See W. Elliot Brownlee, *Federal Taxation in America: A Short History,* 176; and "Reflections on the History of Taxation," in *Funding the Modern American State, 1941–95,* ed. Brownlee, 8.

52. See Brownlee, "Reflections," in *Modern American State,* 19, 27–28.

53. See Brownlee, *Federal Taxation,* 35; and "Reflections," in *Modern American State,* 18, 36.

54. Brownlee, *Federal Taxation,* 173; "Reflections," in *Modern American State,* 7.

55. See Brownlee, *Federal Taxation,* 40; and "Tax Regimes, National Crisis, and State-Building in America," in *Modern American State,* 55.

56. Brownlee, *Federal Taxation,* 35–36.

57. See Brownlee, "Reflections," in *Modern American State,* 22; *Federal Taxation,* 5; and "Tax Regimes," in *Modern American State,* 38.

58. See Brownlee, *Federal Taxation,* 6–7, 34; "Reflections," in *Modern American State,* 25; and "Tax Regimes," in ibid., 39, 68.

59. Brownlee, *Federal Taxation,* 4–5; "Tax Regimes," in *Modern American State,* 37–38.

60. Brownlee, *Federal Taxation,* 7; "Tax Regimes," in *Modern American State,* 40.

61. See Brownlee, *Federal Taxation,* 5–8; and "Tax Regimes," in *Modern American State,* 39, 40.

62. Brownlee, *Federal Taxation,* 174; "Reflections," in *Modern American State,* 8.

63. See Brownlee, "Reflections," in *Modern American State,* 53; *Federal Taxation,* 5, 7; and "Tax Regimes," in *Modern American State,* 40.

64. Brownlee, *Federal Taxation,* 7–8, 114; "Tax Regimes," in *Modern American State,* 40.

65. See Brownlee, *Federal Taxation,* 3–6, 75, 174–75; "Tax Regimes," in *Modern American State,* 8, 37; and "Reflections," in ibid., 8, 29–30, 35.

66. Brownlee, "Reflections," in *Modern American State,* 20.

67. See Brownlee, *Federal Taxation,* 38, 175; "Tax Regimes," in *Modern American State,* 53–54; and "Reflections," in ibid., 8.

68. For an explanation of this method, see Edward A. Shils and Henry A. Finch, trans. and eds., *Max Weber: The Methodology of the Social Sciences.*

1. A Nation in Transition

1. For an account of social and economic developments leading to enactment of the income tax, see Ratner, *Taxation and Democracy;* and Edwin R. A. Seligman, *The Income Tax: A Study of the History, Theory, and Practice of Income Taxation at Home and Abroad,* 494–95. For a more general overview of social and economic developments in the latter part of the nineteenth century, see W. Elliot Brownlee, *Dynamics of Ascent: A History of the American Economy;* Harold Underwood Faulkner, *American Economic History;* Louis M. Hacker, *The Course of American Economic Growth and Development;* and Robert L. Heilbroner and Aaron Singer, *The Economic Transformation of America: 1600 to the Present.*

2. "There have arisen conditions out of our civil war that have made great changes in the condition of individuals. Probably the most important tendency since the war is the concentration of men and women in cities at the expense of the country. The cities have grown enormously, the most remarkable growth being that of Chicago" (*Cong. Rec.,* 53d Cong., 2d sess., 1894, 26, pt. 7:6695 [statement of Sherman]). See also Hacker, *Course of Growth,* 239–42.

3. Hacker, *Course of Growth,* 217, 224.

4. See *Cong. Rec.,* 53d Cong., 2d sess., 1894, 26, pt. 9:272 (statement of Richardson).

5. See Faulkner, *American Economic History,* 379. During the period 1884–94, annual interest rates on loans to residents of the South and West, excluding bank commissions and other incidental charges, averaged 8 percent per annum (*Cong. Rec.,* 53d Cong., 2d sess., 1894, 26, pt. 7:6634 [statement of Peffer]).

6. See Hacker, *Course of Growth,* 321. According to one source, so extensive was this activity that by 1894, more than 50 percent of U.S. farms had been mortgaged for more than 60 percent of their value (*Cong. Rec.,* 53d Cong., 2d sess., 1894, 26, pt. 2:1667 [statement of Maddox]).

7. *Cong. Rec.,* 53d Cong., 2d sess., 1894, 26, pt. 9:272 (statement of Richardson).

8. See Heilbroner and Singer, *Economic Transformation,* 189–91; Mansel G. Blackford and K. Austin Kerr, *Business Enterprise in American History;* Glenn Porter, *The Rise of Big Business, 1860–1920;* David O. Whitten, *The Emergence of Giant Enterprise, 1860–1914;* and George Heberton Evans Jr., *Business Incorporations in the United States.*

9. See Brownlee, *Dynamics of Ascent,* 300–301. Remarked Missouri senator George Vest on June 27, 1894: "Why are corporations created? Why have they increased so marvelously in this country with the increase of wealth? It is because corporate powers and privileges are peculiarly favored by capital. Corporations to-day are thicker almost, I was about to say, than individual investors. The vast body of the wealth of the country is in their hands, and it is because of the peculiar privileges given them by the terms of their creation which are favored as I have said especially by capitalists" (*Cong. Rec.,* 53d Cong., 2d sess., 1894, 26, pt. 7:6867).

10. *Cong. Rec.,* 53d Cong., 2d sess., 1894, 26, pt. 7:6867(statement of Hoar).

11. On the proliferation of financial instruments and the growth of capital markets, see Brownlee, *Dynamics of Ascent,* 293–97; and Hacker, *Course of Growth,* 236.

12. Remarked Michigan representative George Richardson on Jan. 29, 1894: "Almost all of the factories were operated by corporations, and frequently the principal directors of these concerns were also officers of banks which carried a heavy line of discounts for these factories and other corporations" (*Cong. Rec.,* 53d Cong., 2d sess., 1894, 26, pt. 9:272).

13. Ibid., pt. 7:6866.

14. On labor and the labor movement, see Brownlee, *Dynamics of Ascent,* 319–38; Faulkner, *American Economic History,* 449–51; Hacker, *Course of Growth,* 188–89; and Heilbroner and Singer, *Economic Transformation,* 219–46.

15. The data shown in table 7 were reported by the *New York Sun* on Sept. 10, 1893.

16. See Faulkner, *American Economic History,* 371, 378.

17. *Cong. Rec.,* 53d Cong., 2d sess., 1894, 26, pt. 7:6686 (statement of Kyle).

18. "The last thirty years marks a very important period in our history, in fact the most important one that we as a nation have ever known. . . . There have been greater changes in the condition of our people during that time than ever before in our history. Thousands have become

Table 7
Crop Value per Acre Based on Average Yields at 1893 Prices

Staple	1866–1870	1871–1875	1876–1880	1881–1885	1886–1890	1893
Corn	$12.84	$11.30	$9.62	$10.25	$8.81	$8.35
Wheat	13.16	11.90	12.00	10.20	9.07	6.00
Oats	10.92	9.81	8.58	9.17	7.50	5.75
Hay	13.28	14.38	11.57	11.15	10.19	10.00
Cotton	28.01	28.55	17.65	15.63	13.84	10.65
Total	$78.21	$75.94	$59.42	$56.40	$49.44	$40.75
Average	15.64	15.19	11.88	11.28	9.89	8.15

Source: Cong. Rec., 53d Cong., 1st sess., 1893, 25, pt. 3:690 (app.) (quoted in statement of Jones).
Note: Data for the years 1866–1890 are historical. Data for 1893 are then-current estimates.
See also Brownlee, *Dynamics of Ascent,* 339–40; Faulkner, *American Economic History,* 369–71; and Blakey and Blakey, *The Federal Income Tax,* 9.

millionaires. Millions have become paupers. Our advancement in each respect is perhaps without parallel in the world's history" (ibid., pt. 9:506 [statement of Baker]).

19. See Brownlee, *Dynamics of Ascent,* 286–87.

20. Thomas Gaskell Shearman, 1834–1900. A disciple of Henry George, Shearman wrote *Natural Taxation* (1895) in support of George's theories. In 1873, he and John W. Sterling established a law firm that specialized in corporate reorganizations. See *Dictionary of American Biography,* s.v. "Shearman, Thomas Gaskell." Shearman reported his statistical extrapolations in "The Owners of the United States." These extrapolations were cited in a letter dated Jan. 25, 1894, from People's Party chairman H. E. Taubeneck to Colorado representative Lafe Pence. See *Cong. Rec.,* 53d Cong., 2d sess., 1894, 26, pt. 9:606 (statement of Pence).

21. Shearman, "Owners," 271. Shearman also extrapolated figures on U.S. wealth distribution from British income statistics. See also 268.

22. George Kirby Holmes, 1856–1927. A native of Massachusetts and a member of its bar, Holmes had served as special agent in charge of the Division of Farms, Homes, and Mortgages, U.S. Census of 1890. See *Who Was Who in America,* s.v. "Holmes, George Kirby." Holmes reported his findings in "The Concentration of Wealth." These findings were cited in a letter dated Jan. 25, 1894, from People's Party chairman H. E. Taubeneck to Colorado representative Lafe Pence. See *Cong. Rec.,* 53d Cong., 2d sess., 1894, 26, pt. 9:606 (statement of Pence). On Holmes's study, see also Ratner, *Taxation and Democracy,* 189–90.

23. Holmes, "The Concentration of Wealth," 593; also quoted in *Cong. Rec.,* 53d Cong., 2d sess., 1894, 26, pt. 7:6687 (statement of Kyle). See also Lee Soltow, "Evidence on Income Inequality in the United States, 1866–1965."

24. Quoted in *Cong. Rec.,* 53d Cong., 2d sess., 1894, 26, pt. 7:6686 (statement of Kyle).

25. "The question to-day is, who owns this enormous increase of wealth which we as a nation have accumulated within the last thirty years?" wrote Populist Party chairman H. E. Taubeneck to Congressman Lafe Pence on Jan. 25, 1894. "Does it belong to the farmer? No. Because

the price of his products for years has been below the cost of production, and we have more tenant farmers and mortgaged farms in the United States to-day than we had at any other period in the history of our country. Do the laborers, the men who dig in mines and toil in workshops, own this wealth? No. Because their wages, in spite of a high-protective tariff, have been coming down every year, until to-day strikes, lockouts, and boycotts have become to be part of the regular order between the employed and employer. It is a sad fact that those who have created and dug this wealth out of the earth own but a trifle of it" (ibid., pt. 9:606 [speech of Pence]).

26. For example, Nebraska representative Omer Kem referred to Shearman as an "authority" on economics and statistics (ibid., 297).

27. See Hacker, *Course of Growth,* 180; and Lawrence M. Friedman, *A History of American Law,* 497. Some states, however, had already instituted an income tax. See Seligman, *Income Tax,* 399–406.

28. See Brownlee, *Dynamics of Ascent,* 354–58; Ratner, *Taxation and Democracy,* 159–60; and Frank W. Taussig, *The Tariff History of the United States,* esp. chap. 5.

29. See Faulkner, *American Economic History,* 550; and *Cong. Rec.,* 53d Cong., 2d sess., 1894, 26, pt. 5:4064 (statement of Aldrich) and pt. 8:7809 (statement of Gorman).

30. On Sept. 10, 1893, the *New York Sun* explained why: "For more than fifteen years—1878 to 1893—all the great primary agricultural staples have been declining in price, although there have been periods when the price of some was high for a limited time. . . . In the meantime, there has been no material reduction in the cost of production, the self-binder, the gang plow, mower, hay tedder, and hay loder, and all other great improvements in agricultural machinery having come into use prior to 1878. Subsequent modifications and improvements have been in the direction of greater facility in operation rather than of lessened cost. . . . *While the cost of production can not have been lessened as much as 5 per cent since 1875,* prices for the staple products of the farm averaged 82 per cent greater during the five years ending with 1875 than now" *(Cong. Rec.,* 53d Cong., 1st sess., 1893, 25, pt. 3:689 [app.] [quoted in statement of Jones]). See also Blakey and Blakey, *The Federal Income Tax,* 9; Faulkner, *American Economic History,* 366–67; and Hacker, *Course of Growth,* 266.

31. Remarked Illinois representative James R. Williams on Jan. 30, 1894: "For more than thirty years the farmers of my district have been paying high tribute to the Eastern manufacturers in order to build up a home market for their products, and to-day in that home market, which has cost them so much, they can sell their wheat for but 50 cents a bushel, and many other products in the same proportion" *(Cong. Rec.,* 53d Cong., 2d sess., 1894, 26, pt. 9:212). Added Representative Richardson on Jan. 30, 1894: "[F]arm products have fallen in value and will continue to fall, out of proportion considering the labor required in their production, to the fall in prices of articles and commodities produced in other industries, which are kept up by legislation and by organized combinations. . . . The policy of restricting trade has been ruinous to the interests of agriculture. The home market has been made, but not for the farmers. The products of the factories, with less than half the labor, producing nearly three times the value, has had a home market for nearly all its products at prices which yielded a net income averaging in 1860, 64 per cent; in 1870, 62 per cent; in 1880, 50 per cent; and in 1890, 24 per cent" (ibid., 271).

32. See ibid., 287, 290 (speech of Coffeen). A similar condition seems to have existed in

1913: "No one can deny that excessively high tariffs have helped to enable great corporations to put wages down and prices up, and thus reap a far too wide margin of profit" *(Cong. Rec.,* 63d Cong., 1st sess., 1913, 50, pt. 2:1251 [statement of Kelly]).

33. *Accord,* Blakey and Blakey, *The Federal Income Tax,* 11.

34. Shearman, "Owners," 272; also quoted in *Cong. Rec.,* 53d Cong., 2d sess., 1894, 26, pt. 2:1673 (statement of Talbert). Remarked West Virginia representative James Capehart on Jan. 31, 1894: "This paternal Government has gone on protecting the industries of the land until our farmers who owned in 1850 60 per cent of the assessed wealth, now own but about 17 per cent. Yet, though his share of property has shrunk to such an insignificant figure, he pays still one-half of the taxes to maintain the Government. . . . Bowed down with taxes and debts, he no longer has a dollar to loan, his credit gone, his lands depreciated 50 per cent or more in value, and this during the period of highest protection; he can see no hope for bettering his condition unless some part of the great burdens now borne by him can be shifted to the shoulders of those who profited by his misfortunes, who have grown fat on the taxes he has been paying to every conceivable monopoly" (ibid., 1734–35). Capehart added that the U.S. farmer paid a premium of 50 to 100 percent on goods bought from "protected trusts" (ibid., 1735).

35. On the decline of land values, see Faulkner, *American Economic History,* 367. Significantly, the value of farm machinery, which was rarely taxed, more than doubled between 1860 and 1890. See ibid., 371.

36. See Seligman, *Income Tax,* 495.

37. *Cong. Rec.,* 53d Cong., 2d sess., 1894, 26, pt. 6:5382. Walsh added: "Under our system of Federal taxation it is possible for a citizen to be worth millions of dollars and not to contribute any more to the support of the General Government than the man who is worth but a few thousand dollars. There is no equity in our system of levying taxes for the support of the Government" (ibid.).

38. Ibid., pt. 7:6685 (quoted in statement of Kyle). On Jan. 29, 1894, Tennessee representative Benton McMillin remarked on the House floor: "Take for example estates that are invested in United States bonds. I remember once to have had my attention called to one where there was more than $50,000,000 bonds owned by one man. And yet upon all that colossal accumulation—that estate beside which that of Croesus would be small—the possessor did not contribute one cent to the country in which he lived, the State in which he lived, nor of the General Government in ten years. The man who drinks one cup of sweetened coffee, the man who wears one suit of clothes, the man who wipes his face once on an imported towel contributes more in that one simple act to the support of the general Government than this individual did upon his many millions in a whole decade" (ibid., pt. 1:418).

39. Ibid., pt. 2:1611. Cf. the statement of Tennessee Democrat Cordell Hull in Jan. 1914: "[T]here are 30,000 Americans residing in France alone—most of them wealthy—who draw their incomes from this country. Many nonresident Americans annually receive as much as $5,000 income from interest on our corporate bonds alone. No tax method has heretofore been devised that would reach this class of persons or that would successfully reach the resident owners of our more than $40,000,000,000 of intangible personalty" ("Address of the Honorable Cordell Hull, of Tennessee, Before the New York Bar Association," in *Cong. Rec.,* 63d Cong., 1st sess., 1913 [1914], 50, pt. 7:102 [statement of Burgess]).

40. *Cong. Rec.*, 53d Cong., 2d sess., 1894, 26, pt. 9:182 (statement of Hunter).

41. See Blakey and Blakey, *The Federal Income Tax,* 9; and Ratner, *Taxation and Democracy,* 160–61.

42. On the 1892 presidential campaign, see Ratner, *Taxation and Democracy,* 160, 165–67; and Taussig, *Tariff History,* 284–85. In the aftermath of this campaign, the Populists captured 37 percent of the vote in Alabama, 24 percent in Texas, 19 percent in Georgia and Mississippi, 16 percent in North Carolina, and 14 percent in Florida. In the West, numerous Populists were elected to state office and drew most of their support from former Republicans. See Stanley, *Dimensions of Law,* 107.

43. From 1890 to 1892, the Senate was dominated by a Republican majority; Republican Benjamin Harrison served as president. For his part, President Cleveland advocated not an end to the tariff system, but rather a fairer distribution of the tariff burden. See Stanley, *Dimensions of Law,* 110.

44. See Blakey and Blakey, *The Federal Income Tax,* 11; and Ratner, *Taxation and Democracy,* 164–65.

2. The Impetus to Change

1. For a more detailed account of the genesis of the crisis, see Faulkner, *American Economic History,* 519–22; Rendigs Fels, *American Business Cycles, 1865–1897,* 179–209; Charles Hoffman, *The Depression of the Nineties: An Economic History;* and Ratner, *Taxation and Democracy,* 168–69.

2. *Cong. Rec.,* 53d Cong., 2d sess., 1894, 26, pt. 9:272 (speech of Richardson).

3. Hoffman, *Depression of the Nineties,* 206.

4. "By the mismanagement of a large number of banks through heavy loans to favorite corporations and bank officials, and by a failure to properly distribute their loans, further weakened by withdrawals for the World's Fair, an unusual number of banks failed early in the season" *(Cong. Rec.,* 53d Cong., 2d sess., 1894, 26, pt. 9:272 [statement of Richardson]). See also ibid., pt. 3:2573 (statement of Bryan). The most notable banks to fail were the Maverick Bank of Boston and the Keystone Bank of Philadelphia. In both cases, bank officers and the cashier had tapped deposits to speculate in stocks. See ibid., 1st sess., 1893, 25, pt. 3:2567, 2570 (statements of Cox), 2611 (statement of Bingham), and 2612 (statement of Draper).

5. See Fels, *American Business Cycles,* 184–85; and Hoffman, *Depression of the Nineties,* 54. Detailed contemporaneous accounts of the crisis are provided in the following periodicals, excerpts from which are found in *Public Opinion: Atlanta Constitution, Atlanta Journal, Baltimore Herald, Baltimore Manufacturer's Record, Boston Advertiser, Boston Globe, Boston Transcript, Bradstreet's, Chicago Evening Journal, Chicago Journal, Cleveland Plain Dealer, Financier, Manufacturer's Record, Minneapolis Tribune, New Orleans Picayune, New Orleans Times-Democrat, New York Financier, New York Journal of Commerce and Commercial Bulletin, New York Mail and Express, New York Recorder, New York Tribune, New York World, Philadelphia Inquirer, Philadelphia Press, Philadelphia Record, Springfield (Mass.) Republican, St. Louis Globe-Democrat, St. Louis Republic,* and *St. Paul Pioneer Press.* See *Public Opinion* 15 (Apr.-Oct. 1893): 7, 32, 54, 82, 108, 132, 155, 178, 202, 227, 250, 274, 297, 311, 320, 343, 365, 387, 411, 436, 466, 491, 514, 538, 562, 586, 612; and 16

(Oct. 1893-Apr. 1894): 13, 14, 38, 63, 87, 112, 135, 159, 183, 207, 230, 254, 279, 303, 326–27, 350, 375, 399, 422, 469, 492, 516, 541, 565, 587, 613.

6. Remarked New York congressman Daniel Lockwood on Oct. 17, 1893: "A great business and financial panic came suddenly over the country, and a few of these institutions . . . found themselves unable to meet the sudden and universal demand of their depositors. Suspension followed. Among them a few . . . were found to have been wrecked by their officers" *(Cong. Rec.,* 53d Cong., 1st sess., 1893, 25, pt. 3:2609).

7. *Cong. Rec.,* 53d Cong., 2d sess., 1894, 26, pt. 9:272 (statement of Richardson). Representative Richardson further commented: "The failure of these banks was published in every paper in the country with scare heads, until the depositors generally lost confidence. Frightened with the idea that if banks in an adjoining state or city failed, perhaps the one in which their money was deposited might be the next to go down, and so the run was started. The banks were compelled to refuse discount and were in no condition to meet a run, in consequence of which failures kept increasing until over seven hundred banking concerns had closed their doors from the beginning of May to July" (ibid.). Fels notes that as time went on, failures became more and more associated with the deteriorating financial system *(American Business Cycles,* 185).

8. Hoffman, *Depression of the Nineties,* 58. Fels tells us that for all of 1893, more than six hundred banks and other financial institutions with liabilities of more than $200 million failed *(American Business Cycles,* 187). Representative Richardson put the latter figure at seven hundred *(Cong. Rec.,* 53d Cong., 2d sess., 1894, 26, pt. 9:272).

9. "Every bank had to contract its loans and strengthen its reserve by crowding collections and refusing discount. Panic stricken depositors kept on withdrawing their funds until $400,000,000 had been retired from the banks" *(Cong. Rec.,* 53d Cong., 2d sess., 1894, 26, pt. 9:272 [statement of Richardson]).

10. Fels gives us this account: "Gold exports ceased early in June when Cleveland announced a special session of Congress for September to repeal the Sherman Purchase Act. This allayed fears that the United States would go off the gold standard, but the New York banks were forced to continue contracting credit. Their reserves declined because of a drain to the interior caused by numerous bank failures in the rest of the country, which in turn were the consequence of business failures. The bank failures were due mainly to violations of law and imprudent policies, so that their closing was merely hastened and bunched by the general situation. . . . Loan contraction continued all over the country, with reserve ratios outside New York rising as individual banks attempted to improve their own positions at the expense of accelerating the contraction of business. All the usual phenomena were present—hoarding, runs, credit rationing as well as high interest rates, and forced liquidation of inventories" *(American Business Cycles,* 186).

11. *Cong. Rec.,* 53d Cong., 2d sess., 1894, 26, pt. 9:272 (statement of Richardson). Noted economist Fels: "Early in May the National Cordage Co. failed because it lacked working capital. Ordinarily this did not matter, but in the conditions then prevailing in the money market the company could not raise sufficient funds to meet its obligations. The credit contraction forced an apparently sound company of great prominence into failure. This precipitated panic on the stock market. There was a rash of failures largely confined to unsound firms" *(American Business Cycles,* 186).

12. See, for example, Spaulding, Jennings, and Company to Senator John Sherman, Jersey

City, N.J., Apr. 20, 1894, in *Cong. Rec.,* 53d Cong., 2d sess., 1894, 26, pt. 6:5513 (statement of Sherman); and ibid., pt. 5:4976 (statement of Sen. Gallinger). Fels reports that by the third week of July, bank suspension of cash payments quickly spread throughout the country, intensifying the depression by making it hard to meet payrolls *(American Business Cycles,* 186–87).

13. "Southern Financial Situation," *Manufacturer's Record,* in *Public Opinion* 15 (Apr.-Oct. 1894): 388. Remarked Senator Gallinger: "The factories were in no condition to continue the purchase of material and the employment of labor to manufacture goods for which there was practically no market. Their line of discounts at the banks could not be increased. So it transpired that factories had to be closed down, and the laboring men had to go out, who without wages became poor customers of shops and markets that sold the products of the factory and the farm. Thus it was that factories stopped running, laboring men were forced to idleness, and trade everywhere stagnated. Failures increased at a fearful rate" *(Cong. Rec.,* 53d Cong., 2d sess., 1894, 26, pt. 5:4976).

14. During the year, freight ton miles fell to 80 percent of capacity. See Hoffman, *Depression of the Nineties,* 13. According to *Bradstreet's,* in 1893, seventy-two railroad corporations with a total capitalization of $1,288 million were placed in receivership, compared to thirty-six railroad corporations with a total capitalization of $358 million in 1892 ("Railroad Receiverships in 1893," *Bradstreet's,* in *Public Opinion* 16 [Oct. 1893-Apr. 1894]: 303). See also "Railroad Earnings in 1893," *Louisville Courier-Journal,* in ibid., 541; and Faulkner, *American Economic History,* 520.

15. The average price of farm products declined by 10 percent from the previous year. See Hoffman, *Depression of the Nineties,* 235. On the rise in interest rates, see ibid., 213.

16. *Cong. Rec.,* 53d Cong., 2d sess., 1894, 26, pt. 5:4976 (statement of Gallinger). Stanley estimates the annual decline in gross national product to be 10 percent *(Dimensions of Law,* 111).

17. Hoffman, *Depression of the Nineties,* 165.

18. "Business Failures in 1893," *Bradstreet's,* in *Public Opinion* 16 (Oct. 1893-Apr. 1894): 327.

19. Hoffman, *Depression of the Nineties,* 203. *Bradstreet's* reported that 370 out of more than 600 financial institutions suspended their operations in 1893 ("Business Failures in 1893," 327).

20. Hoffman, *Depression of the Nineties,* 260–61.

21. *Cong. Rec.,* 53d Cong., 2d sess., 1894, 26, pt. 5:4976 (statement of Gallinger). As might be expected, the principal casualty of the crisis was the American worker. His livelihood threatened, his savings depleted, he and his family faced destitution. Those individuals without work turned to soup kitchens and public charities. Those citizens without hope turned to violence. Reported one New Jersey manufacturer on Apr. 20, 1894: "Little by little the business dropped off, until we were obliged to discharge the hands employed on the night turn early in August. . . . Wages have been reduced and the reduction accepted without a murmur. Many of our oldest and most reliable men are walking the streets, without any means of support for their families; what little they have been able to earn has been consumed, as well as what had been laid aside for a 'rainy day'. The American workingman . . . is suffering. He and his family have denied themselves, first, the comforts of life, then the necessities, and finally have endured a degree of pinching and deprivation that is simply heroic before he or they should become objects of charity. His whole nature revolts against the thought of becoming a beggar, and no one who has not peered in behind the scenes of many of the neatly furnished and once comfortable little homes of this coun-

try can realize the awful misery which these people are enduring and the dreadful uncertainty which is confronting them" (Spaulding, Jennings, and Company to Senator John Sherman, Jersey City, N.J., Apr. 20, 1894, in ibid., pt. 6:5513 [statement of Sherman]).

22. *Cong. Rec.,* 53d Cong., 2d sess., 1894, 26, pt. 9:272 (statement of Sherman). In May 1894, former congressman William R. Moore of Memphis wrote to Ohio senator John Sherman: "[M]ore than 3,000,000 of American citizens are to-day without employment; soup houses and charitable organizations are everywhere taxed to their utmost capacity to satisfy the hunger of the starving poor and cover the nakedness of the ragged masses" (ibid., 5513 [quoted in statement of Sherman]). Fels reports that in 1893, one-sixth of the railroads, measured in terms of either capital or mileage, went into bankruptcy; some thirty-two iron and steel companies suffered a similar fate *(American Business Cycles,* 187). According to Stanley, the ensuing depression increased the rate of unemployment to an estimated 20 percent and intensified a decade-long price decline in agriculture *(Dimensions of Law,* 111).

23. "Business Failures in 1893," 327. "Taking it in all respects, 1893 was the most awful and depressing since we became a nation," lamented New Hampshire senator Jacob Gallinger. "More than one-half of our mills and factories either had closed down or were running on parttime; freights, both by land and water, had fallen off tremendously, and a large proportion of our railroads in the United States were bankrupt and in the hands of receivers, because they had not enough business to pay the expenses of operating them; our manufacturers and builders found but very little to do; our merchants were all buying only for the day or week; all business men were afraid of to-morrow; more than two millions (Gompers says three millions) of workers were idle, because there was no work; and as many more were working from one to three days per week" *(Cong. Rec.,* 53d Cong., 2d sess., 1894, 26, pt. 5:4976).

24. "Business Embarrassments for Nine Months," *Bradstreet's,* in *Public Opinion* 15 (Oct. 1893-Apr. 1894): 14. The comparisons are based on data for the first nine months of the year. For the entire year, business failures in the middle Atlantic states rose by more than one-third, failures in New England by about one-third. See "Business Failures in 1893," 327.

25. "Business Embarrassments," 14. See also "Business Failures in 1893," 327. For the entire year, business failures in the South rose by more than one-quarter; failures in the Midwest more than doubled; failures in the north-central states rose by more than two-thirds; failures in the Pacific states rose by about one-third.

26. Hoffman, *Depression of the Nineties,* 219. See also Ratner, *Taxation and Democracy,* 170.

27. *Cong. Rec.,* 53d Cong., 2d sess., 1894, 26, pt. 5:4976 (statement of Gallinger). In early 1894, according to Representative Tarsney, monthly government expenditures were exceeding revenues by a margin of $6 to $7 million (ibid., pt. 9:186).

28. It also sparked widespread civil unrest, most notably the march of Coxey's Army on Washington, the strike of the United Mine Workers, and the revolt of the American Railway Union in the spring and summer of 1894. See Samuel Rezneck, "Unemployment, Unrest, and Relief in the United States During the Depression of 1893–97"; and Fels, *American Business Cycles,* 190.

29. Address of President Cleveland to the Fifty-third Congress, Dec. 4, 1893, in *Cong. Rec.,* 53d Cong., 2d sess., 1894, 26, pt. 1:9. On Dec. 20 in a report to Congress, Treasury secretary Carlisle recommended the imposition of new taxes on legacies, successions, and incomes derived

from corporate investments as a means of raising $50 million in additional government revenues. See Ratner, *Taxation and Democracy,* 174; Seligman, *Income Tax,* 496; and Stanley, *Dimensions of Law,* 112.

30. "We demand a graduated income tax" ("Populist Platform of 1892," in *National Party Platforms,* edited by Donald B. Johnson, 1:91). The economic crisis strengthened the hand of the Populists. The sharp rise in unemployment exacerbated disparities in wealth. Greater disparities, in turn, underscored the inequities of the existing tax system. The Populists proposed to institute a new tax system that would substantially reduce these disparities. This proposal had won the support of the National Grange, the Farmers' Alliance, the Knights of Labor, and the National Federation of Labor. See *Cong. Rec.,* 53d Cong., 2d sess., 1894, 26, pt. 2:1609 (statement of Hall).

31. See *Cong. Rec.,* 53d Cong., 2d sess., 1894, 26, pt. 5:4064 (statement of Aldrich); and pt. 8:7809 (statement of Gorman). The Wilson Bill would reduce the average rate on "articles in common use" from about 35 percent to 16.8 percent. See ibid., pt. 5:4914 (statement of Aldrich); Ratner, *Taxation and Democracy,* 175; and Taussig, *Tariff History,* esp. chap. 6.

32. See *Cong. Rec.,* 53d Cong., 2d sess., 1894, 26, pt. 2:1251 (speech of Springer).

33. See "An Income Tax Caucus," *Washington Post,* Jan. 26, 1894, 1; Blakey and Blakey, *The Federal Income Tax,* 13; Ratner, *Taxation and Democracy,* 173; and Stanley, *Dimensions of Law,* 113. Within the Ways and Means Committee, eight out of eleven Democrats supported the income tax; all six Republicans opposed it. The eight Democrats had been elected from the South and West. The three Democrats that opposed the measure were Chairman Wilson; Representative Bourke Cockran, a Tammany orator; and Representative Moses Stevens, a former Massachusetts banker. See "An Income Tax Caucus," *Washington Post,* Jan. 26, 1894, 1.

34. See Ratner, *Taxation and Democracy,* 172.

35. The Democrats were McMillin, Alexander Montgomery of Kentucky, and William Bynum of Indiana. The Republicans were Albert Hopkins of Illinois and Sereno Payne of New York. See House Committee on Ways and Means, *Honorable Thomas G. Shearman Before Ways and Means Subcommittee on Internal Revenue,* 53d Cong. 1 (1893).

36. See *Cong. Rec.,* 53d Cong., 2d sess., 1894, 26, pt. 2:1666 (statement of Maddox); and House Committee on Ways and Means, *Report of the Committee on Ways and Means,* 53d Cong., 2d sess., 1894, H. Rept. 53–276, 6. This report is hereinafter referred to as "H. Rept. 53–276."

37. Hull, *Memoirs of Hull,* 49.

38. See House Committee, *Honorable Thomas G. Shearman,* 1. Under Shearman's proposal, only the following items would have been subject to taxation: corporate interest and dividends, rents, and monopoly profits. The tax would have been withheld, reported, and paid exclusively by corporations and tenants. See ibid., 11–14.

39. See *Cong. Rec.,* 53d Cong., 2d sess., 1894, 26, pt. 2:1672 (statement of Talbert), pt. 7:6687 (statement of Kyle), and pt. 9:606 (speech of Pence).

40. See H. Rept. 53–276, 5.

41. See *Cong. Rec.,* 53d Cong., 2d sess., 1894, 26, pt. 1:584 (statement of Bryan); and "Answers to Questions Submitted May 20, 1893, to Hon. Alvey A. Adee, Second Assistant Secretary of State, and by Him Submitted to the United States Consuls in Foreign Countries Where an Income Tax Is Collected," in ibid.

42. "Answers to Questions." See also Seligman, *Income Tax,* 65.

43. *Cong. Rec.,* 53d Cong., 2d sess., 1894, 26, pt. 1:584–85. See also Seligman, *Income Tax,* 79, 90, 102, 177.

44. *Cong. Rec.,* 53d Cong., 2d sess., 1894, 26, pt. 1:588.

45. Ibid., pt. 2:1655 (statement of Rep. Bryan). See also Seligman, *Income Tax,* 251–52.

46. *Cong. Rec.,* 53d Cong., 2d sess., 1894, 26, pt. 1:588, 590. See also Seligman, *Income Tax,* 237, 248–49, 252. In Bremen, incomes greater than 6,000 marks were subject to a special surcharge.

47. Seligman, *Income Tax,* 330; *Cong. Rec.,* 53d Cong., 2d sess., 1894, 26, pt. 1:591.

48. *Cong. Rec.,* 53d Cong., 2d sess., 1894, 26, pt. 1:591.

49. Ibid. See also Seligman, *Income Tax,* 344. There was also a 1.2 percent surcharge earmarked for a special war fund. In addition, under the Italian scheme, incomes greater than 400 lire, but less than 500 lire, were allowed a 250 lire abatement. This abatement was phased down to 100 lire for incomes greater than 700 lire. The Italian law excluded income derived from land. See *Cong. Rec.,* 53d Cong., 2d sess., 1894, 26, pt. 1:591; and Seligman, *Income Tax,* 344.

50. See H. Rept. 53–276, 2.

51. See *Cong. Rec.,* 53d Cong., 2d sess., 1894, 26, pt. 9:610 (speech of Pence). The Civil War schemes were developed in a context distinct from the context of the Income Tax of 1894. They bear only a loose causal connection with the latter scheme. *Accord* Blakey and Blakey, *The Federal Income Tax,* 1.

52. *The Revenue Act of 1862,* chap. 323, sec. 90, *U.S. Statutes at Large* 12 (1862): 433. See also secs. 81, 82, 90, 91.

53. Ibid., secs. 80, 82, 84, 88, 92.

54. *The Revenue Act of 1864,* chap. 173, secs. 116–17, *U.S. Statutes at Large* 13 (1864): 223. See also secs. 104, 107, 108, 111, 120, 122.

55. *The Revenue Act of 1865,* chap. 78, *U.S. Statutes at Large* 13 (1865): 469, 479; *The Revenue Act of 1866,* chap. 184, *U.S. Statutes at Large* 14 (1866): 137–39; *The Revenue Act of 1867,* chap. 169, sec. 13, *U.S. Statutes at Large* 14 (1867): 471; *The Revenue Act of 1870,* chap. 255, sec. 6, *U.S. Statutes at Large* 16 (1870): 257.

56. See H. Rept. 53–276, 2.

57. *Report of the Wells Commission,* June 1865, in ibid. The commission asked in its final report: "Assuming, then, that the policy indicated, which we may here restate in brief, to be the abolition or speedy reduction of all taxes which tend to check development, and the retention of all those which like the income tax, fall chiefly upon realized wealth, is accepted as the desirable future revenue policy of the country, . . .in what manner and to what extent can it be carried out?" Referring to the income tax, the commission noted, "Although in many respects an obnoxious tax yet, falling as it does mainly on accumulation, it will probably be sustained with less detriment to the country than any other form of taxation" (ibid.).

58. Representative Montgomery did not join in the recommendation. He advocated a more limited tax on corporate investment income. In the full committee, he voted against taxing individual incomes. See "History of the Law," *New York Sun,* Apr. 9, 1895, 3; and "A Tax upon Incomes," *Washington Post,* Jan. 3, 1894, 1. On the floor, however, Montgomery voted in favor of the income tax proposal. See *Cong. Rec.,* 53d Cong., 2d sess., 1894, 26, pt. 2:1795–96; and ibid., pt. 9:207 (speech of Dunn).

59. See *Cong. Rec.,* 53d Cong., 2d sess., 1894, 26, pt. 9:666 (speech of Peffer); 601 (speech of Pence); and pt. 8:7804 (statement of Jones). "Many of the Democrats think that it is unsatisfactory in particulars which relate to their districts" ("$60,000,000 Deficit," *Washington Post,* Dec. 6, 1893, 1). "Half a dozen Democrats are making an active and earnest effort to crystalize the opposition in the House so as to compass the defeat of the bill. At the head of this endeavor is Congressman Sperry, of Connecticut, who has the misfortune to have located in his district almost every interest affected by the tariff bill" ("Talk on the Tariff," ibid., Dec. 15, 1893, 1). "As is well known, there is among the Democrats in the House a coterie of members who are bitterly opposed to the provisions of the new tariff bill. They object to it, mainly, because it lowers the duties on articles manufactured in their districts which have hitherto enjoyed a high degree of protection. They have announced their intention of antagonizing the bill at every stage and they began yesterday to put their plan of campaign into operation" ("Democrats Sit Silent," ibid., Jan. 4, 1894, 1). See also "The Tariff Bill in Danger," *New York Times,* Jan. 26, 1894, 1; and Ratner, *Taxation and Democracy,* 171.

60. On Dec. 19, Populist John Davis of Kansas introduced an income tax bill, as did Democrat John Bretz of Indiana. Their initiatives were followed on Jan. 3 by Democrat Tom Johnson of Ohio. See House Bills nos. 4861, 4898, 4955 in *Cong. Rec.,* 53d Cong., 2d sess., 1894, 26, pt. 1:425, 461.

61. Ibid., pt. 9:207 (speech of Dunn) and 666 (speech of Peffer). See also "The Tariff Bill in Danger," *New York Times,* Jan. 26, 1894, 1. Reported the *Washington Post* on Jan. 22, 1894: "The expressed opposition, as evidenced by talk in the cloak rooms, is estimated to be confined to thirty-five Democrats. Should the income tax be attached to the tariff bill as an amendment, doubt on the subject in the minds of nearly all these Democratic members will be resolved in favor of the pending measure, and the actual opposition will probably not exceed five. To offset the most liberal estimate which the friends of the income tax have formed of the strength of the opposition, they say they can rely upon ten Populist votes for the Wilson bill, if the income tax is incorporated with it" ("May Pass Both Houses," 2).

62. Reported the *Washington Post* on Jan. 7, 1894: "The Populist members of the House are acting with the Republicans in declining to aid the Democrats in making a quorum. A proposition was made to them by some of the Democratic managers that if they voted and made the quorum the income tax feature would be brought in as part of the tariff bill and they would be given three hours of the general debate" ("To Arrest Absentees," 1). Noted Populist senator William Peffer months later: "I think it may safely be said that the income-tax feature is to a very large extent of Populist origin. If my information was correct, the friends of the tariff bill in the House of Representatives, when the bill was pending, were unable to get it before the body for action until they procured the assistance of the Populists, and in order to procure that assistance this change was required; that is to say, instead of making two separate bills, one for tariff reform and the other an income-tax bill, so that the income-tax bill might be defeated and the other one passed, the Populists required that before their vote could be had even to consider the tariff proposition their income-tax bill should be incorporated and it was so finally determined. Then a quorum was had and the bill was proceeded with" *(Cong. Rec.,* 53d Cong., 2d sess., 1894, 26, pt. 9:666). See also ibid., 601 (speech of Pence) and 351 (speech of Wheeler).

63. Reported the *Washington Post* on Jan. 6, 1894: "The Democrats of the House are bound hand and foot. They are completely at the mercy of the Republicans and of a handful of their own

party. Four times was a call of the House made yesterday, and as many as 273 members answered to their names. Four times was the roll call on a yea and nay vote, and the highest aggregate response was 170, of whom 169 were Democrats. Even while the business of the House was paralyzed because the majority could not get within seven of a quorum, there were over 180 Democrats in and around the House. . . . [T]he situation for the Democrats, instead of improving during the day, grew worse, so that on the last roll-call, only 166 Democrats voted, a net falling off of three. . . . If this was a concerted scheme to keep the tariff bill out of the House until after the caucus, it was successful" ("Bound Hand and Foot," 1). See also "For Lack of a Quorum," ibid., Jan. 3, 1894, 1; "Democrats Sit Silent," Jan. 4, 1894, 1; "To Arrest Absentees," Jan. 7, 1894, 1; "When a Quorum Comes," Jan. 8, 1894, 1; and "Only Democrats to Blame," *New York Times*, Jan. 8, 1894, 1.

64. In the absence of a quorum, debate on the Wilson Bill was delayed four days. A quorum was finally reached on Jan. 8, when the deputy sergeant at arms arrested about thirty representatives, who, rather than face contempt charges, cast their votes. See "The Tariff Bill Is Up," *Washington Post*, Jan. 8, 1894, 1.

65. See "Bound Hand and Foot," 1.

66. Including two independents and one Free Silverite. The ten were William Baker (Kans.), John Bell (Colo.), Haldor Boen (Minn.), John Davis (Kans.), William Harris (Kans.), Omer Kem (Neb.), William McKeighan (Neb.), Francis Newlands (Nev.), Lafe Pence (Colo.), and Jerry Simpson (Kans.)

67. See "An Income Tax Caucus," ibid., Jan. 26, 1894, 1; and "The Tariff Bill in Danger," *New York Times*, Jan. 26, 1894, 1. On Jan. 2, a majority of Democrats on Ways and Means, convening in caucus, had endorsed the subcommittee's proposal. Voting in favor were Representatives McMillin (Tenn.), Tarsney (Mo.), Bynum (Ind.), Bryan (Neb.), Turner (Ga.), and Whiting (Mich.). Voting against were Representatives Wilson (W.Va.), Stevens (Mass.), Montgomery (Ky.), Cockran (N.Y.), and Breckinridge (Ark.). See "A Tax upon Incomes," *Washington Post*, Jan. 3, 1894, 1; "Decided on an Income Tax," *New York Times*, Jan. 3, 1894, 1; and "History of the Law," *New York Sun*, Apr. 9, 1895, 3. This endorsement bound all committee Democrats to the same affirmative vote. Later, on the House floor, Breckinridge, Montgomery, and Wilson voted in favor of the income tax proposal. See *Cong. Rec.*, 53d Cong., 2d sess., 1894, 26, pt. 2:1795–96.

68. Quips Ratner: "Most of the Republicans were, in tariff matters at least, like the Bourbons, who never forgot anything and never learned anything" *(Taxation and Democracy,* 171).

69. See *Cong. Rec.*, 53d Cong., 2d sess., 1894, 26, pt. 7:7134 (statement of Hill).

70. Opposing the income tax were the nation's chambers of commerce and boards of trade, as well as bankers, manufacturers, and businessmen. See ibid., pt. 2:1616 (statement of McDannold) and pt. 7:6612 (statement of Hill). On criticism by labor unions and farmers' cooperatives, see ibid., pt. 2:1609 (statement of Hall).

3. The Legislative Process

1. Some historians have credited William Jennings Bryan with this drafting. See, for example, Louis William Koenig, *A Political Biography of William Jennings Bryan*, 130; and Paolo E. Coletta, *William Jennings Bryan*, vol. 1, *Political Evangelist, 1860–1908*, 56. However, members of the Fifty-third Congress consistently credited McMillin. See *Cong. Rec.*, 53d Cong., 2d sess.,

1894, 26, pt. 7:6835 (statement of Vest) and 6880 (statement of Chandler). In all probability, McMillin, as subcommittee chair, worked closely with Bryan, who had gathered data on the European tax systems. See "A Tax upon Incomes," *Washington Post,* Jan. 3, 1894, 1.

2. See *Cong. Rec.,* 53d Cong., 2d sess., 1894, 26, pt. 7:6835 (statement of Vest), 6880 (statement of Chandler); and Seligman, *Income Tax,* 508.

3. See "Text of Income Tax Bill," *Washington Post,* Jan. 27, 1894, 7.

4. H. Rept. 53–276, 6.

5. See *Cong. Rec.,* 53d Cong., 2d sess., 1894, 26, pt. 2:1737 (statement of Van Voorhis) and pt. 7:6620 (statement of Hill). Remarked Ohio representative Tom Johnson: "The great feature of the exemption is that it is purposely made high enough to exempt the great mass of voters" (ibid., pt. 2:1652). See also "Tariff Bill Had to Wait," *New York Times,* Jan. 4, 1894, 1; and "Democrats Grow Serious," ibid., Jan. 27, 1894, 1.

6. "The committee think that too large a portion of the taxes are collected from the necessaries of life, and consequently too small a part from the wealth of the people, which has been accumulated and is held in excess of what is necessary for their comfort" (H. Rept. 53–276, 7).

7. *Cong. Rec.,* 53d Cong., 2d sess., 1894, 26, pt. 9:315. Cf. the statement of Maryland Democrat David Lewis in the Sixty-third Congress: "[I]f any exemption is equitable, the exemption should be just such an amount as is necessary to the purpose of exemption—the maintenance of the individual for mere living. This in order that he may not be doubly taxed. It is upon that great army of unfortunate citizens . . . that taxation principally falls. They must pay upon their bread a bread tax, upon their meat a meat tax, upon their shoes the tax of the Shoe Trust, upon their garments the tax of the Woollen Trust. . . . The theory is that those people should be exempt from this income tax in order that they may not be doubly taxed. First, the indirect tax on all their needs, by high tariff, making high prices; then on the wages coming in to pay the prices" *(Cong. Rec.,* 63d Cong., 1st sess., 1913, 50, pt. 4:4082).

8. "The wealth of this country amounts to more than $65,000,000,000, and the question arises whether it is not just and fair that a portion of this money should be raised by a tax on the earnings of wealth instead of imposing it all or nearly all on consumption. The committee believe that it is eminently just and proper that the amount proposed by this bill should be collected from a tax on incomes instead of placing all of it on the necessaries of life, which are consumed by all but are not used in proportion to their ability to pay taxes, but according to the necessities of existence. . . . The committee sees no hardship in requiring those who have incomes of more than $4,000 a year to pay 2 per cent of all in excess of that amount to carry on the Government under which it has been accumulated and by which it is protected" (H. Rept. 53–276, 3).

9. Joseph S. Miller to Benton McMillin, Nov. 23, 1893, in ibid., 7. In 1913, according to one congressional source, roughly 325,000 individuals earned incomes in excess of $3,000. See *Cong. Rec.,* 63d Cong., 1st sess., 1913, 50, pt. 4:3817 (statement of Bristow). In deriving the $32 million figure, Miller had used a rate of 4 percent. The committee, however, opted for a more politically palatable 2 percent. It realized that applying the lower rate would result in a $16 million revenue shortfall. See Miller to McMillin, Nov. 23, 1893, in H. Rept. 53–276, 6. By all indications, rather than eliminate this shortfall by reducing the exemption amount, the committee decided to fund it through a tax on corporations.

10. On the various features of the tax, see Seligman, *Income Tax,* 508–11.

11. See *Tariff Act of 1894,* 53d Cong., 2d sess., H.R. 4864, secs. 54, 59. Southern and western Democrats on Ways and Means initially proposed a rate of 4 percent. In light of Republican and eastern Democratic opposition to the tax, however, they settled for a rate of 2 percent. See "A Tax upon Incomes," *Washington Post,* Jan. 3, 1894, 1.

12. See *Tariff Act of 1894,* secs. 54, 55, 58, 59, 61. Section 55 provided that gains from the sale of realty would be taxable only if the realty had been purchased within two years of the year of sale. This provision parallels Section 13 of the Revenue Act of 1867. See *The Revenue Act of 1867,* chap. 169, sec. 13.

13. See *Tariff Act of 1894,* secs. 56, 59, 63, 65, 66.

14. The 1870 law had achieved a certain degree of rate uniformity. See *The Revenue Act of 1870,* chap. 255, sec. 6. This uniformity, however, stemmed from the repeal of the gross receipts tax, not a deliberate attempt to standardize the corporate rate schedule.

15. See *Cong. Rec.,* 53d Cong., 2d sess., 1894, 26, pt. 4:3561, 3567 (statements of Hill), pt. 7:6693 (statement of Teller), and pt. 10:1393 (speech of Morrill). As a concession to tax opponents, however, proponents agreed to limit the operation of the 1894 tax to the five-year period ending Jan. 1, 1900. See ibid., pt. 7:6631.

16. Explained Senator Morrill, who sponsored the 1864 legislation: "This is intended as a war measure, a temporary measure, and we must as such give it our support. The present bill is not likely to suit everybody, and I regard it only as a temporary measure, fit to be introduced because of the imperious necessities of our present condition" (ibid., pt. 9:185 [quoted in speech of Tarsney]). See also Blakey and Blakey, *The Federal Income Tax,* 559.

17. Before this vote, Democrats on the committee caucused. By a vote of six to five, they decided to endorse the income tax proposal. Voting in favor were McMillin (Tenn.), Tarsney (Mo.), Bynum (Ind.), Bryan (Neb.), Turner (Ga.), and Whiting (Mich.). Voting against were Wilson (W.Va.), Stevens (Mass.), Montgomery (Ky.), Cockran (N.Y.), and Breckinridge (Ark.). This vote bound all committee Democrats to the same affirmative vote. Following the caucus, the full committee convened. All eleven Democrats cast their votes in favor of the income tax proposal; all six Republicans cast their votes against. These Republicans were Reed (Maine), Burrows (Mich.), Payne (N.Y.), Dalzell (Pa.), Hopkins (Ill.), and Gear (Iowa). See "The Income Tax," *Washington Post,* Jan. 13, 1894, 2.

18. See "An Income Tax Caucus," ibid., Jan. 26, 1894, 1. The House debate commenced on Jan. 29 and ended on Jan. 31.

19. See *Cong. Rec.,* 53d Cong., 2d sess., 1894, 26, pt. 2:1730; and Ratner, *Taxation and Democracy,* 179. On June 21, Populist William Peffer introduced a similar amendment in the Senate. At the urging of President Pro Tem Harris, the Senate tabled this amendment so as not to delay passage of the main measure. See *Cong. Rec.,* 53d Cong., 2d sess., 1894, 26, pt. 7:6633, 6637, 6639.

20. See *Cong. Rec.,* 53d Cong., 2d sess., 1894, 26, pt. 2:1730.

21. See ibid., 1730, 1732. Sibley added: "It requires more of the strength of this Government to protect a man who has accumulated a million dollars than it does to protect a million men with a dollar apiece. Let each bear the burden in proportion to the demand he makes upon the Government for protection" (ibid., 1730).

22. Cf. the statement of Connecticut Republican Frank Brandegee in the Sixty-third Con-

gress: "I do not think in the passage of a tariff bill we should attempt to utilize it as a vehicle to float through any propositions to tax corporations out of existence or to penalize the rich or to reduce swollen fortunes or to accomplish any other collateral purpose, no matter how desirable" *(Cong. Rec.,* 63d Cong., 1st sess., 1913, 50, pt. 4:3837). Added Massachusetts Republican Henry Cabot Lodge: "But to have the Government undertake, for vindictive reasons, to punish a man simply because he has succeeded and has accumulated property by thrift and intelligence and character, or has inherited it honestly under the law, is entering upon a dangerous path. It would convert this tax from the imposition of a tax to the pillage of a class" (ibid., 3840).

23. See *Cong. Rec.,* 53d Cong., 2d sess., 1894, 26, pt. 2:1736, 1737, 1738. The insertion of a reference to "choses in action" was made at the request of Representative McMillin (ibid., 1737).

24. See ibid., 1795; and Ratner, *Taxation and Democracy,* 181.

25. The Republicans who voted in favor of the provisions were William Bowers of California, Loren Fletcher of Minnesota, Charles Hartman of Montana, Benjamin Marsh of Illinois, John Pickler of South Dakota, Willis Sweet of Idaho, and William White of Ohio. The two Democratic representatives from the industrial East were Michael McEttrick of Boston and James Pigott of New Haven. As used herein, "industrial East" refers to congressional districts that lay north of the Potomac River and east of the Allegheny Mountains, "West" refers to districts that lay to the west of the Allegheny Mountains, and "South" refers to districts that lay south of the Mason-Dixon line. These references comport with the views of members of the Fifty-third Congress.

26. See *Cong. Rec.,* 53d Cong., 2d sess., 1894, 26, pt. 2:1796. The adoption of McMillin's amendment to the Wilson Bill prompted the withdrawal of all other income tax amendments. See Ratner, *Taxation and Democracy,* 177.

27. See *Cong. Rec.,* 53d Cong., 2d sess., 1894, 26, pt. 2:1804; and Ratner, *Taxation and Democracy,* 182. The bill lay in committee until Mar. 20. See *Cong. Rec.,* 53d Cong., 2d sess., 1894, 26, pt. 8:7887 (statement of Vilas).

28. See *Cong. Rec.,* 53d Cong., 2d sess., 1894, 26, pt. 7:6623 (statement of Hill).

29. See ibid., pt. 8:7746 (statement of Blanchard) and 7802 (statement of Gorman).

30. See ibid., 7804 (statement of Jones). On political divisions within the Senate over the Wilson Bill, see Ratner, *Taxation and Democracy,* 181–82.

31. See *Cong. Rec.,* 53d Cong., 2d sess., 1894, 26, pt. 8:7803 (statement of Vest).

32. Grover Cleveland to William Wilson, July 2, 1894, in *Letters of Grover Cleveland, 1850–1908,* ed. Allan Nevins, 354, 357. See also "No Vote Was Taken," *Washington Post,* Jan. 2, 1894, 2; and "A Tax upon Incomes," ibid., Jan. 3, 1894, 1.

33. See *Cong. Rec.,* 53d Cong., 2d sess., 1894, 26, pt. 7:6623, 7134 (statements of Hill), pt. 8:7735–36 (statement of Vest), and 7802 (statement of Gorman).

34. See ibid., 7804 (statement of Jones), 7805 (statement of Harris), 7887 (statement of Vilas); and Ratner, *Taxation and Democracy,* 32. The average rate would increase from 35.51 percent to 38.68 percent. See *Cong. Rec.,* 53d Cong., 2d sess., 1894, 26, pt. 8:7809 (statement of Gorman). The amendments restored all items but raw wool to the duty list; increased the rates on woolen and cotton goods, manufactured iron, and glass; and restored the McKinley bounty to Louisiana sugar planters. See Stanley, *Dimensions of Law,* 113.

35. *Tariff Act of 1894,* sec. 54 in *Cong. Rec.,* 53d Cong., 2d sess., 1894, 26, pt. 7:6632.

36. See *Tariff Act of 1894,* sec. 58.

37. *Cong. Rec.,* 53d Cong., 2d sess., 1894, 26, pt. 7:6632–33.

38. Ibid., 6633.

39. "We declare it to be a fundamental principle of the Democratic party that the Federal Government has no constitutional power to impose and collect tariff duties, except for the purpose of revenue only" ("Democratic Platform of 1892," in *National Party Platforms,* edited by Johnson, 87). "We affirm the American doctrine of protection. We call attention to its growth abroad. We maintain that the prosperous condition of our country is largely due to the wise revenue legislation of the Republican congress" ("Republican Platform of 1892," in ibid., 93).

40. See *Cong. Rec.,* 53d Cong., 2d sess., 1894, 26, pt. 7:6633.

41. See Robert A. Green, "The Future of Source-Based Taxation of the Income of Multinational Enterprises," 18, 29, 71; Nancy H. Kaufman, "Fairness and the Taxation of International Income," 145, 153; and Rutsel Silvestre Martha, *The Jurisdiction to Tax in International Law: Theory and Practice of Legislative Fiscal Jurisdiction,* 45.

42. See *Cong. Rec.,* 53d Cong., 2d sess., 1894, 26, pt. 7:6772. Hill pointed out that the imposition of the tax would be unconditional, even when the enterprise was insolvent, and that in some circumstances, it would render a financially weak corporation insolvent (ibid.).

43. This issue had been considered earlier by Ways and Means, which failed to resolve it. See ibid., pt. 9:420 (speech of McMillin).

44. See ibid., pt. 7:6690 (statement of Vest). In 1913, the Sixty-third Congress reinstituted collection at the source. Representative Cordell Hull, the principal architect of the 1913 tax, argued that this withholding mechanism would both reduce fraud in tax reporting and be less annoying to the taxpayer *(Cong. Rec.,* 63d Cong., 1st sess., 1913, 50, pt. 2:1302–3).

45. *Cong. Rec.,* 53d Cong., 2d sess., 1894, 26, pt. 7:6831. New Section 59 was offered as a substitute for original Sections 59–61.

46. The Senate viewed the proposed changes in a positive light. On June 26, it approved new Section 59 by unanimous vote. See ibid., 6832.

47. Ibid., 6887–88. Vest added: "But out of an abundance of caution the word 'business' was added, which seems to me would clearly cover all the legitimate expenses attending the business" (ibid., 6888).

48. See *Tariff Act of 1894,* sec. 32.

49. See *Cong. Rec.,* 53d Cong., 2d sess., 1894, 26, pt. 7:6678, 6827–28.

50. Ibid., 6705.

51. Ibid., 6865.

52. Two other amendments are worth mentioning. The first pertained to those corporations that would be subject to the income tax. Under the House version of the bill, only *domestic* corporations organized for profit would have been subject to the tax. The Finance Committee broadened the scope of this provision to encompass *all* corporations, foreign and domestic, organized for profit doing business in the United States. The full Senate endorsed the Finance Committee measure on June 21, 1894. See ibid., 6832. The second amendment concerned the definition of taxable income. After the specific enumeration of items made subject to the tax, the Finance Committee added "or from any other source whatever." On June 21, the Senate endorsed this addition. See ibid., 6633.

53. See note 8 to this chapter.

4. What Is a "Corporation"?

1. *Cong. Rec.,* 53d Cong., 2d sess., 1894, 26, pt. 7:6865 (statement of Hill). See also ibid., 6868–69 (statement of Allison).

2. Ibid., 6870.

3. See ibid., 6870, 6832–34.

4. See ibid., 6866–67, 6879.

5. Ibid., 6868. Delaware Republican Anthony Higgins shared this vision. "The fact is," remarked Higgins, "that corporations are but aggregations of the capital of individuals for joint profit, with joint liability and joint loss, conveniently divided into shares for the purposes of distribution and management" (ibid., 6874).

6. See ibid., 6869, 6879.

7. Ibid., 6879.

8. Ibid.

9. See ibid., 6882.

10. See ibid., 6833, 6835. In offering his amendment, Hoar professedly had in mind the numerous Massachusetts grocers and mechanics who had formed joint stock companies (ibid., 6877).

11. See ibid., 6866. In Vest's own words: "But when you enter into this maze and labyrinth of details and undertake to go into the counting house of a corporation and examine into all their business in order to frame a statute, you are simply piling up perplexity, and doubt, and difficulty" (ibid., 6868).

12. Ibid., 6866. Earlier in the session, the Ways and Means Committee had considered a proposal granting a corporate exemption, but rejected it. Reasoned Representative McMillin: "Here are artificial parties; here are creatures of the law that have peculiar privileges. They have in some instances the right of eminent domain; they have the right to sue and be sued as individuals . . . the right to go to the courts. They have the right to be exempt from personal liability. As the Government has to keep its courts in existence for the benefit of many of these corporations, as all or a majority of them are presumed to be founded upon surplus, we have thought that an exemption might be made in their case, and that the exemption need not apply; therefore, the net income of the corporation would be liable" (ibid., pt. 9:420).

13. See ibid., pt. 7:6878.

14. See ibid., 6867, 6872–73, 6875, 6878.

15. See ibid., 6867–68, 6872, 6875–76, 6879. In Vest's own words: "It seems to me it makes intricate and complex the business of all these corporations, and opens the door to great indirection, if not to fraud" (ibid., 6868).

16. This definition comports with that set forth by Chief Justice John Marshall in *Trustees of Dartmouth College v. Woodward:* "A corporation is an artificial being, invisible, intangible, and existing only in contemplation of law. Being the mere creature of law, it possesses only those properties which the charter of its creation confers upon it, either expressly, or as incidental to its very existence" (17 U.S. [4 Wheat.] 518, 536 [1819]). The Fifty-third Congress's conception of the corporation as a taxable entity was ultimately endorsed by members of subsequent Congresses. For example, in the debate over the Revenue Act of 1918, Tennessee Democrat Cordell Hull re-

marked: "The income tax law only defines two taxable entities, the individual and the corporation. It prescribes systems of deductions for those two business entities in computing their income for taxation" *(Cong. Rec.,* 65th Cong., 2d sess., 1918, 56, pt. 10:10420). See also the tax treatment prescribed in Section 38 of the Corporation Tax Act of Aug. 5, 1909, which was modeled after the 1894 Act *(Cong. Rec.,* 61st Cong., 1st sess., 1909, 44, pt. 4:4016 [statements of Shively and Root]).

17. See *The Revenue Act of 1864,* chap. 173, sec. 117. Only the undistributed profits of those corporations not specifically enumerated in the act were attributable to their respective owners.

18. Old Section 55 provided that "in estimating the gains, profits, and income of any person there shall be included . . . the share of any person of the gains or profits of all companies, whether incorporated or partnership, who would be entitled to the same if divided, whether divided or otherwise" *(Tariff Act of 1894,* sec. 55).

19. See *Cong. Rec.,* 53d Cong., 2d sess., 1894, 26, pt. 7:6777, 6833, 6865.

20. Ibid., 6704.

21. Ibid., 6876. Added Aldrich: "A corporation is simply an aggregation of individuals. Many of the corporations that have been chartered under the various State governments are simply cooperative associations" (ibid.).

22. Ibid., 6774.

23. Ibid., 6874. In Hill's own words: "If corporations are injurious to the country, if corporations have violated their charters, then the law can proceed against them and abolish them; but so long as they are permitted to exist, so long as people are allowed to make corporate investments, they should be treated like citizens" (ibid., 6873).

24. Ibid., 6704.

25. Ibid., 6705.

26. Ibid., 6881. Chandler continued: "If the Senator from Missouri had wished to provide a symmetrical and logical and a decent tax upon incomes, he would have provided simply that the incomes of individuals should be taxed, with a suitable exemption. . . . Having thus taxed according to equity and justice, if an income tax is required by the exigencies of the country, the income of individuals, then a simple tax upon the surplus profits of the corporations of the country, a simple tax upon such portion of the profits of a corporation as should not be paid out to its stockholders or its bondholders either as dividend or interest, would have made a tax which could have been defended, if the necessities of the country required such a tax" (ibid.).

27. Ibid., 7136. As might be expected, Senator Hill voted against the measure because of its income tax feature. Populist William Peffer of Kansas rejected the measure because he believed that the duties that it imposed on imported wool were not high enough (ibid., pt. 9:666).

28. The recorded vote was 182 yeas to 106 nays (ibid., pt. 8:8482).

29. See ibid., 7732, 8666; and Ratner, *Taxation and Democracy,* 184. Under the new law, all U.S. citizens and resident aliens would be taxed on their worldwide income. Nonresident aliens would be taxed only on income derived from a business or property located in the United States. "Income" was to include profits and gains derived from any source whatever. See Section 27. It was to exclude dividends paid out of earnings on which the tax had previously been assessed. Partnership profits, whether distributed or not, were to be taxed to the partners. Only corporate profits distributed to stockholders were to be taxed to the stockholders. See Section 28. These

stockholders would be responsible for collecting and remitting the tax to the government. The individual and corporate collection schemes were to be distinct. In computing their taxable income, individuals would be allowed a statutory exemption. They would also be allowed deductions for interest, business expenses, business and casualty losses, taxes, and worthless debts. See Section 27. All corporations organized for profit and doing business in the United States would be subject to the corporate tax. They were to be treated as "artificial beings," not "aggregations of individuals." In deriving their taxable income, they would be allowed deductions for losses and operating expenses. Such expenses were to include taxes, interest, and the cost of trade or manufacturing inventory. See *Wilson-Gorman Tariff Act of 1894,* chap. 349, secs. 27–37, *U.S. Statutes at Large* 28 (1894): 509, 553.

5. The Rationale

1. See *Cong. Rec.,* 53d Cong., 2d sess., 1894, 26, pt. 2:1566 (statement of Cooper), 1607 (statement of Hall), pt. 4:4029 (statement of Mills), pt. 6:5381 (statement of Walsh), pt. 7:6685 (statement of Kyle), pt. 9:183 (speech of Hunter), and 503 (speech of Baker).

2. Ibid., pt. 2:1674.

3. Ibid., 1656.

4. Ibid., pt. 9:293. Added the Committee on Ways and Means: "The committee believe that it is eminently just and proper that the amount proposed by this bill should be collected from a tax on incomes instead of placing all of it on the necessaries of life, which are consumed by all but are not used in proportion to their ability to pay taxes, but according to the necessaries of existence. . . . Here we have 'a Government of the people, by the people, and for the people.' We boast that our motto is 'Equal rights to all and special privileges to none.' Here we claim that the burdens of Government ought to be borne in proportion to the ability of each citizen who is protected by it. Yet under our peculiar system there are citizens of great wealth who, by our method of taxing what we must consume rather than what we have accumulated, pay little more to the support of the Government than is paid by the day laborer, who has nothing" (H. Rept. 53–276, 5). Cf. the Report of the Committee on Ways and Means, Sixty-third Congress: "The amount each citizen contributes is governed not by his ability to pay tax but by his consumption of the articles taxed. It requires as many yards of cloth to clothe, and as many ounces of food to sustain, the day laborer as the largest holder of invested wealth; yet each pays into the Federal Treasury a like amount of taxes upon the food he eats, while the former at present pays a larger rate of tax upon his cheap suit of woollen clothing than the latter upon his costly suit. The result is that the poorer classes bear the chief burden of our customhouse taxation. The tax upon incomes is levied according to ability to pay, and it would be difficult to devise a tax fairer or cheaper of collection" (House Committee on Ways and Means, *Report of the Committee on Ways and Means,* 63d Cong., 1st sess., 1913, H. Rept. 63–5, 37).

5. "Equality of taxation, therefore, as a maxim of politics, means equality of sacrifice. It means apportioning the contribution of each person towards the expenses of government, so that he shall feel neither more nor less inconvenience from his share of the payment than every other person experiences from his" (John Stuart Mill, *Principles of Political Economy: With Some of Their Applications to Social Philosophy,* 398).

6. *Cong. Rec.,* 53d Cong., 2d sess., 1894, 26, pt. 2:1731.

7. Ibid., 1605 (incorporating remarks of University of Wisconsin economist Richard T. Ely). In the following example, Williams illustrates what constitutes "inequality of sacrifice": "Suppose you levy an income tax of 10 per cent upon the man who has an income of $100, upon the man who has $5,000, and upon the man who has an income of $100,000. What have you done? You have taken from the man with $100 income, $10, but what have you taken? Not money, but what money could buy, and what he would have bought with it. You have taken from him fuel, flannels, medicines—the necessaries of life. Suppose you take $500 from the man who has an income of $5,000. What have you taken? You have taken from that man some of the comforts of life, a higher degree of education for his children perhaps, lithographs or engravings, books that he might have wanted. That is his sacrifice. It is a sacrifice of comforts, of refinements of life, but not of prime necessaries. Suppose you take $10,000 from the man in possession of a hundred thousands dollars a year. What have you taken from him? Not necessaries, not comforts, not even refinements, but luxuries. I might go further and say you have simply taxed out of his surplus, over and above luxuries even, a part of what was his, for purposes of display or of charity" (ibid., 1606).

8. Ibid., 1617.

9. "[I]t is in the interest of the public quiet, and by consequence it concerns the duty of the magistrate, to see that the public burthens be equally borne. . . . Now in this place we understand an equality, not of money, but of burthen; that is to say, an equality of reason between the burthens and the benefits" (Thomas Hobbes, *De Cive* [1642], pt. 7, p. 11).

10. *Cong. Rec.,* 53d Cong., 2d sess., 1894, 26, pt. 2:1566. In a similar vein, Illinois Democrat Edward Lane remarked: "Every just citizen should be willing to pay his just proportion for the expenses of the Government, and the rich requiring more protection than the poor, should be willing to pay more than the poor. I regard the income tax the fairest form of taxation, for it makes every one contribute to the wants of the state in proportion to the revenue he enjoys under its protection" (ibid., 1755). Adding a political-economy twist to the argument was Illinois Democrat James Williams: "So bold and daring has accumulated wealth become in its efforts to control the affairs of our Government, until to-day there is nothing in my judgment which so threatens the rights and liberties of the American people as these rising pyramids of fortune. . . . Now, sir, if wealth is to have such representation, why should it not have its fair share of taxation? If wealth has become such a power in the politics of our country; if wealth, centralized wealth, is able to substitute itself for statesmanship, enter the halls of legislation and other high positions of public trust, where it may wield a mighty influence in its own behalf, why, in the name of all that is just, should it not pay a reasonable rate of taxation?" (ibid., pt. 9:213).

11. Ibid., pt. 9:185.

12. Ibid., 276–77. Asked Illinois Democrat James Williams: "Why should not men pay taxes in proportion to the amount of property which they enjoy under our Government? What is government for but to protect life, liberty, and property? What does it cost to protect the property of the poor man whose all is less than $1,000, as compared with the amount that it costs to protect the property of the great railroad king whose possessions reach from one ocean to the other, and who is furnished a court in every locality in which to litigate his rights and the rights of those he wrongs? What does it cost to protect the property of the farmers of Illinois, as compared with that

which it costs to protect the vast accumulations of property gathered from the earnings of the people by the millionaires of New England?" (ibid., 212).

Referring to Holmes's statistical report on rich and poor families, Nebraska Democrat William Jennings Bryan queried: "Is it unfair or unjust that the burden of taxation shall be equalized between these two classes? Who is it most needs a navy? Is it the farmer who plods along behind the plow upon his farm, or is it the man whose property is situated in some great seaport where it could be reached by an enemy's guns? Who demands a standing army? Is it the poor man as he goes about his work, or is it the capitalist who wants that army to supplement the local government in protecting his property when he enters into a contest with his employees? For whom are the great expenses of the Federal Government incurred? Why, sir, when we ask that this small pittance shall be contributed to the expenses of the Federal Government, we are asking less than is just rather than more" (ibid., pt. 2:1657). Cf. the statement of Illinois Democrat Robert Fowler in the Sixty-third Congress: "A tariff tax carries with it burdens and benefits. Only those who have property on which a tariff can be laid can ever hope to share in the benefits. So the producer of raw material and the producer of the finished product are the only classes who can hope to share in the benefits of such taxation. But the toiling millions, constituting more than three-fourths of the population of this country, bear the great burdens of taxation, and yet they never have had an opportunity to share in the benefits of such taxation. The income tax stands out like a great emancipator, with a proclamation to the world declaring that the time has come when the unequal burdens of taxation shall no longer rest upon the shoulders of the laboring classes of this country, but that, instead thereof, these burdens shall be placed upon the backs of the rich" *(Cong. Rec.*, 63d Cong., 1st sess., 1913, 50, pt. 2:1250).

13. Although it also may be said that partnerships derived many of the same benefits, members of the Fifty-third Congress offered no similar arguments in favor of taxing the partnership.

14. H. Rept. 53–276, 3. Committee member William Jennings Bryan commented: "I need not give all the reasons which led the committee to recommend this tax, but will suggest two of the most important. The stockholder in a corporation limits his liability. When the statute creating the corporation is fully complied with the individual stockholder is secure, except to the extent fixed by the statute, whereas the entire property of the individual is ordinarily liable for his debts. Another reason is that corporations enjoy certain privileges and franchises. Some are given the right of eminent domain, while others, such as street-car companies are given the right to use the streets of the city—a franchise which increases in value with each passing year. Corporations occupy the time and attention of our Federal courts and enjoy the protection of the Federal Government, and as they do not ordinarily pay taxes the committee felt justified in proposing a light tax on them" *(Cong. Rec.,* 53d Cong., 2d sess., 1894, 26, pt. 2:1655). In a similar vein, Senator Vest argued: "[C]orporations, in consideration of their corporate privileges and the protection given to their property, should bear their proportion of this common tax placed upon all the people of the United States" (ibid., pt. 7:6866).

15. Of course, the problem with this argument is that it erroneously assumes that "state" and "federal government" are one and the same. In the socioinstitutional view, "state" refers to the collective and objectified will of members of the polity; "federal government" refers to the administrative apparatus of the state. The raison d'être of the federal government is to serve the state.

16. *Cong. Rec.,* 53d Cong., 2d sess., 1894, 26, pt. 2:6618. On the benefit principle as applied to corporations, Hill argued: "The theory that the General Government . . . protects corporations, that the General Government gives them powers and privileges, is a mere fiction. The General Government can not punish crime in the State; it can not interfere with the local government, because it has no jurisdiction. . . . The State governments, therefore, are the authorities to regulate corporations; are in the main the proper authorities to tax them" (ibid., 6873). See also ibid., pt. 4:3558, pt. 7:6619.

17. Ibid., pt. 7:6866.

18. Ibid., pt. 9:305.

19. Ibid., pt. 2:1650. In a similar vein, Pennsylvania Democrat Frank Beltzhoover remarked: "An income tax is an imposition on energy, enterprise, and accumulation—the greatest of all the sinews of wealth, power, and progress in the Republic. It is an insidious and communistic leveler which exacts sufficient penalty from the thrifty, sober and laborious to make up for the delinquencies of the idle dissolute and improvident" (ibid., 1298).

20. Ibid., 1648.

21. Ibid., pt. 7:6767. Remarked Republican senator Jacob Gallinger of New Hampshire: "Mr. President, we have heard a great deal in this discussion from our Populist friends in regard to the accumulation of wealth and the necessity for distributing the wealth of the country. . . . I should like to ask the question, if the wealth of this country were equally distributed to-day how could we possibly keep it distributed?" (ibid., 6771).

22. Ibid., pt. 4:3559, pt. 7:6620. Declared New Jersey Democrat James Smith: "Discrimination between classes or individuals in apportioning the burdens of government is manifestly unjust. And that this scheme does make such discrimination in the most wanton manner does not admit of question. As between individuals it exempts the man who earns $75 a week and taxes the man who earns $80 a week. Then, if by harder work he can increase his income to $100 a week, he must pay $24 for the privilege, and ever thereafter one-fiftieth part of all that he receives in excess of $4,000" (ibid., pt. 4:3780).

23. Ibid., pt. 9:439. Asked Kansas Populist William Baker: "Why are the strong more successful in accumulating wealth than the weak? Many reasons might be given, but the two principal ones are natural abilities and greater opportunities. The state is not responsible for the ability of her subjects, but she is for their opportunities, for their education, and for the development of their God-given powers" (ibid., 503).

24. Ibid., 207, 397.

25. Ibid., pt. 4:3560. Seconded Senator Smith: "Neither the President of the United States, nor the Supreme Court, nor the Senate, nor the House of Representatives, nor all combined have authority equal to this. Understand: The deputy collector or agent, a local politician inevitably, 'may increase the amount of any list or return if he has reason to believe that the same is understated.' What 'reason' is required to enable a representative of the United States to thus pronounce a citizen guilty of perjury? Only that which is sufficient unto himself. Nothing more. It may be the libel of a rival. It may be a personal grudge. It may be refusal to contribute to a campaign fund. The officer is the judge" (ibid., 3784). The Committee on Ways and Means addressed the first of these issues by adding to the Wilson Bill a provision that would subject any agent who improperly disclosed taxpayer information to removal, plus fine or imprisonment. See

H. Rept. 53–276, 3; and *Wilson-Gorman Tariff Act of 1894,* chap. 349, sec. 3167. By all indications, the committee did not address the second of these issues.

26. Reported the Committee on Ways and Means: "Of course the collection of any tax presupposes inquiry into the value of the thing taxed. Without this no tax, whether governmental or State, could be collected, and if all taxes are to be abolished which make inquiry into the nature and value of the estate of the taxpayer, the vocation of the tax-gatherer must cease" (H. Rept. 53–276, 3). Added committee member Tarsney: "Mr. Chairman, another objection urged against this measure is that it is harsh and drastic in the provisions for its administration and enforcement; that it is inquisitorial in its character. What tax measure is not? What would be the value of a measure imposing taxes that did not provide administrative details and compulsory methods for ascertaining what should be paid or that omitted to provide means to enforce payment? What idealist has yet dreamed of a government supported by the voluntary contributions of its citizens? What theoretical statesman has suggested that each and every citizen, without coercion or the compelling force of law, will voluntarily contribute his just share of the cost of the support of his government?" *(Cong. Rec.,* 53d Cong., 2d sess., 1894, 26, pt. 9:185).

27. *Cong. Rec.,* 53d Cong., 2d sess., 1894, 26, pt. 9:298. Kem added: "In my opinion, the more searching the law the better; the more wealth will be driven from under cover and compelled to bear its part of the burden. . . . Without inquiry no tax can be properly levied" (ibid.).

28. With considerable foresight, Senator Hill argued that individuals could successfully evade the tax by inflating their operating expenses and by engaging in related-party transactions. "Is there reason why a gentleman of wealth with a great stock farm, having a large family of boys coming up between 18 and 25 years of age shall not give them a large salary upon the ground of services rendered in the raising of cattle, in the raising of wool, in the raising of cotton? Can he not give his wife a salary too? Can he not give it to his hired man, his nephew, living with him? Can he not have an arrangement with those people whereby he has some drawbacks?" (ibid., pt. 7:6766).

29. Milliken added: "Taking this fact for an excuse, how much taxable property do you think capitalists will remove beyond the reach of all taxation if this law shall be enacted? They may remove it out of the country or dispose of it in other ways" (ibid., pt. 9:306).

30. Ibid., pt. 4:3784.

31. Remarked Illinois Democrat James Williams: "But they say this will lead to fraud, and tempt these poor infants of morality into perjuring their own souls in order to evade the payment of such taxes. My answer is, if in the enforcement of this law we find those who are so unscrupulous and dishonest as to swear falsely in order to beat the Government out of that which is just, send them, as you would other rascals, to the penitentiary" (ibid., pt. 9:213). Commented Ways and Means Committee member William Jennings Bryan: "Instead of abandoning just measures for fear somebody will perjure himself, let them be enacted into law, and then if anyone perjures himself we can treat him like any other felon, and punish him for his perjury" (ibid., pt. 2:1657). Omer Kem added: "But, says one, it is a breeder of perjurers, makes liars of men, and is therefore a corrupter of morals. Allow me to say in reply that the individual who is only waiting for an opportunity to perjure himself is already a perjurer" (ibid., pt. 9:297).

32. Ibid., pt. 9:186. Stated Georgia Democrat John Maddox: "Yet it is a fact that one of the main objections urged against this bill is that the tax can not be collected; that it will be evaded. Is there any law in existence or has there ever been one that was not violated? Murder is a crime and

against the law of both God and man, and yet these laws are violated every day, and so are hundreds of other statutes violated and evaded, but a man who would undertake to repeal these laws because they are violated or evaded would have up-hill business" (ibid., pt. 2:1667). Finance Committee chairman Voorhees added: "We are gravely informed that such a tax can not be collected because of the wholesale perjury which income owners will commit in order to evade the law. . . . If the criminal classes of the country or those of assumed respectability can defeat the enactment of laws by threatening to commit crime in their violation, then, indeed, have we have reached a depth of degradation far beyond the hand or the power of resurrection" (ibid., pt. 4:3398).

33. On its being a "direct tax," see ibid., pt. 2:1643–44 (statement of Bartlett), 1653 (statement of Johnson), pt. 4:3561 (statement of Hill), pt. 7:6627 (statement of Higgins), and 6638 (statement of Hoar). On its being sectional, see ibid., pt. 4:3562 (statement of Hill), 3780 (statement of Smith), pt. 7:6627 (statement of Higgins), and 6630 (statement of Hoar). On being unnecessary in a time of peace, see ibid., pt. 4:3778 (statement of Smith), pt. 7:6619 (statement of Hill), and pt. 9:306 (speech of Milliken).

34. 102 U.S. 586 (1880).

35. *Cong. Rec.,* 53d Cong., 2d sess., 1894, 26, pt. 7:6707.

36. As discussed in the epilogue, many of the same arguments were propounded in the income tax debates of 1909 and 1913.

37. See ibid., 4:3564–65.

38. Ibid., 3565.

39. Ibid., 3564, pt. 7:6616.

40. H. Rept. 53–276, 2. Significantly, the committee's view of a consumption tax emphasizes the present *demand* for goods and services and the future *demand* for labor. By contrast, Hill's view of a consumption tax emphasizes the present *supply* of capital and the future *supply* of goods and services. Likewise, the committee's objection to a consumption tax emphasizes *subjective need;* in other words, the tax fails to adequately address the individual's need to consume basic commodities. By contrast, Hill's support for a consumption tax emphasizes *objective result;* in other words, the tax burdens all citizens without discrimination.

6. Pollock

1. The account that follows is based on reports, for the days of the hearing, from the *Chicago Daily Tribune, New York Sun, New York Daily Tribune, New York World,* and *Washington Post.* For an analysis of the *Pollock* decision, see Blakey and Blakey, *The Federal Income Tax;* Edward S. Corwin, *Court over Constitution: A Study of Judicial Review as an Instrument of Popular Government,* esp. chap. 4; Henry H. Ingersoll, *The Revolution of 20th May 1985: Read Before Tennessee Bar Association, July 19, 1895;* Sidney Ratner, *American Taxation: Its History as a Social Force in Democracy,* esp. chap. 10; Stanley, *Dimensions of Law;* and Arnold M. Paul, *Conservative Crisis and the Rule of Law,* esp. chaps. 7 and 9.

2. Robert T. Swaine, *The Cravath Firm and Its Predecessors,* 519–20.

3. *New York Sun,* Dec. 18, 1894, and *Cincinnati Commercial Gazette,* May 18, 1895, as quoted in ibid., 518–19; editorial, *New York World,* May 21, 1895, 4.

4. Swaine, *Cravath Firm,* 520–21.

5. Motion to Advance, in the Supreme Court of the United States, October Term 1894, *Charles Pollock v. Farmers' Loan & Trust Company,* no. 893; and *Lewis H. Hyde v. The Continental Trust Company,* no. 894, 4, 6–8.

6. See Swaine, *Cravath Firm,* 521. It was an unauthorized agreement that would ultimately cost Maxwell his job (ibid.).

7. Under the provision of an 1891 procedural statute, U.S. district court decisions involving a constitutional question could be appealed directly to the Supreme Court. See *U.S. Statutes at Large* 26 (1891): 826, 827–28. This provision was repealed in 1925. See *U.S. Statutes at Large* 43 (1925): 936.

8. *Pollock v. Farmers' Loan & Trust Company,* 158 U.S. 601 (1895).

9. See Ingersoll, *Revolution of 20th May 1895,* 7; and "The Law Swept Away," *Washington Post,* May 21, 1895, 1.

10. See *Pollock v. Farmers' Loan & Trust Company,* 158 U.S. 601, 618–21, 626–27, 629, 633, 637 (1895).

11. See ibid., 621–25, 630, 634–35.

12. See ibid., 632.

13. See ibid., 636–37.

14. Ingersoll, *Revolution of 20th May 1895,* 8.

15. Arnold M. Paul, *Conservative Crisis,* 2, 4–5. Corwin presents a more cynical view: "The real motive of the Court in the Pollock Case was to convert the 'direct tax' clauses *into positive protections of wealth.* That is just what Mr. Choate contended they were meant to be, and a majority of the Justices agreed with him" *(Court over Constitution,* 192). In a subsequent passage, he notes, "In a word, the Court ceased to be a part of the democratic process for the time being, and set itself against that process, in behalf of a powerful interest which deserved no such intervention" (ibid., 209).

16. See Stanley, *Dimensions of Law,* 138–39, 141, 155–56, 163, 171, 173–74.

17. Editorial, *New York World,* Apr. 12, 1895, 4.

18. Ibid.; editorial, *Richmond Dispatch,* as quoted in "The Income-Tax Decision," *New York World,* May 23, 1895, 4; editorial, *St. Louis Post-Dispatch,* as quoted in ibid.; editorial, *Syracuse News,* as quoted in ibid. For detailed accounts of public reaction to the *Pollock* decision, see Ratner, *American Taxation,* 214; and Stanley, *Dimensions of Law,* 165–69. Additional press reports relating to the *Pollock* decision are found in *Public Opinion* 18 (1895): 563, 594–96.

19. "New-Yorkers Pleased," *New York Daily Tribune,* May 21, 1895, 3.

20. First paragraph of quote: "Speech of Senator Hill," *New York Sun,* May 25, 1895, 2. Subsequent paragraphs: "Senator Hill Gratified," *New York Daily Tribune,* May 21, 1895, 3; "Senator Hill Gratified," *New York Sun,* May 21, 1895, 2; "Hill Highly Pleased," *Washington Post,* May 21, 1895, 1.

21. Editorial, *New York Sun,* May 21, 1895, 6.

Epilogue: The Vitality of Ideas

1. See Blakey and Blakey, *The Federal Income Tax,* 22; and Hull, *Memoirs of Hull,* 48.

2. See Hull, *Memoirs of Hull,* 49. "This new tax was wholly indispensable in time of war

while, by lifting vast tax burdens in consumption taxes from the backs of the poor and the masses generally, it became the one great equalizer of the tax burden and therefore a tremendous agency for the improvement of social conditions" (ibid., 71).

3. Ibid., 58.

4. See ibid., 70–71; *Cong. Rec.,* 63d Cong., 1st sess., 1913, 50, pt. 2:1254 (statement of Tavenner), pt. 4:3766 (statement of Williams), pt. 7:90 (speech of Moore); Blakey and Blakey, *The Federal Income Tax,* 74; and Ratner, *American Taxation,* 272, 324.

5. See U.S. Senate, *Opinion of the Honorable John K. Shields,* 14; and Hull, *Memoirs of Hull,* 48. For references to the 1894 tax in the 1913 debates, see *Cong. Rec.,* 63d Cong., 1st sess., 1913, 50, pt. 2:1251 (statement of Palmer), 1257 (statement of Scott), and 1309 (statement of Rupley).

6. For example, remarked Illinois Democrat Robert Fowler on May 6, 1913: "The man who is the most able to pay has escaped the burden of high taxation, and the man who is the least able to pay is carrying its greatest burden. . . . The income tax stands out like a great emancipator, with a proclamation to the world declaring that the time has come when the unequal burdens of taxation shall no longer rest upon the shoulders of the laboring classes of this country, but that, instead thereof, these burdens shall be placed where they properly belong—upon the backs of the rich" (*Cong. Rec.,* 63d Cong., 1st sess., 1913, 50, pt. 2:1250). See also ibid., pt. 4:3807 (statement of Borah) and 3812 (statement of Works); and H. Rept. 63–5, 37.

7. See *Tariff Act of 1913,* chap. 16, sec. E, *U.S. Statutes at Large* 38 (1913): 114, 115.

8. *Cong. Rec.,* 63d Cong., 1st sess., 1913, 50, pt. 2:1252 (statement of Murdock). See also Ratner, *American Taxation,* 307–8.

9. H. Rept. 63–5, 37.

10. *Cong. Rec.,* 63d Cong., 1st sess., 1913, 50, pt. 2:1253 (statement of Tavenner). See also ibid., pt. 4:3820 (statements of Borah and La Follette) and 4082 (statement of Lewis).

11. Ibid., 3772 (statement of Williams). See also ibid., pt. 2:1250 (statement of Fowler) and 1252 (statement of Kelly).

12. See Blakey and Blakey, *The Federal Income Tax,* 30; and Ratner, *American Taxation,* 282.

13. In 1909, President Taft utilized the window of opportunity created by *Pollock* to propose an unapportioned "excise tax" on corporate earnings. See "Message from William H. Taft to the Senate and House of Representatives, June 16, 1909," in *Cong. Rec.,* 61st Cong., 1st sess., 1909, 44, pt. 4:3344–45. On the Republican attempt to preempt passage of a comprehensive tax package, see ibid., 3929 (statement of Aldrich); Blakey and Blakey, *The Federal Income Tax,* 40; and Ratner, *American Taxation,* 285–86.

14. As suggested in the following dialogue on the floor of the Sixty-first Congress, between Democratic senator Benjamin Shively of Indiana and Republican senator Elihu Root of New York: "Mr. Shively: 'Then, to speak accurately, the tax is exactly the same in substance and result in both cases [that is, the Corporations Tax of 1909 and the Income Tax of 1894], and only the peculiar language of the statute describing it differentiates this amendment . . . from the Pollock case?' Mr. Root: 'Precisely' " (*Cong. Rec.,* 61st Cong., 1st sess., 1909, 44, 4:4016). Root served as chairman of the Finance Committee.

15. See Blakey and Blakey, *The Federal Income Tax,* 47–50; and Ratner, *American Taxation,* 287. The Corporations Tax of 1909 imposed a 1 percent "excise" on the net income of all corporations organized for profit and doing business in the United States. These corporations were al-

lowed five deductions: for all ordinary and necessary business expenses; business losses; interest paid; federal, state, and local taxes; and dividends received. The most significant difference between the Republican-sponsored 1909 scheme and the Democrat-sponsored 1894 scheme was a $5,000 corporate exemption provided in the former scheme. See *Payne-Aldrich Tariff Act of 1909,* chap. 6, secs. 38–39, *U.S. Statutes at Large* 36 (1909): 11, 112.

16. See Blakey and Blakey, *The Federal Income Tax,* 60–61; and Ratner, *American Taxation,* 298.

17. On Taft's proposal, see Ratner, *American Taxation,* 298; and Blakey and Blakey, *The Federal Income Tax,* 60. On the ratification process, see Blakey and Blakey, *The Federal Income Tax,* 68; and Ratner, *American Taxation,* 304–7. On institution of the new tax and the merger, see *Cong. Rec.,* 63d Cong., 1st sess., 1913, 50, pt. 4:3773 (statement of Williams).

18. See Blakey and Blakey, *The Federal Income Tax,* 77–94; and Ratner, *American Taxation,* 327.

19. *Cong. Rec.,* 53d Cong., 2d sess., 1894, 26, pt. 6:5519.

20. Ibid., pt. 9:467.

21. Moreover, to the extent that the pretax cost of dutiable merchandise fell, import duties, being specific, absorbed a greater proportion of this cost. On the wage and price declines of 1878 and 1893, see Fels, *American Business Cycles,* 90, 109–10, 162–63, 188–91.

22. Blakey and Blakey, *The Federal Income Tax,* 1; Ratner, *American Taxation,* 13–17.

23. According to data compiled by Witte, the percentage of federal revenues raised from customs duties and excise taxes fell from more than 80 percent in 1914 to less than 10 percent in 1980; the percentage of revenues raised from income taxation rose from roughly 2 percent in 1914 to about 60 percent in 1980. See Witte, *Politics and Development,* 80. According to Brownlee, the percentage of general revenues raised from indirect taxes (principally, the tariff) fell from almost 75 percent in 1902 to about 25 percent in the 1920s; during the same period, the percentage of revenues raised from income taxation rose from nil to nearly 50 percent ("Tax Regimes," in *Modern American State,* 69).

24. *Cong. Rec.,* 63d Cong., 1st sess., 1913, 50, pt. 4:3772. Remarked Senator Borah on Aug. 27, 1913: "I am not in favor of trying to equalize the fortunes of this country through taxation. I am not in favor of punishing people who, through one method or another, have acquired fortunes which it is almost beyond man's mental conception to measure. . . . But it is a known rule of taxation, and one which we profess to follow, that men ought to pay taxes in accordance with their ability to pay, or pay them on the principle of causing them the least possible inconvenience when they part with their money" (ibid., 3807). See also *Cong. Rec.,* 53d Cong., 2d sess., 1894, 26, pt. 2:1730 (statement of Hall).

Appendix B: *Pollock v. Farmers' Loan & Trust Company*

1. By Mr. Worthington C. Ford in The Nation, April 25, 1895; republished in 51 Albany Law Journal, 292.

Bibliography

Records

Cleveland, Grover. Papers. Washington, D.C.: Library of Congress, 1958 (microfilm).

Congressional Directory. Washington, D.C.: Government Printing Office, 1893 (Fifty-second Congress); 1894 (Fifty-third Congress); 1909 (Sixty-first Congress); 1913 (Sixty-third Congress).

The Congressional Globe. Washington, D.C.: Congressional Globe Office, 1862 (Thirty-seventh Congress); 1864 (Thirty-eighth Congress); 1866 (Thirty-ninth Congress).

Congressional Record. Washington, D.C.: Government Printing Office, 1893–1894 (Fifty-third Congress); 1895 (Fifty-fourth Congress); 1909 (Sixty-first Congress); 1913 (Sixty-third Congress).

U.S. Supreme Court Briefs and Records. Washington, D.C.: [The Court?], 1895 (microfilm).

United States Congressional Serial Set. Washington, D.C.: Government Printing Office, 1893–1895 (committee reports, tax-related documents).

Books

Beth, Laren P. *John Marshall Harlan: The Last Whig Justice.* Lexington: Univ. Press of Kentucky, 1992.

Blackford, Mansel G., and K. Austin Kerr. *Business Enterprise in American History.* 2d ed. Boston: Houghton Mifflin, 1990.

Blakey, Roy G., and Gladys C. Blakey. *The Federal Income Tax.* New York: Longmans, Green, 1940.

Brown, Henry Billings. *Memoir of Henry Billings Brown: Late Justice of the Supreme Court of the United States: Consisting of an Autobiography.* New York: Duffield, 1915.

Brownlee, W. Elliot. *Dynamics of Ascent: A History of the American Economy.* 2d ed. New York: Knopf, 1979.

———. *Federal Taxation in America: A Short History.* Washington, D.C.: Woodrow Wilson Center Press; Cambridge: Cambridge Univ. Press, 1996.

———, ed. *Funding the Modern American State, 1941–95.* Washington, D.C.: Woodrow Wilson Center Press; Cambridge: Cambridge Univ. Press, 1996.

Buenker, John D. *The Adoption of the Income Tax Amendment: Urban Liberalism and Progressive Reform.* New York: Norton, 1973.

———. *The Income Tax and the Progressive Era.* New York: Garland, 1985.

Coletta, Paolo E. *William Jennings Bryan.* Vol. 1, *Political Evangelist, 1860–1908.* Lincoln: Univ. of Nebraska Press, 1964.

Corwin, Edward S. *Court over Constitution: A Study of Judicial Review as an Instrument of Popular Government.* New York: P. Smith, 1938.

Ely, Richard Theodore. *An Introduction to Political Economy.* New York: Swan, Sonnenschein, 1891.

———. *Taxation in American States and Cities.* New York: Crowell, 1888.

Evans, George Heberton, Jr. *Business Incorporations in the United States.* New York: National Bureau of Economic Research, 1948.

Faulkner, Harold Underwood. *American Economic History.* 7th ed. New York: Harper, 1954.

———. *Politics, Reform, and Expansion, 1890–1900.* New York: Harper, 1959.

Fels, Rendigs. *American Business Cycles, 1865–1897.* Chapel Hill: Univ. of North Carolina Press, 1959.

Foster, Roger, and Everett V. Abbot. *A Treatise on the Federal Income Tax of 1894.* Boston: Boston Book, 1895.

Friedman, Lawrence M. *A History of American Law.* New York: Simon and Schuster, 1973.

Friedman, Leon, and Fred L. Israel, eds. *The Justices of the United States Supreme Court: Their Lives and Major Opinions, 1789–1969.* New York: Chelsea House in Association with Bowker, 1969.

Furer, Howard B. *The Fuller Court, 1888–1910.* Millwood, N.Y.: Associated Faculty Press, 1986.

Hacker, Louis M. *The Course of American Economic Growth and Development.* New York: Wiley, 1970.

Hall, Kermit L., ed. *The Oxford Companion to the Supreme Court of the United States.* New York: Oxford Univ. Press, 1992.

Heilbroner, Robert L., and Aaron Singer. *The Economic Transformation of America: 1600 to the Present.* New York: Harcourt Brace Jovanovich, 1977.

Highsaw, Robert B. *Edward Douglas White: Defender of the Conservative Faith.* Baton Rouge: Louisiana State Univ. Press, 1981.

Hobbes, Thomas. *De Cive.* Oxford: Clarendon Press, 1983.

Hoffman, Charles. *The Depression of the Nineties: An Economic History.* Westport, Conn.: Greenwood, 1970.

Hughes, Charles Evans. *The Supreme Court of the United States.* New York: Columbia Univ. Press, 1928.

Hull, Cordell. *The Memoirs of Cordell Hull.* New York: Macmillan, 1948.

Ingersoll, Henry H. *Revolution of 20th May, 1895: Read Before Tennessee Bar Association, July 19, 1895.* N.p., 1895.

Johnson, Donald B., ed. *National Party Platforms.* Rev. ed. Urbana: Univ. of Illinois Press, 1978.

Josephson, Matthew. *The Politicos.* New York: Harcourt, Brace, 1938.

King, Willard L. *Melville Weston Fuller: Chief Justice of the United States, 1888–1910.* New York: Macmillan, 1950.

———. *The Wealth and Income of the People of the United States.* New York: Macmillan, 1915.

Klinkhamer, Marie Carolyn (Sister). *Edward Douglas White: Chief Justice of the United States.* Washington, D.C.: Catholic Univ. of America Press, 1943.

Koenig, Louis William. *A Political Biography of William Jennings Bryan.* New York: Putnam, 1971.

Kurland, Philip B., and Gerhard Casper, eds. *Landmark Briefs and Arguments of the Supreme Court of the United States: Constitutional Law.* Vol. 12, *Pollock v. Farmers' Loan and Trust Co. (1895).* Arlington, Va.: Univ. Publications of America, 1975.

Latham, Frank B. *The Great Dissenter: John Marshall Harlan, 1833–1911.* New York: Cowles Book, 1970.

Martha, Rutsel Silvestre. *The Jurisdiction to Tax in International Law: Theory and Practice of Legislative Fiscal Jurisdiction.* Boston: Kluwer Law and Taxation Publishers, 1989.

Martin, Edward S. *The Life of Joseph Hodges Choate.* New York: C. Scribner's Sons, 1920.

Mill, John Stuart. *Principles of Political Economy: With Some of Their Applications to Social Philosophy.* 7th ed. New York: D. Appleton, 1896.

The National Cyclopaedia of American Biography: Being the History of the United States As Illustrated in the Lives of the Founders, Builders, and Defenders of the Republic. New York: J. T. White, 1898.

Nevins, Allan. *Grover Cleveland.* New York: Macmillan, 1936.

———, ed. *Letters of Grover Cleveland, 1850–1908.* Boston: Houghton Mifflin, 1933.

Paddock, Lisa. *Facts about the Supreme Court of the United States.* New York: H. W. Wilson, 1996.

Paul, Arnold M. *Conservative Crisis and the Rule of Law.* Ithaca: American Historical Association, Cornell Univ. Press, 1960.

Paul, Randolph E. *Taxation in the United States.* Boston: Little, Brown, 1954.

Perry, Arthur Latham. *Principles of Political Economy.* New York: Scribner's Sons, 1891.

Porter, Glenn. *The Rise of Big Business, 1860–1920.* 2d ed. Arlington Heights, Ill.: Harlan Davidson, 1992.

Ratner, Sidney. *American Taxation: Its History as a Social Force in Democracy.* New York: Norton, 1942.

———. *Taxation and Democracy in America.* New York: Wiley, 1967.

Schlesinger, Arthur M., Jr., and Fred L. Israel, eds. *History of American Presidential Elections, 1789–2001.* Philadelphia: Chelsea House Publishers, 2001.

Seligman, Edwin R. A. *Double Taxation and International Fiscal Cooperation.* New York: Macmillan, 1928.

———. *The Income Tax: A Study of the History, Theory, and Practice of Income Taxation at Home and Abroad.* New York: Macmillan, 1914.

———. *Studies in Public Finance.* New York: Macmillan, 1925.

Semonche, John E. *Charting the Future: The Supreme Court Responds to a Changing Society, 1890–1920.* Westport, Conn.: Greenwood, 1978.

Shils, Edward A., and Henry A. Finch, trans. and eds. *Max Weber: The Methodology of the Social Sciences.* Glencoe, Ill.: Free Press, 1949.

Shiras, George. *Justice George Shiras, Jr., of Pittsburgh: Associate Justice of the United States Supreme Court, 1892–1903.* Pittsburgh: Univ. of Pittsburgh Press, 1953.

Simons, Henry. *Personal Income Taxation.* Chicago: Univ. of Chicago Press, 1938.

Smith, Adam. *An Inquiry into the Nature and Causes of the Wealth of Nations.* London: W. Strahan and T. Caddell, 1776.

Sobel, Robert, and John Raimo, eds. *Biographical Directory of the Governors of the United States, 1789–1978.* Westport, Conn.: Meckler Books, 1978.

Stanley, Robert. *Dimensions of Law in the Service of Order.* New York: Oxford Univ. Press, 1993.

Strong, Theron George. *Joseph H. Choate: New Englander, New Yorker, Lawyer, Ambassador.* New York: Dodd, Mead, 1917.

Sumner, William Graham. *Science of Society.* New Haven: Yale Univ. Press, 1927.

Swaine, Robert T. *The Cravath Firm and Its Predecessors.* 1946. Reprint, New York: privately printed at Ad Press, 1948.

Swisher, Carl B. *American Constitutional Development.* Boston: Houghton Mifflin, 1954.

———. *Historic Decisions of the Supreme Court.* New York: Van Nostrand Reinhold, 1969.

———. *Stephen J. Field: Craftsman of the Law.* Washington, D.C.: Brookings Institution, 1930.

Taussig, Frank W. *The Tariff History of the United States.* 6th ed. New York: G. P. Putnam's Sons, 1914.

Walker, Francis Amasa. *Political Economy.* New York: H. Holt, 1883.

Waltman, Jerold L. *Political Origins of the U.S. Income Tax.* Jackson: Univ. Press of Mississippi, 1985.

Warren, Charles. *The Supreme Court in United States History.* Boston: Little, Brown, 1928.

Whitten, David O. *The Emergence of Giant Enterprise, 1860–1914.* Westport, Conn.: Greenwood, 1983.

Who Was Who in America. Chicago: Marquis–Who's Who, 1966.

Wilson, James G., and John Fiske, eds. *Appleton's Cyclopaedia of American Biography.* New York: D. Appleton, 1888–1901.

Witte, John F. *The Politics and Development of the Federal Income Tax.* Madison: Univ. of Wisconsin Press, 1985.

Yarbrough, Tinsley E. *Judicial Enigma: The First Justice Harlan.* New York: Oxford Univ. Press, 1995.

Articles

Adams, T. S. "Ideals and Idealism in Taxation." *American Economic Review* 18 (1928): 1.

Brownlee, W. Elliot. "The Transformation of the Tax System and the Experts, 1870–1930." *National Tax Journal* 32 (1979): 47.

Dunbar, Charles F. "The New Income Tax." *Quarterly Journal of Economics* 9 (1894): 26.

Farrelly, David G. "Justice Harlan's Dissent in the Pollock Case." *Southern California Law Review* 24 (1951): 175.

Fels, Rendigs. "American Business Cycles, 1865–79." *American Economic Review* 41 (1951): 325.

Graetz, Michael J. "The 'Original Intent' of U.S. International Taxation." *Duke Law Journal* 46: 1021.

Green, Robert A. "The Future of Source-Based Taxation of the Income of Multinational Enterprises." *Cornell Law Review* 79 (1993): 18.

Guthrie, William D. "The Income Tax Cases." *American Lawyer* 3 (1895): 239.

Holmes, George K. "The Concentration of Wealth." *Political Science Quarterly* 8, no. 4 (1893): 589.

Kaufman, Nancy H. "Fairness and the Taxation of International Income." *Law and Policy in International Business* (1998): 145.

Miller, A. C. "National Finance and the Income Tax." *Journal of Political Economy* 3, no. 3 (1895): 255.

Public Opinion. Washington, D.C.: Public Opinion. Various articles from vol. 15 (Apr.–Oct. 1893) and vol. 16 (Oct. 1893–Apr. 1894).

Rezneck, Samuel. "Unemployment, Unrest, and Relief in the United States During the Depression of 1893–97." *Journal of Political Economy* 61, no. 4 (1953): 324.

Schumpeter, Joseph. "The Crisis of the Tax State." In *The Economics and Sociology of Capitalism,* edited by Richard Swedberg. Princeton: Princeton Univ. Press, 1991.

Seligman, Edwin R. A. "Is the Income Tax Constitutional and Just?" *Forum* 19 (1895): 48.

———. "The Theory of Progressive Taxation." *Political Science Quarterly* 8 (1893): 220.

Sewell, Robert. "The Income Tax: Is It Constitutional?" *American Law Review* 28 (1894): 808.

Shearman, Thomas G. "The Owners of the United States." *Forum* (Nov. 1889): 262.

Soltow, Lee. "Evidence on Income Equality in the United States, 1866–1965." *Journal of Economic History* 29 (1969): 279.

Tunnell, George. "Legislative History of the Second Income-Tax Law." *Journal of Political Economy* 3, no. 3 (1895): 311.

Wells, David A. "An Income Tax: Is It Desirable?" *Forum* 17 (1893): 1.

———. "Is the Existing Income Tax Unconstitutional?" *Forum* 18 (1895): 537.

Whitney, Edward B. "The Income Tax and the Constitution." *Harvard Law Review* 20 (1906–1907): 280.

Newspapers

Chicago Daily Tribune. Mar. 20–May 25, 1895.

New York Daily Tribune. Mar. 20–May 25, 1895.

New York Sun. Mar. 20–May 25, 1895.

New York Times. Mar. 20–May 25, 1895.

New York World. Mar. 20–May 25, 1895.

Washington Post. Mar. 20–May 25, 1895.

Index